The Mother-Blame Game

EDITED BY

Vanessa Reimer and Sarah Sahagian

DEMETER

DEMETER PRESS

Funded by the Government of Canada | **Canada**
Financé par la gouvernement du Canada

Demeter Press
140 Holland Street West
P. O. Box 13022
Bradford, ON L3Z 2Y5
Tel: (905) 775-9089
Email: info@demeterpress.org
Website: www.demeterpress.org

Demeter Press logo based on the sculpture "Demeter" by
Maria-Luise Bodirsky <www.keramik-atelier.bodirsky.de>

Front cover photograph: Alice Keeler.

Printed and Bound in Canada

Library and Archives Canada Cataloguing in Publication

The mother-blame game / editors, Vanessa Reimer and Sarah Sahagian.

Includes bibliographical references.
ISBN 978-1-926452-14-2 (paperback)

1. Motherhood. 2. Mothers. 3. Feminists. 4. Feminism. I. Reimer, Vanessa, 1986-, author, editor II. Sahagian, Sarah, 1986-, author, editor

HQ759.M6648 2015   306.874'3   C2015-907448-7

The Mother-Blame Game

Dedication from Sarah:
For my grandmother, Anna Laidlaw. Even though you are
no longer with us, you will always be one of the loves of my life.
Thank you for telling me I was clever and capable. You gave me
the confidence to do unusual yet awesome things, like pitch
a book to Demeter Press at a launch party, in between
downing glasses of wine. I am fortunate to have had you in my
life for the first twenty-seven years.

Dedication from Vanessa:
For all my indomitable kinswomen whose wisdom, love, and
labour have nourished and sustained me throughout my life.

Table of Contents

II: BLAMING "OTHERED" MOTHERS

Acknowledgements

This book had numerous caregivers who helped transform it from a rough idea to the robust volume you now hold in your hands. In light of this, we have prepared an extensive list of acknowledgments for everyone who helped produce *The Mother-Blame Game*. We know these are just words on a page and that we can never convey our gratitude enough to everyone who dedicated their time and energy to making this book what it is. As such, this is our attempt to articulate the immense affection and appreciation we feel for our colleagues.

First of all, we would like to thank the entire team at Demeter Press. Without them, we may have given up long ago. We must give a very special thank you to Alice Keeler for the use her original photograph as the cover image of this book. It is often said that a picture is worth a thousand words, and this is certainly the case here. We would also be remiss if we did not give a special thanks to Katherine Barrett for her detailed copy editing of this manuscript. Our book would not be the same without your deft hand and keen insight.

Of course, we could never overstate our gratitude to the incomparable Andrea O'Reilly. After hearing a short summary of our idea two years ago at the book launch for our first Demeter Press collection, Andrea generously put her faith in us again. Without her guidance, support, and brilliant example as an academic, we could not have taken our little embryo of a book to the point of delivery. There are no words to capture how honoured we are by Andrea believing in us not once, but twice!

Next, we would like to offer our considerable thanks to the people who generously offered to act as peer reviewers for this collection. We thank you for your thoughtful suggestions and your encouragement. You were an indispensable part in the completion of *The Mother-Blame Game*.

Finally, we must thank our contributors, who bravely trusted us with their work. We learned much from reading your insightful pieces on an impressively wide range of topics. This book is richer for each and every chapter we were lucky enough to receive. We thank you for your diligence, your creativity, and, most importantly, your patience. Putting together a book is an arduous task, but our desire to share your important work with the world inspired us every day.

Introduction

Contextualizing *The Mother-Blame Game*

VANESSA REIMER AND SARAH SAHAGIAN

W E LIVE IN A CULTURE where mother-blame is omni-present. Whether it manifests as bloggers critiquing Kim Kardashian's ability to mother her daughter, news media speculating if Adam Lanza's mother could have prevented the Sandy Hook mass shooting, or medical professionals shaming women for the decision not to breastfeed, mother-blame is largely unavoidable—to the extent that many of us perpetuate it in our daily attitudes and interactions and mothers themselves often internalize it.

Despite the widely held assumptions that mothers are to blame for all that is perceived to go "wrong" in their children's lives, we know that mothers do not have a monopoly on influencing their children's behaviour. Family members, peers, and social institutions such as schools, churches, and media play varying roles in children's lives as they grow. Yet as the chapters in this anthology will show, mother-blame is a very real, very common, and very gendered phenomenon.

This book is a piece of feminist activism that is written from a place of frustration and anger, but also from one of optimism. This collection of essays explores what mother-blame means and how it operates in our world, just as it seeks to challenge mother-blame by deconstructing it and envisioning empowering possibilities for moving forward. We, the editors of this anthology, do not have children of our own. We came to Motherhood Studies as child-free PhD students with an academic interest in the topic but no "on-the-job" training. Now, privileged enough to have studied with renowned maternal theorist Andrea O'Reilly, even we two non-mothers can see that mother-blame is both unfair and everywhere.

We ourselves have never been mother-blamed, and yet, like many people, we have both been guilty of *mother-blaming*. Before our exposure to maternal theory, there were times when we begrudged the harsh words our mothers occasionally had for us or times our mothers fell short of our expectations. It is now, armed with a critical lens informed by feminist politics and maternal theory, that we realize how wrong it was to judge our mothers against standards so onerous no human being could ever live up to them. This book is thus an exercise in critical analysis as well as a form of personal repentance on our part. In compiling this anthology, we hope to atone for our own histories of mother-blame as well as empower and embolden readers by naming and problematizing a dysfunctional cultural rubric that never fails to find mothers lacking.

THE PATRIARCHAL ROOTS OF MOTHER-BLAME

Of course, no introduction to the topic of mother-blame is complete without first examining the roots of maternal oppression. To do so, we turn to Adrienne Rich, the Ovarian maternal theorist, and her writing on the patriarchal institution of motherhood. Rich defines patriarchy as follows:

> Patriarchy is the power of the fathers; a familial-social, ideological, political system in which men—by force, direct pressure, or through ritual, tradition, law and language, customs, etiquette, education, and the division of labor, determine what part women shall or shall not play, and in which the female is everywhere subsumed under the male. (57)

She further explains that the "core of patriarchy is the individual family unit which originated with the idea of property, and the accompanying desire to see one's property transmitted to one's biological descendants" (60); she also contextualizes it as a "cross-cultural" phenomenon that oppresses women everywhere

(56). To that end, a patriarchal society assumes that women are "natural mothers" who have "no further identity" beyond that of nurturer to their children (22). This of course opens up space for mothers to be found inadequate when they fall short of behaving like perfect, self-sacrificing beings who never fail to put their children first.

Much of Rich's theory on patriarchal motherhood certainly has the potential to leave us feeling disheartened; crucially, however, she also writes: "I try to distinguish between two meanings of motherhood, one superimposed on the other: the *potential relationship* of any woman to her power of reproduction and to children; and the *institution*, which aims at ensuring that that potential—and all women—shall remain under male control" (13).

It is this optimistic potential to dismantle patriarchal motherhood that inspires this volume. We hope that this work will contribute meaningfully to the growing body of motherhood scholarship by naming and problematizing harmful mother-blame practices as well as discussing empowering strategies that mothers already utilize in their day-to-day lives to resist the cultural forces that constrain them.

WHAT IS THE MOTHER-BLAME GAME?

The title of this collection refers to a concept we believe affects how mothers experience blame in society. Simply put, the mother-blame game is our term for describing how the world is structured to persecute mothers. Mothers are blamed for everything from a nine-year-old child's lack of proficiency in math to the horrific crimes committed by adult serial killers. We hope to resist this larger phenomenon in part by naming it so prominently on our book's cover.

Of course, many motherhood scholars before us have contemplated the vilification and scapegoating of mothers. In their work, Molly Ladd-Taylor and Lauri Umansky argue that U.S. culture is obsessed with "bad" mothers, citing such examples as "the welfare mother, the teen mother, the career woman who has no time for her kids, the drug addict who poisons her fetus, the pushy stage mother, the overprotective Jewish mother" and others (2). Unfortunately for mothers themselves, Ladd-Taylor and Umansky also explain how the "bad mother" concept is dangerously adaptable, thus resulting in mothers being blamed "for everything, pure and simple" (2).

In her pioneering research, Paula J. Caplan also addresses mother-blame's adaptability and versatility. Caplan recounts to her readers: "I became interested in mother blaming when I was working in a clinic where we were evaluating families, and I noticed that no matter what was wrong, no matter what the reason for the family's coming to the clinic, it turned out the mother was always assumed to be responsible for the problem" (592). From her real world experience as a health professional, Caplan observes how children's problems are consistently held up as evidence of inadequate mothering.

According to Caplan, mothers are not only blamed for anything that goes wrong in their children's lives, but they are also frustratingly unappreciated when they supposedly do things "right." She posits, "Important work that a mother does goes largely unnoticed, except when she doesn't do it, as when she is sick and can't make dinner" (593). Mothers are therefore rendered invisible when they are succeeding but are berated for any work they fail to do—or cannot do—in a perfect manner. Ultimately, Caplan argues that these standards of motherhood are so onerous and contradictory that, to her, "it seemed there was nothing that a mother could do that was right" (592). This insight informs the basic premise of this text, and in this capacity *The Mother-Blame Game* is more than a title. We would like to offer it up as a theoretical concept—as a widespread cultural "game" that is rigged against mothers no matter what they do.

WHICH MOTHERS ARE TO BLAME?

We recognize that mothering is not synonymous with biology. To discuss the meaning of motherhood and how one becomes a mother, we turn to the definition of mothering developed by renowned maternal theorist Sara Ruddick. In her ground-breaking work, Ruddick contends that the practice of mothering "is to take upon oneself the responsibility of child care, making its work a regular and substantial part of one's working life" (17). Ruddick also expresses her position that mother-work does not begin until after a child is born. She contends, "Birthgiving and mothering really are two distinct activities" (xiii). We find this definition of what it means to be a mother particularly useful because of its inclusivity. Rather than privilege biological mothers, Ruddick theorizes motherhood as "work" that can be done by anyone should they so choose (14). While conceiving and giving birth to children can be entry points into motherhood for some, these experiences are not necessary for one to do the work of mothering.

Motherhood is thus a catchall phrase that describes an endless array of work, from the physical task of changing diapers to the emotional labour of consoling a teenager after a falling-out with friends. Ruddick attempts to categorize this sort of work with her contention that the practice of motherhood is shaped by three major demands: preservation, growth, and acceptability (19-21). While these categories may describe various types of maternal labour, the red thread that unites them all is the demand on the mother's time and energy to ensure none of this work is left undone.

Of course, there are many obstacles to performing the work of mothering. For instance, Ruddick reminds us that "war, poverty, and racism twist a mother's best efforts. These are not sorrows brought on by mothering; they are socially caused and politically remediable" (29). Even though these structural barriers are beyond any individual mother's control, too often mothers are blamed when their children's life outcomes are thwarted by oppressive societal structures. Indeed, after being tasked with all this work of keeping a child alive and making sure they can function in society, the mother receives the gift of being "blamed" if a child is deemed unsatisfactory (Ruddick 110). It would thereby seem that mothers must be ever-vigilant and ready to absorb blame like a punching bag. To that end, perhaps a fourth category could be added to Ruddick's three demands—that of internalizing and mitigating maternal failure. This work materializes as anticipating and preventing a child's potential failures and accepting responsibility for the child's life outcomes—all while deeply embedded patriarchal ideologies and systemic inequalities continue to operate unnoticed.

WHY DO WE NEED THIS BOOK NOW?

In the Canadian Broadcasting Corporation's 2014 documentary *The Motherload*, Andrea O'Reilly argues that it is more difficult to be a mother now than at any other time in history. Indeed, while mothers have always been blamed when they fall short of patriarchal ideals, contemporary "good mothering" standards demand more of them than ever before. Sharon Hays refers to this trend, which has unfolded over the past thirty years or so, as "intensive mothering" and argues that this approach to motherhood makes "the underlying assumption that the child absolutely requires consistent nurture by a single primary care-taker and that the mother is the best person for the job" (414). As such, while Sara Ruddick defines motherhood as a concept that has been historically defined by work, intensive mothering expands on this definition by emphasizing how motherhood is characterized by a call to *overwork*.

Susan J. Douglas and Meredith Michaels refer to the rise of this intensive mothering trend as "the New Momism" and explain how this paradigm "redefines all women, first and foremost, through their relationships to children" (633). They further argue that, particularly since the 1980s, mothers are now expected to "acquire professional-level skills such as those of a therapist, pediatrician ('Dr. Mom'), consumer products safety inspector, and teacher" (620). As if this were not enough, mothers must also spend all of their emotional energy and "the monetary equivalent of the gross domestic product of Australia" on their children (620-621).

As Melinda Vandenbeld Giles similarly expresses in her timely anthology *Mothering in the Age of Neoliberalism*, intensive mothering standards are inextricably linked to neoliberal economics and ideologies. David Harvey defines neoliberalism as "a theory of political economic practices that proposes that human well-being can best be advanced by liberating individual entrepreneurial freedoms and skills within an institutional framework characterized by strong private property rights, free markets, and free trade" (2). The neoliberal state thus values self-sufficiency, autonomy, and a capitalist commitment to generating monetary wealth above all else. Giles further notes how neoliberalism gained prevalence in the same decades as intensive modes of mothering became commonplace and argues, "It is no coincidence that the height of global neoliberal restructuring in the mid-1990s coincided with a returned interest in mothering given how the neoliberal paradigm necessitates mothers take on the primary role of caregiving with the depletion of state resources" (8). In an era where citizens are tasked with absorbing the economic shocks of a dissipating social safety net, mothers—and women more generally—are increasingly called upon to perform intensive care work for their children and anyone else who cannot care for themselves.

TALKING BACK TO MOTHER-BLAME: OUR CHAPTERS

In light of these socioeconomic and ideological barriers that constrain maternal practice and maternal relationships, this anthology provides space to talk back to mother-blame. The chapters that follow not only work to contextualize and critique the pervasive cultural practice of mother-blame but also highlight empowering strategies for actively challenging and transforming patriarchal motherhood ideologies. We have organized the chapters into four thematic sections, each of which addresses one particular—albeit fluid—facet of mother-blame: Mother-Blame and the Body, Blaming "Othered" Mothers, Mother-Blame in Popular Culture, and, finally, Sharing Mother-Blame Stories: Strategies for Resistance.

Our first section addresses how the cultural practice of mother-blame stigmatizes women's bodies by constructing them as sites of shame. We begin with "Mothers, Daughters, Blame, and the Body" wherein Marie Hansen, Heather Reel, Tasha Muresan, and Aurélie Athan examine how the popular and academic psychological gaze naturalizes mother-blame by addressing the mother-daughter relationship in unilateral terms through an attachment-theory paradigm. In doing so, this research holds individual mothers responsible for perpetuating the dominant patriarchal ideologies that stigmatize female bodies and subject them to social scrutiny, surveillance, and control. The authors accordingly call for future psychological research to focus on the qualitative experiences of mothers themselves as well as to honour the mother-daughter bond while acknowledging the social forces that constrain it.

The next two chapters elucidate how mothers are shamed when their bodies and experiences deviate from the norms prescribed by dominant infant and maternal health discourses. In "Breast-feeding Shame and the Birth of the Mother," Catherine Robinson draws from her own experiences with "breastfeeding failure" to problematize the medical, political, and social prescriptions that "breast is best." She argues that the intensive promotion of exclusive infant breastfeeding as the only acceptable form of infant nutrition is symptomatic of neoliberal risk culture wherein women are held individually responsible for their children's health and well-being. The chapter further explores how the singular focus on infant rights to receive the health benefits associated with breast milk ultimately overlooks mothers themselves, many of whom may be unable to breastfeed for various physiological and socioeconomic reasons.

In a similar vein, Tracy Royce draws from fat studies scholarship to examine how mothers are blamed and shamed for perpetuating North America's "obesity epidemic" in "Unfit Mothers? Moth-er-Blame and the Moral Panic over 'Obesity.'" She refers to case studies and news media stories to illustrate how fat mothers and mothers of fat children are subject to social scrutiny and state regulation because they are perceived as incompetent caregivers. The chapter further elucidates how the broader cultural prac-tice of fat-shaming affects women who wish to adopt, just as it problematizes the practices that stem from the hegemonic—and inaccurate—conflation of fatness with ill-health and maternal incompetence.

Our second section addresses how mother-blame manifests as social surveillance and institutional regulation of women who are marginalized by intersecting identity markers of "Otherness." In "Fated Fate? Fated Fate? Patriarchal Ethics and Reproductive Politics in Southwest China," Fang-Tzu Yen draws from her re-search with ethnic minority Kam women in China to reveal how their reproductive agency is constrained by multiple systems of oppression. She explains how the Chinese government has re-sponded to high infant mortality rates by implementing a medical modernization program that stigmatizes Kam women's traditional birthing and mothering practices. These mother-blame discourses are exacerbated by the patriarchal Kam belief in "fated fate," which presumes that individual women with "bad fate" are at fault when they experience infertility, pregnancy and birth complications, or the death of a child. The chapter argues that substantive political and economic changes are needed to empower Kam women in their fight for improved reproductive agency and maternal health.

The next two chapters examine how young mothers are marginalized and stigmatized within U.S. socioeconomic contexts. In "'I Was the One Who Opened My Legs': The Tropes and Consequences of Blaming Pregnant and Mothering Teens," Jenna Vinson and Sally Stevens draw from their research with young mothering and pregnant women to problematize the larger cultural practice of teen mother-blame in the U.S. The chapter reveals how teenaged mothers internalize discriminatory societal norms that hold them solely responsible for "opening their legs" and becoming pregnant, thereby excusing fathers from responsibility in the childrearing process. The authors further argue that the taken-for-granted "consequences" of teen pregnancy, such as social isolation and poverty, are actually symptomatic of patriarchal ideologies and oppressive socioeconomic structures. While this chapter explores how the teen mother-blame game perpetuates the larger patriarchal devaluation and control of women's bodies, it also draws attention to how young mothers challenge and resist these sexist double standards.

Vanessa Reimer similarly examines how a selection of 2013 U.S. teen pregnancy prevention campaigns operationalizes neoliberal discourses of individual risk management in "'Because You Had Me as a Teen': Neoliberalism and the 'Problem' of Teen Pregnancy." Reimer argues that the societal "problems" of young motherhood and single motherhood are perpetuated by neoliberal policies that demand the privatization of social reproductive work and construct childrearing as inimical to "real" productivity in the market. This chapter problematizes these campaigns for blaming and shaming young mothers as the individual causes and perpetuators of poverty in their communities and society at large, just as it considers how young mothers and their allies have worked to challenge the dominant discourses that stigmatize and devalue their maternal practice.

This section closes with two chapters that examine mothering in relation to criminal justice systems. Kaley M. Ames explores how legal discourses contrast with popular perceptions of women who kill their children in "From the Court of Law to the Court of Public Opinion: The Role of Mother Blame in Canadian Infanticide Cases." Here the author draws from Paula Caplan's mother-blame myths to highlight how patriarchal structures and beliefs perpetuate a larger mother-blaming culture that regards women who commit infanticide with unique contempt. The chapter explores how Canada's historically sympathetic infanticide laws have been replaced with harsher sentences as the cultural practice of mother-blame grows increasingly pervasive. It accordingly argues for a paradigm shift that focuses on the larger circumstances and structures—and, importantly, the lack of resources and societal awareness—that exacerbate maternal crises, rather than singularly demonizing individual mothers who commit violent acts.

In "'*We* Want to Consistently Address *Their* Needs': Explorations of the Perceptions, Practices, Experiences, and Challenges of Parenting Interventions for Incarcerated Mothers," Talia Esnard similarly explores how incarcerated mothers and their children are aided and constrained by parent intervention programs in Trinidad and Tobago. Drawing from interviews with external facilitators of parent intervention programs, the chapter considers how incarcerated mothers' maternal identities are often rendered invisible by their criminal status, and it problematizes the lack of resources dedicated to facilitating access and communication between incarcerated mothers and their children. The chapter argues that additional research and augmented resources have the potential to aid and empower incarcerated mothers in the Caribbean.

Our third section analyzes how mother-blame manifests in mass media and popular culture. In "Blaming the Mother: The Politics of Gender in Cindy Sheehan's Protest of the Iraq War," Linda Pershing explores how the prominent U.S. peace activist's protests against the Bush administration were represented in media and taken up in public discourse. She recounts how Sheehan's detractors utilized the sexist tropes of "loud-mouthed bitch" and "bad mother" to discredit and dismiss her. Despite the vitriolic opposition that Sheehan garnered for her activism, her subversion of "good woman" and "good mother" ideologies also received considerable public support, and she contributed significantly to a shifting national paradigm that would eventually recognize the U.S. occupation of Iraq as illegal and unjust.

In the next chapter, "Tiger Mothers and the Birth of a New Maternal Epithet: A Feminist Critical Discourse Analysis of Popular Responses to Amy Chua's *Battle Hymn of the Tiger Mother*," Sarah Sahagian problematizes public reactions to Chua's popular text that construct her as a bad mother of "monstrous" proportions. She explains how, even though Chua invests the time, energy, and material resources required of "good" intensive mothering, she is still publicly reviled for her refusal to relinquish her authority and selfhood in accordance with patriarchal standards of sacrificial motherhood. In this way, the popular backlash against Chua demonstrates how mother-blame operates as a dominant paradigm wherein women are blamed for all that is perceived to go "wrong" in their children's lives yet are also criticized when they do things "right."

This section closes with two chapters that address how popular texts propagate various facets of mother-blame. In "Because My Mother Was a Liar and a Whore: Adulterous Mothers and Paternity Uncertainty in Jo Nesbø's *The Snowman*," Berit Åström explores how the myth of widespread paternity fraud is utilized as a plot device in popular crime fiction. She notes how there is little scientific evidence to support the belief that women often dupe their male partners into raising children they have conceived with other men of "superior" genes; nevertheless, this trope is widely perpetuated by evolutionary psychologists and men's rights activists. *The Snowman* naturalizes this stereotype by inviting readers to empathize with a male protagonist who murders women that commit this "social crime" against their husbands and children. Åström explains how this novel re-enforces patriarchal assumptions that all women are potential liars and "whores," and she further problematizes how it constructs women as "deserving" when they are victims of male violence.

In the next chapter, "*Lean In* or Leave before You Leave? False Dichotomies of Choice and Blame in Public Debates about

Working Motherhood," Jennifer Borda outlines how the "choice feminism" rhetoric employed in Sheryl Sandberg's popular 2013 text overlooks the structural barriers and intensive mothering ideologies that constrain women's abilities to achieve "work-life balance." She explains how this text blames individual women for internalizing sexist stereotypes, just as it encourages readers to adopt a patriarchal and neoliberal corporate ethos that devalues mothering and parenting more generally. The chapter highlights how praise for Sandberg's text has been tethered by critical voices that draw attention to women's complex and diverse experiences, therein shaping a constructive alternative discourse that calls for collective advocacy that will benefit everyone who does the work of parenting.

Our fourth and final section addresses the importance of sharing diverse maternal narratives in resisting patriarchal mother-blame practices. In "Twice Shamed and Twice Blamed: Assumptions, Myths, and Stereotypes about 'Giving Up a Child' and 'Taking In a Child,'" Lee Murray and Kerri Kearney refer to popular adoption literature and their personal narratives to problematize the cultural assumptions that mothers who "give up" their children for adoption, as well as those who adopt their children, should experience pain, shame, and remorse. The authors address how they are both "twice-shamed" for their maternal experiences—first for subverting the normative framework wherein women birth and raise their "real" biological children and again for not feeling the intense failure and loss that are presumed to shape such experiences. They highlight how the dominant discursive framework for such "Othered" mothering experiences leaves little space for women to affirm their complex and diverse maternal narratives, and they further consider how sharing alternative narratives is vital for eliminating the stigmas and stereotypes associated with adoption and infertility.

In the next chapter, "What My Buddhist Son Taught Me about Blame," Rosie Rosenzweig shares how her emotionally tumultuous relationship with her mother caused her to judge both of them against the mythical "good mother" ideal. Her own feelings of maternal inadequacy were further compounded when her adult son seemingly rejected their family's Jewish cultural and religious heritage by becoming a Buddhist monk. The author recounts joining her son on a trip to meet his spiritual teachers, which inspired her to undertake studies in Buddhist Psychology. She explains how these spiritual practices have helped her to let go of her "mother-blame mind habits" by cultivating compassion toward her own mother as well as by relinquishing the "stories" that foster feelings of personal guilt and inadequacy.

Next, Alison Quaggin Harkin blends life writing with creative fiction to highlight how mothers are blamed and shamed when they give birth to children with disabilities. Her chapter, "'Disabling' Motherhood in 1914 and 2014: Stories of Two Women," begins with a fictional narrative of mother "Alice" raising her "feeble-minded" son in the early twentieth century, a time when eugenics and mass institutionalization were the primary solutions for managing "damaged" children. She then contrasts this narrative with her own experience raising a son with a cognitive disability and problematizes how dominant maternal health discourses suggest that mothers who plan adequately can guarantee the birth of healthy and "normal" children. Such advice not only perpetuates the cultural practice of mother-blame but also devalues children and adults with disabilities. The chapter highlights the importance of sharing personal mothering stories in resisting such harmful cultural practices.

We conclude with Lorinda Peterson's piece "Loving Miss JBP: Writing/art as Mothering Practice in a Mother-Blaming Culture." Here the author reflects on how life writing and sequential art have helped her navigate her complex relationship with her non-biological adolescent daughter. Writing from the standpoint of a lesbian single mother who is bound to her daughter through a shared story of trauma, she recounts how engaging in collaborative writing has helped her re-interpret her mothering experiences. She further elucidates how creating her own "trauma comics" as an act of feminist art activism has helped her create new stories wherein trauma and agency, like mothering practice itself, are fluid experiences that often defy coherent temporal and spatial structures. Doing so has also helped her critically address—and ultimately reject—the pervasive cultural practice of mother-blame.

CONCLUDING THOUGHTS

While we take pride in the diverse topics discussed here, we also acknowledge this anthology's limitations. It does not definitively represent every facet of mother-blame in our contemporary globalized society, nor does it represent each diverse geographic, cultural, or interpersonal context in which mother-blame occurs. In this capacity, we hope this collection inspires readers to engage in passionate and introspective dialogue regarding the many ways that the ubiquitous mother-blame game manifests in social institutions as well as daily personal attitudes and interpersonal interactions.

As these chapters illustrate, there is much work to be done in dismantling the deleterious material and ideological systems that constrain maternal practice. However, these pieces also demonstrate how mothers in diverse cultural, geographic, and socioeconomic contexts *do* recognize and resist patriarchal motherhood ideologies. We accordingly invite our readers to join us in daily, purposeful efforts that will continue to debunk—and finally end—the mother-blame game. Whether our activism occurs in private interactions or on public platforms—or anywhere in between—our work is equally crucial to cultivating the conditions that will empower everyone who performs and benefits from the indispensable work of mothering.

WORKS CITED

Caplan, Paula J. "Don't Blame Mother: Then and Now." *Maternal Theory: Essential Readings*. Ed. Andrea O'Reilly. Toronto: Demeter Press, 2007. 592-600. Print.

Douglas, Susan J., and Meredith Michaels. "The New Momism." *Maternal Theory: Essential Readings*. Ed. Andrea O'Reilly. Toronto: Demeter Press, 2007. 617-639. Print.

Giles, Melinda Vandenbeld. Introduction. *Mothering In the Age of Neoliberalism*. Ed. Melinda Vandenbeld Giles. Toronto: Demeter Press, 2013. 1-30. Print.

Harvey, David. *A Brief History of Neoliberalism*. Oxford: Oxford University Press, 2007. Print.

Hays, Sharon. "Why Can't a Mother Be More Like a Business-man?" *Maternal Theory: Essential Readings*. Ed. Andrea O'Reilly. Toronto: Demeter Press, 2007. 408-430. Print.

Ladd-Taylor, Molly and Lauri Umansky. Introduction. *"Bad" Mothers: The Politics of Blame in Twentieth-Century America*. Ed. Molly Ladd-Taylor and Lauri Umansky. New York: New York University Press, 1998. 1-28. Print.

The Motherload. Dir. Cornelia Principe. Canadian Broadcasting Corporation, 2014. Film.

Rich, Adrienne. *Of Woman Born: Motherhood as Experience and Institution*. New York: Norton, 1976. Print.

Ruddick, Sara. *Maternal Thinking*. 2nd Ed. Boston: Beacon Press, 1995. Print.

I.
Mother-Blame and the Body

1.
Mothers, Daughters, Blame and the Body

TASHA MURESAN, HEATHER REEL, MARIE HANSEN
AND AURÉLIE ATHAN

THE FEMALE BODY IS A site of contested, conflicting, and ever-changing meanings, existing at the intersection of multiple conceptual grids. In the Western[1] imagination, the female body is at once revered and reviled. Perceptions of the female form vary from powerful, awe-inspiring and sensual, to messy, obscene, unpredictable and dangerous. While vacillating between the extremes of disdain and desire, the female body's material functions are often regarded as detached from more nuanced psychic processes. Australian psychologist Jane Ussher uses the term "monstrous feminine" (1) to describe the social condition of the reproductive female body. She argues that, in contrast to the male body, the female form is seen as leaky, unruly, and grotesque; it is an object that needs to be controlled and regulated. As a result, women's lived experiences of the body are often disrupted. Seeking to reconcile their subjective bodily experiences with these objectifying cultural practices, women often live within what may be considered a form of "double consciousness"—a phrase coined by W.E.B. DuBois to describe the peculiar bind faced by African Americans, which results from living in one's body while simultaneously "looking at one's self through the eyes of others, of measuring one's soul by the tape of a world that looks on in amused contempt and pity" (3).

While the mother-daughter relationship has been scrutinized for reproducing women's distorted bodily experiences, the larger patriarchal context in which such relationships exist seems to have been largely obviated. Mothers are held as the primordial source of criticism, rejection, shame, and modelling that leads to experiences of bodily discord—from disordered eating patterns to sexual dissatisfaction. The implicit answer to the question, "Why do women have trouble with their bodies?" has become, "Because our mothers have taught us so." This chapter accordingly examines mother-blame through the mother-daughter relationship as it is contextualized through the body. We will begin by describing the current literature on mother-daughter relationships and the female reproductive system and the ways in which the mother-daughter bond shapes the lived experience of the physical body in a North American context. We will then explore how mothers are implicated in reproducing bodily discord throughout daughters' reproductive life cycles, focusing specifically on menstruation, sexuality, and pregnancy. In doing so, we will examine the role of mother-blame in body-shaming discourses, particularly those that perpetuate shame. We will then analyze the expression of sexual attitudes, behaviours, and subjectivities, including sexual body-esteem, entitlement to pleasure, sexual self-reflection, and sexual agency, in relation to the mother-daughter relationship. Lastly, we will consider how the narrative of mother-blame operates vis-a-vis the pregnant body and is invoked to explain away a multitude of pregnancy outcomes.

THE MOTHER-DAUGHTER MATRIX

It is largely taken as uncontested truth that contentious relational dynamics exist between mothers and daughters. Indeed, within Western cultural discourse, the mother-daughter relationship is considered to be one of the most salient in the journey toward adulthood. Over the past several decades, scholars from a handful of disciplines have engaged with the topic of motherhood and the mother-daughter relationship to a considerable degree.[2] Despite this increased scholarly attention, little work has been done in the realm of psychology to treat the mother-daughter relation-ship outside the context of correlational questions such as, "Are alcoholic mothers likely to have alcoholic daughters?" (Caplan 3). These correlational questions lend themselves quite easily to the "mother-blame game"—the common practice of linking life outcomes, whether optimal or suboptimal, to maternal variables.

Outside the domain of academic literature, a multitude of voices continually weigh in on how body image is cultivated through the mother-daughter relationship. The majority of these sources assert that mothers have the strongest influence on their daughters' developing bodies and self-perceptions. Unfortunately, while many of these conversations seek to instill a sense of responsibility in the collective maternal cohort, their tone more often than not elicits a sense of shame and blame. Vander Ven and Vander Ven explore the trend of mother blaming in anorexia scholarship, for example, and highlight the co-occurrence of mother-blame and women's social roles within these academic discourses. They refer to the mother-daughter relationship as a "slippery construct," therein highlighting the dynamism that exists within the mother-child matrix (97). To that end, maternal qualities such as jealousy, competition, and hyper concern with daughters' behaviours are implicated repeatedly in the development of eating pathology and distorted body image (Fassino et al. 293). However, such evaluations fail to recognize that mothering is a subjective experience that subverts the power of expert discourse and defies comprehensive measurement. To measure mothers' supposed successes and failures based on their daughters' psychological, physical, and social outcomes is as much an exercise in futility as it is disruptive to healthy mutual engagement between mothers and daughters. So how can the mother-daughter relationship be both honoured and freed from the trap of the mother-blame game? How might we problematize the way mothers are blamed for their daughters' experiences and struggles?

Historically, the use of mother-blame as a device for explaining the existence of psychopathology has been a staple of clinical literature. Most notorious is Frieda Fromm-Reichmann's "schizophrenogenic mother," a term used to describe a form of mother-child communication that purportedly led to the development of schizophrenia (Fromm-Reichmann 265). However, despite the claims that psychology has moved beyond mother-blame (Seeman 284), many mental health professionals have confessed that mother-blaming messages are embedded in their training (Caplan 50). These contemporary messages are often more subtle than those of the past; for example, recent developmental literature, despite an emphasis on "bidirectionality," still places the onus on the mother,[3] potentially because of the obvious power-differential between mother and child. When the mother is suffering from psychological distress, these messages become more overt. For example, maternal schizophrenia is believed to cause behavioural problems in children (Malhotra, Deepak and Verma) and maternal postnatal depression is believed to cause adolescent depression (Stein).

In a similar vein, Margaret Mahler advised therapists to note whether mothers carried their child "like a part of herself," thus revealing her inability to separate from the child, or "like an inanimate object," thus revealing her cold demeanour (Caplan 51). Statements such as these eventually led to the popularization of concepts such as "refrigerator mothers" and "helicopter mothers," women who are deemed responsible for their children's autism and ADHD respectively. Psychoanalyst Nancy McWilliams also rationalizes the existence of mother-blame in clinical literature by acknowledging that it is often easier to focus blame on the active and involved mother rather than the uninvolved and often emotionally distant father (McWilliams 150). In sum, despite the influence of feminist thinkers on clinical psychology and psychoanalytic theory, mother-blame is still largely intertwined with child psychopathology outcomes.

MOTHER-BLAME AND MENSTRUATION

Menstrual shame is perhaps the sine qua non in the development of the "monstrous feminine" framework of the female body and psyche. The existence of menstrual shame is particularly relevant to women's psychological wellbeing. As menstruation and the reproductive cycle are so inherent to the physical form and structure of the female body, the incorporation of such shame delves deeply into the very essence of what it means to be a female subject. As Elizabeth Grosz contends, "The body and its various sensations are projected onto the world, and conversely the world and its vicissitudes are introjected into the body of the subject-to-be" (74). Puberty, like birth, is a time of "coming-to-be," as girls begin to address issues related to their sexuality and identity while changes to their body provoke further questions.

Likewise, the culture in which these bodily and psychological issues are embedded also begins to renegotiate the girl's social role as she becomes an adult reproductive subject. Throughout this process, mothers are seen as having a strong effect on their daughters' psychological wellbeing. Mothers and daughters are also linked through what Greer Litton Fox calls a "time-lagged mutuality of shared sexual experience," which encompasses the events of menarche, menstruation, conception, gestation, birth, and menopause (21). Since it is presumed that mothers and daughters share female physicalities, mothers are often called upon to be guides and confidants as their daughters' bodies change and develop. This experience has been indicated cross-culturally, such as in the Jewish cultural practice of *niddah* and the Tamil cultural practice of *Manjal Neerattu Vizha*. However, in North America, menarche is often represented as a medical event wherein mothers' roles are reduced to imparting lessons on concealment and hygiene maintenance (Ussher 20).[4] Mothers are thus implicated in perpetuating their daughters' internalized sense of menstrual shame and stigma.

Is it possible to problematize the existence of such "menstrual mother-blame" while still honouring mothers' roles in their daughters' physical development? To begin addressing this question, it is important to understand the various facets of menstrual shame. Beginning in girlhood, the time of menstruation in Western culture is often equated with hassle and annoyance. While in school, the menstruating body becomes a highly regulated secret, and girls often struggle to hide all signs of menstruation from their classmates. For example, teen magazines such as *Seventeen* commonly contain stories of "school menstrual exposure" under columns about readers' most embarrassing moments (Houppert 86).

Johnston-Robledo and Chrisler accordingly describe menstruation through Goffman's concept of "social stigma" (9). Menstruation becomes a marker of female "Otherness,"[5] which women internalize as they learn that an intimate aspect of themselves is disgusting and disgraceful. This can have a major impact on young girls' self-esteem, body image, and confidence. Research has also found that menstrual shame has a strong effect on sexual deci-

23

sion-making. Women who are uncomfortable with menstruation have lower levels of body comfort than those women who report being comfortable with menstruation. In turn, women who have high levels of body comfort exhibit greater sexual assertiveness and less sexual risk. This relationship suggests a "cycle of shame" whereby discomfort with menstruation has a global effect on shameful views of the body (Schooler et al. 324). Later, during childbearing years, women who have shameful attitudes towards menstruation have also been shown to have shameful attitudes towards breastfeeding (Johnston-Robledo et al.). These findings suggest that the same shame felt about menstruation is pervasive and extends into other areas of life.

In much of the literature on menstrual shame, the mother's role in the creation and perpetuation of menstrual stigma has been heavily analyzed. The mother-daughter bond is considered by many authors to bear a significant relationship to a daughter's perception of her own body, as the different-but-shared aspects of their corporeality speak to a sense of mutuality and learning. Mothers are seen as contributors to their daughters' negative conceptions of menstruation as well as perpetrators of menstrual secrecy and taboo. Perhaps one of the most researched areas of menstrual stigma has been "menarche communication," or the experience of mother-daughter dialogue during a girl's first menstrual period. Although many Western cultures do not have formalized rituals associated with menarche, the mother-daughter "talk"—or lack thereof—is often regarded as a girl's entry point into womanhood. Analyses of mother-daughter menarche communications have shown that the majority of messages that mothers impart to their daughters are negative, often in the form of a "grin and bear it" paradigm (Costos, Ackerman and Paradis 49).

To that end, Joyce McFadden's study of 450 women saw many participants report menarche as a symbol of distance between themselves and their mothers (50). Similarly, Lee and Sasser-Coen found that a great deal of women's menarche narratives focused on their relationships with their mothers and were "filled with ambivalence, conflict and confusion" (114). Stubbs and Costos also identify mother-daughter menarche communication as a key area for therapeutic intervention as well as an important avenue for repairing mother-daughter relationships more broadly (37).

Although the potential lack of communication during menarche is seen as a key causal factor in this perceived distance between mothers and daughters, it could also be a marker of the natural progression from parental control to teenage autonomy, thus complicating cultural assumptions about the importance of menarche communications. As early as 1944, Helene Deutsch found that daughters would often censure mothers who attempted to be more open about menarche communications, preferring instead to be instructed by their sisters and friends (161). In this sense, perhaps the lack of communication between mothers and daughters during menarche is a form of "good enough" mothering (Winnicott) wherein mothers allow their daughters to discover what menstruation means on their own terms. Arguments for and against this new twist on silence are difficult to navigate, as menarche communications are embedded with cultural and historical significance. Although mother-daughter menarche communication is important, the emphasis on this communication in the literature does a disservice to the complexity of the issue at hand as well as to the broader dyadic nature of the mother-daughter relationship. Without societal structures in place that support alternative views of menstruation, mothers' attempts to resist the social code will be significantly constrained.[6]

Furthermore, such attempts to transgress this social code through fostering open menarche communication may be possible only for a select few. Bobel draws a connection between the ability to transgress mothering norms and Bourdieu's concept of "cultural capital." Referring to the white, middle-class privileges enjoyed by most people engaged in "high risk" forms of activism, Bobel states, "Their privilege not only affords them access to the world of alternativity, but also protects them from the public censure that women with less cultural capital stand exposed to" (136). It is thus necessary to acknowledge socio-cultural and historical power dynamics in conversations about mother-daughter menarche communications. For example, current literature places the same expectations on mothers without regard for the power structures that constrain their maternal practice. Here, the burden of sexual and reproductive health literacy is too narrowly placed on the shoulders of individual women, while other avenues toward developing body knowledge are given far less attention.

MOTHERS, DAUGHTERS, AND SEXUAL BEHAVIOUR

On the whole, developmental literature in psychology has largely focused on attachments established between mothers and daughters prior to puberty. This early maternal relationship is thought to set the stage for bonding, intimacy, and sexual behaviour in adulthood. Thus, a child's relationship with her mother is evaluated based on its potential to affect future bodily experiences as well as her abilities to form other attachments. In this way, physical, sensory, and emotional intimacy between mother and infant is regarded as the early foundation of more mature forms of physical intimacy and love that accompany sexual development. The importance of the mother-daughter relationship stems in large part from the centrality of this dyad as a socialization structure in the female life course (Fox 21). The work of Lipman-Blumen, among others, has established the centrality of mothers' values, attitudes, and behaviours as determinants of their daughters' sexual attitudes and behaviours (34-52). Research in this area has also generally concluded that mothers' attitudes and self-care behaviours play a significant role in daughters' sexual socialization (Inazu and Fox 81-84).

Although the relationship between maternal variables and sexual expression has been studied at length, such research has been largely confined to evaluations of mother-daughter communication about sex and the influence that mothers have on adolescent sexual behaviour. For instance, correlations have been found between measures of the mother-daughter relationship and daughters' sexual behaviour and birth control attitudes (Jaccard et al. 159-185). Other findings have shown that adolescent daughters' satisfaction with their maternal relationships may be related to sexual abstinence and more consistent use of contraceptives (159-185). Similar to the research on menarche communications, a noteworthy pattern emerges that characterizes the mother-daughter relationship as non-transactional, unidirectional, and devoid of social context. Increased attention must be paid to the larger ecology of mother-daughter relationships as well as to the multi-directional nature of influence.[7] Macrolevel ideologies, political influences, historical trends, and the contexts of media, neighbourhoods, and schools, for instance, must also be considered.

While the maternal variables described thus far can be useful predictors of daughters' sexual behaviour, we still know very little about how mothers influence intergenerational reproductive and sexual experiences. As such, although the mother-daughter relationship may be a legitimate area for continued enquiry into determinants of sexual behaviour, the preoccupation with the correlational nature of this relationship—rather than its qualitative value—seems to tightly circumscribe the boundaries of the existing scholarship. Additionally, most of the work dealing with daughters' sexual behaviour remains beholden to the pervasive grip of attachment theory, which tends to position maternal relationship patterns as the sole or primary focus of numerous developmental processes. This singular focus on the mother-daughter relationship, although important, may naturally lend itself to mother-blame.

Reproductive behaviours are similarly drawn into this pervasive web of mother-blame. In popular discourse, a purported surge in teen pregnancies over the last several decades has sometimes been conceptualized as a balm for adolescent low self-esteem or an affirmation of independence. This narrative is represented by the image of the adolescent girl on popular television programs such as *16 and Pregnant* and *Teen Mom*. She may feel rejected by her parents and thus begin to seek attention through "promiscuous" sexual behaviour. The same narrative was used to suggest that Jamie Lynn Spears became pregnant because her mother was preoccupied with her more famous older sister ("Spears Tells"). Similarly, since mothers are often charged with imparting knowledge of female physiology and contraception, a daughter's unwanted pregnancy may be thought to be rooted in her mother's psychological illiteracy and inability to foster effective communication (Murcott). A teenage daughter's pregnancy is cited as primary evidence of the lack of trust and mutual understanding between mother and daughter. In this sense, much like menarche communication, mothers may be blamed for failures in contraceptive communication when their teenage daughters become pregnant.

In a similar vein, perceived sexual dysfunction in women—on both sides of the coin, from "promiscuity" to "frigidity"—has also been associated with the mother-daughter relationship. Clinically, the mental health field continues to reference the "mother-wound," at least in practice if not always in name. This so-called "wound" is the consequence of an unhealthy early relationship with one's mother, which in turn causes sexual shame or submissiveness. Clinician Pamela Madsen has written about daughters dealing with "mother-wounds" as such:

> They keep themselves sexually small because they don't want to threaten other women or call too much attention to themselves. There is this fear that something bad will happen to them that they will not be able to control. Or worse—that they will be blamed. They compete endlessly with other women and have this feeling that they cannot trust other women. After all, some feel that they couldn't trust their mother to protect them or see them as they truly were/are. (n.p.)

As the discourse of the "mother-wound" might have us believe, a mother is largely responsible for her daughter's feelings of sexual agency and her ability to feel entitled to sexual pleasure without guilt and shame. Herein we encounter the complex nature of mother-blame, as mothers are implicated in both promoting and hindering their daughters' sexual expression.

THE PREGNANT BODY AND THE IMPRESSIONABLE FETUS

Popular conceptions of the pregnant body are similarly varied and contradictory. On the one hand, the pregnant woman may be revered for her procreative capacity and the unparalleled achievement of gestating new life. On the other hand, the pregnant woman may be perceived as unruly, with "wildly" fluctuating hormones, diminished control of bodily fluids, and endless physical cravings. Hollywood in particular does its part in constructing the pregnant body as abject, gross, awkward, and a source of endless comedy, as the typical film portrayal of a pregnant woman centers on strange cravings and mood swings. Here the insidious power of mother-blame is ever-present: such bodily "unruliness" has become a convenient site of culpability for child outcomes. In this respect, pregnant women are afforded a perilous power over their impressionable young offspring.

The phrase "maternal impressions" refers to the widely held idea that pregnant women possess powerful psychic influences that may produce an impression, physical or otherwise, on the child she is carrying (Mazzoni). Such beliefs about maternal imprinting are often related to food cravings. Thus, a woman who yearns for strawberries during her pregnancy may birth a child who bears a red patch on her forehead. While the development of modern genetic theory has challenged such ideas, an undercurrent of maternal impressions still seems to be manifested, for instance, in a contemporary preoccupation with the fetal origins of adult disease. For example, a 2010 publication titled "Origins: How the Nine Months Before Birth Shape the Rest of Our Lives" synthesizes the various ways that the prenatal environment—particularly maternal nutrition, stress, depression, and drug and alcohol use—appears to influence the fetus and have effects across the lifespan. These ideas are also reproduced, generalized and disseminated in popular parenting magazines (Lende).

A theory of maternal impressions is also contemporarily prevalent in discourses of pregnancy and diet, as evidenced by the pages of pregnancy magazines and advice manuals (Mazzoni). The application of maternal impressions to food choices has particular salience for mothers and daughters as current scientific research emphasizes the influence of the intrauterine environment on a girl child's later relationship with food and body weight (Northrup). While there may be some legitimacy to these claims, they remain largely understudied—yet they are embraced by popular sources and sometimes disguised as folk wisdom (Lende). By focusing on the real and imagined power that a mother has over the child she carries, advice manuals heap blame on pregnant women and collude in perpetuating the regulation of pregnant women's bodies, therein pointing to the insidious potential in her every choice, thought, and feeling.

In this capacity, the womb is imagined as dangerous territory where an impressionable fetus is subject to its mother's physical, emotional, and psychological whims (Mazzoni). Psychiatrist and psychotherapist Rosemary Balsam has attempted to challenge this notion of the womb as a place of peril by pointing to the importance of the pregnant body in a young girl's mental representation of her bodily self (1157). She explains how adult female patients report being impressed with postpubertal adult women as little girls, knowing they model the trajectory that their own bodies could take in adulthood. Thus, according to Balsam, girls frequently envision a future of "being a mommy," therein modelling their physical identities after their mothers' bodies (1158). As adults, women in therapy similarly reveal how their mothers' pregnant bodies are intricately woven into their psyche (1177). This is just one example of how the pregnant mother can be a building block of the female daughter's body image, rather than a hindrance to it.

CONCLUSION

As we have illustrated in this chapter, mothers are routinely scrutinized by the psychological gaze in academia, popular culture, and everyday social relations, all of which contribute to the pathologizing of girls and women of all ages (Burman 4). A myopic focus on mothers as the sole and primary variable in determining their daughters' sexual, reproductive, and psychological development serves to legitimize and perpetuate mother-blame as a widespread cultural practice. In this way, the mother-blame game negates the social, political, and economic barriers that constrain girls' and women's access to bodily knowledge and agency in a patriarchal culture.

In contrast, honouring the empowering potentials of the mother-daughter bond, while acknowledging the social forces that constrain it, is a critical step forward in challenging the prevalence of mother-blame. In the context of academic psychology, researchers can strive to achieve this goal by mindfully and thoroughly contextualizing mother-daughter dialogue within specific cultural and historical contexts, just as they may resist simplistic discourses which construct mothers as the key determinants of daughters' life outcomes. Similarly, the mother-daughter relationship needs to be studied as a bi-directional construct wherein a dynamic interaction occurs between mothers and daughter across space and time. Finally, future research must address the qualitative experiences of mothers themselves as they attempt to engage with their daughters concerning matters of health, sexuality, and female corporeality.

ENDNOTES

[1]This essay was written by four women from the United States of varying ethnic and socioeconomic backgrounds. Although using terms such as *the West* can be problematic, we use this term here to contextualize our experiences as women in a particular geographic and cultural context. We acknowledge that our experience is not shared by all women in Western nations.

[2]For examples, see Andrea O'Reilly, Judith Jordan, Andrea Kaplan, Janet Surrey, Paula Caplan.

[3]A striking example of this can be seen in a paper by Mastergeorge et al. which examines how maternal self-esteem predicts infant emotional reactivity (387). Empirical studies such as this are hardly "bidirectional," as the mother's subjectivity is still adversely impacting the infant.

[4]Although there are mothers of various cultural backgrounds that see menstruation as a milestone to be celebrated and an indicator of the transition to motherhood, the overall prevailing discourse in the West views menstruation as a medical event (Hansen 125; Ussher 16).

[5]The term *the Other* is used here to describe what is considered different in juxtaposition to established social norms. If the male form is seen as a "given," the female form is considered alien. In the seminal feminist text *The Second Sex*, Simone de Beauvoir uses the term *the Other* to locate women's bodies within Western cultural discourse. Quoting Michelet she stated, "She is defined and differentiated with reference to man and not he with reference to her; she is the incidental, the inessential as opposed to the essen-

31

tial. He is the Subject, he is the Absolute—she is the Other" (5).
[6]A contemporary and particularly personal example of this is described in author and menstrual activist Chris Bobel's book *New Blood*. There she voices her own attempt to acknowledge and celebrate her daughter's menarche, only to be turned down by her embarrassed daughter.
[7]For more on ecological systems theory and biological theories of human development, see Bronfenbrenner's theory of human development in which an individual's entire ecological system is taken into account, thereby challenging unidirectional flows of influence from mother to daughter.

WORKS CITED

Balsam, Rosemary. "The Vanished Pregnant Body in Psychoanalytic Female Developmental Theory." *Journal of the American Psychoanalytic Association* 51.4 (2003): 1153-1179. Print.

Beauvoir, Simone de. *The Second Sex.* New York: Vintage Books, 2011. Print.

Bobel, Chris. *New Blood: Third-Wave Feminism and the Politics of Menstruation.* New Brunswick: Rutgers University Press, 2010. Print.

Bronfenbrenner, Urie. *Making Human Beings Human: Bioecological Perspectives on Human Development.* Thousand Oaks: Sage, 2005. Print.

Burman, Erica. *Deconstructing Developmental Psychology.* New York: Routledge, 2007. Print.

Caplan, Paula. *The New Don't Blame Mother: Mending the Mother-Daughter Relationship.* New York: Routledge, 2000. Print.

Costos, Daryl, Ruthie Ackerman and Lisa Paradis. "Recollections of Menarche: Communication Between Mothers and Daughters Regarding Menstruation." *Sex Roles* 46 (2011): 49-59. Print.

Deutsch, Helene. *The Psychology of Women: Volume I, Girlhood.* New York: Bantam Books, 1944. Print.

Du Bois, William Edward Burghardt. *The Souls of Black Folk.* Oxford: Oxford University Press, 1903. Print.

Fassino, Secondo, Giovanni Abbate-Daga, Federico Amianto, Federico Facchini and Giovanni Giacomo Rovera. "Eating Psychopathology and Personality in Eating Disorders." *Epidemiologia e Psichiatria Sociale* 12.04 (2003): 293-300. Print.

Fox, Greer Litton. "The Mother-Adolescent Daughter Relationship as a Sexual Socialization Structure: A Research Review." *Family Relations* 29.1 (1980): 21-28. Print.

Fromm-Reichman, Freida. "Notes on the Development of Treatment of Schizophrenics by Psychoanalytic Psychotherapy." *Psychiatry: Interpersonal and Biological Processes* 11.3 (1948): 263-273. Print.

Grosz, E A. *Volatile Bodies: Toward a Corporeal Feminism.* Bloomington: Indiana University Press, 1994. Print.

Hansen, M. "The Subtle Trauma." *Fragments of Trauma and the Social Production of Suffering.* Ed. Michael O'Loughlin and Marilyn Charles. Lanham: Rowman and Littlefield, 2014. 149-168. Print.

Houppert, K. *The Curse: Confronting the Last Unmentionable Taboo: Menstruation.* New York: Farrar, Straus, and Giroux, 1999. Print.

Inazu, Judith K. and Greer Litton Fox. "Maternal Influence on the Sexual Behaviour of Teenage Daughters." *Journal of Family Issues* 1.1 (1980): 81-102. Print.

Jaccard, James, Patricia J. Dittus and Vivian V. Gordon. "Maternal Correlates of Adolescent Sexual and Contraceptive Behaviour." *Family Planning Perspectives* 28.4 (1996): 159-185. Print.

Johnston-Robledo, I. and Joan C. Chrisler. "The Menstrual Mark: Menstruation as Social Stigma." *Sex Roles* 1-2 (2013): 9-18. Print.

Johnston-Robledo, Ingrid, Kristin Sheffield, Jacqueline Voigt and Jennifer Wilcox-Constantine. "Reproductive Shame: Self-Objectification and Young Women's Attitudes Toward their Reproductive Functioning." *Women & Health* 46.1 (2007): 25-39. Print.

Jordan, Judith V., and Janet L. Surrey. "The Self-in-Relation: Empathy and the Mother-Daughter Relationship." *The Psychology of Today's Woman: New Psychoanalytic Visions.* Eds. Toni Bernay and Dorothy Cantor. Hillsdale: Analytic, 1986. 81-104. Print.

Jordan, Judith V., Janet L. Surrey, and Alexandra G. Kaplan. *Women and Empathy: Implications for Psychological Development and Psychotherapy.* Wellesley: Stone Center for Developmental Services and Studies, Wellesley College, 1983. Print.

Lee, Janet and Jennifer Sasser-Coen. *Blood Stories*. New York: Routledge, 1996. Print.

Lende, Daniel. "Fetal Origins: In the Womb, In the News." *Neuroanthropology: Understanding the Encultured Brain and Body*. Public Library of Science (PLOS) Blog. 30 Sept. 2010. Web. 11 Aug. 2015.

Lipman-Blumen, J. "How Ideology Shapes Women's Lives." *Scientific American* 226 (1972): 34-52. Print.

Madsen, Pamela. "Mothers and Daughters: Sexuality and 'The Mother Wound': We Can Break the Legacy and Cycle." *Psychology Today*. 23 Jan. 2014. Web. June 10, 2014.

Malhotra, Mahima, Kumar Deepak and Rohit Verma. "Effect of Psychosocial Environment in Children Having Mother with Schizophrenia." *Psychiatry Research* 226.2. (2015): 418-424. Print.

Mastergeorge, Ann M., Katherine Paschall, Sophie R. Loeb, and Ashley Dixon. "The Still-Face Paradigm and Bidirectionality: Associations with Maternal Sensitivity, Self-Esteem and Infant Emotional Reactivity." *Infant Behaviour and Development* 37.3 (2014): 387-397. Print.

McFadden, Joyce T. *Your Daughter's Bedroom: Insights for Raising Confident Women*. New York: St. Martin's Press, 2011. Print.

McWilliams, Nancy. *Psychoanalytic Case Formulation*. New York: Guilford Press, 1999. Print.

Murcott, Anne. "The Social Construction of Teenage Pregnancy: A Problem in the Ideologies of Childhood and Reproduction." *Sociology of Health & Illness* 2.1 (1980): 1-23. Print.

Mazzoni, Cristina. *Maternal Impressions: Pregnancy and Childbirth in Literature and Theory*. Ithaca: Cornell University Press, 2001. Print.

Northrup, Christiane. *Mother Daughter Wisdom*. Carlsbad: Hay House, 2006. Print.

O'Reilly, Andrea, ed. *Mother Outlaws: Theories and Practices of Empowered Mothering*. Toronto: Women's Press, 2004. Print.

O'Reilly, Andrea. *From Motherhood to Mothering: The Legacy of Adrienne Rich's Of Woman Born*. Albany: SUNY Press, 2012. Print.

Schooler, D., L. M. Ward, A. Merriwether and A. S. Caruthers

"Cycles of Shame: Menstrual Shame, Body Shame, and Sexual Decision Making." *Journal of Sex Research* 42.4 (2005): 324-334. Print.

Seeman, Mary. "The Changing Role of Mother of the Mentally Ill: From Schizophrenogenic Mother to Multigenerational Caregiver." *Psychiatry* 72.3 (2009): 284-294. Print.

"Spears Tells How Jamie Lynn Revealed Pregnancy." *USA Today* 17 Sept. 2008. Web. 11 Aug. 2015.

Stein, Martin. "Developmental Pathway to Depression in Children of Mothers with Postpartum Depression." *Journal Watch: Pediatrics & Adolescent Medicine.* 15 Jun. 2011. Web. 11 Aug. 2015.

Stubbs, Margaret L. and Daryl Costos. "Negative Attitudes Toward Menstruation." *Women & Therapy* 27.3-4 (2004): 37-54. Print.

Surrey, Janet. "The Mother-Daughter Relationship: Themes in Psychotherapy." *Daughtering and Mothering: Female Subjectivity Reanalysed.* Eds. Janneke Van Mens-Verhulst, Karlein Schreurs and Liesbeth Woeterman. London: Routledge. 1993. 114-124. Print.

Ussher, J. M. *Managing the Monstrous Feminine: Regulating the Reproductive Body.* New York: Routledge, 2006. Print.

Vander Ven, Thomas, and Marikay Vander Ven. "Exploring Patterns of Mother-Blaming in Anorexia Scholarship: A Study in the Sociology of Knowledge." *Human Studies* 26.1 (2003): 97-119. Print.

Winnicott, Donald Woods. *The Maturational Processes and the Facilitating Environment.* New York: International Universities Press, 1965. Print.

2.
Breastfeeding Shame
and the Birth of the Mother

CATHERINE ROBINSON

T HIS CHAPTER RESPONDS TO intensifying calls for research on the experience and lived practice of breastfeeding and, in particular, for research engaging with lesser told narratives of breastfeeding *struggle*. These calls emerge at the height of debate about the future of science-based breastfeeding promotion, which has to date gained important ground for women in establishing infants' rights to receive "the best start to life" through exclusive breastfeeding until six months. Growing interest in the unintended *negative* impacts of this infant-focused approach, however, has been in part sparked by a persistent group of scholars prepared to engage with and acknowledge maternal physical, emotional, and psychological suffering associated with breastfeeding struggle. This is a form of maternal suffering sharpened in an environment in which every new mother now knows "breast is best." Contextualized by current debates over breastfeeding promotion, this chapter shifts to a more sustained and personal account of the emotional dynamics of breastfeeding failure.

SET UP TO FAIL? WOMEN AND BREASTFEEDING PROMOTION

Debates in recent academic literature about breastfeeding promotion may be understood to reflect uncertainty about the benefits that breastmilk offers *mothers* (see Hausman "Politics of Feminism"; Taylor; Wolf "Politics of Dissent"). Persistently low rates of exclusive breastfeeding in the United States, the United Kingdom, and Australia have prompted critical reassessment of an historic eagerness to harness scientific evidence in breastfeeding promotion. Such ambivalence has reopened breastfeeding research and advocacy to wider, non-medical input and leadership, including from feminist midwifery, health and women's studies, cultural studies, and the political and social sciences more generally. As a growing range of commentators now discuss, in the context of breastfeeding, scientific evidence has benefited infants but not necessarily the mothers needed to deliver breastmilk. Indeed, the well-intended focus on infants' rights to *receive* the best nutrition, rather than on mothers' rights to *provide* the best nutrition, is understood to frame an explosive political scenario in which the structural capacity of mothers to breastfeed is withheld, but the knowledge that they must strive to do so is not.

The "breast is best" message nonetheless remains a hard-fought platform of infant and maternal health advocacy. In nations such as the United States, Australia, and the United Kingdom, however, a critical analysis of the social, cultural, and political context in which this message proliferates must be taken up. In *Is Breast Best?*, Joan Wolff discusses how individuals shoulder lonely responsibility for delivering scientifically devised and socially beneficial health outcomes in neoliberal contexts. Conditions are thus overripe for individuals to be blamed for poor health outcomes despite the unequal opportunities and support available for them to engage meaningfully in health-promoting behaviour. As argued by Taylor and Wallace, the neoliberal environment frames extremely powerful personal experiences of breastfeeding failure in which mothers who cannot achieve officially recommended breastfeeding goals reconceptualise themselves not only as failed mothers but also as failed *women* (see also Hegney, Fallon and O'Brien; Lee).

Laden with risk-talk, neoliberal breastfeeding culture arguably silences public discussion and public acknowledgement of women's experiences of breastfeeding difficulty, their struggle to meet specified breastfeeding benchmarks, and their rights to choose not to breastfeed at all. As a result, debate has begun to arise about how best to promote breastfeeding and support breastfeeding women without creating a counterproductive and competitive atmosphere in which breastfeeding outcomes at an individual or national scale feed currents of mother-shame and mother-blame.

The field of breastfeeding research addressing nations such as Australia and the United States is currently charged with calls to re-think ageing strategies of breastfeeding promotion on the basis of their limited success in protecting women's bodily autonomy, as well as their lack of sensitivity to women's needs when they struggle to breastfeed (see Schmied, Sheehan and Barclay; Taylor and Wallace; Williams et al.). This is a situation which points to the need to think through how *women's* bodily experiences might count for more in public policy, in the deployment of biomedical evidence, and in multidisciplinary practices of maternal support.

Feminist breastfeeding advocacy offers promising leads in re-orienting public policy away from medically-focused promotion in which the needs of infants' bodies problematically stand in for and elide those of women's bodies. Presumably the invisibility of women's bodies has historically made a physical and political focus on the infant's body an attractive path to pursue—again, there has undoubtedly been recognizable mileage, particularly during the current era of early intervention, in advocating that breast is "best for *baby.*" Nonetheless, the reinforcement of women's invisibility and their reduction to the well-formed breast on pro-motional posters powerfully represents the belief that mothers' bodies only exist to meet their infants' needs; in reality, women's bodies carry a range of responsibilities that radically tie them to *multiple* others. This is a paradoxical situation which promotes breastfeeding but does little to support women in overcoming the physical and structural barriers that may prevent them from breastfeeding their children.

In response to this conundrum, feminist breastfeeding advocacy has developed a clearer focus on reproductive justice for women, that is, a focus on women's social, cultural, and political rights to fully experience the reproductive difference that breastfeeding is. Enabling women's bodily access to their infants through the provision of legally mandated paid maternity leave and more sensi-tively accounting for women's diverse experiences of breastfeeding are both central to current feminist concerns. As I suggest in this chapter, however, a more nuanced account of diverse breastfeed-ing experiences and needs is still required. In turn, it is likely that deeper consideration of breastfeeding diversity will frame a more radical role for the promotion of *inclusive* breastfeeding practices that incorporate alternative feeding strategies—such as the use of expressed milk, donor milk, shared milk, and formula—and that support women to sustain non-exclusive breastfeeding in contexts of physical and emotional struggle, domestic violence, illness, and disability.

Speculation about future breastfeeding advocacy and promotion aside, it is certain that the development of women-focused breastfeeding strategies requires clearer, cross-cultural pictures of the lived realities of infant feeding, including the conflict that infant-focused breastfeeding promotion can produce in mothers' lives. Whilst research has addressed the health, social, cultural, and geographic inequalities that structure feeding possibilities and choices (see Blum), a much smaller body of research documents the experiences of those women who internalize and actively commit to infant-focused breastfeeding goals but who then unexpectedly struggle to breastfeed. While it perhaps seems more likely that this is the fate of a minority group of well-educated women with access to extended maternity leave (for example, of six months or more) or other forms of significant financial support which make the naturalization of breastfeeding possible, these women's stories provide another important insight into the broader social, cultural, and political dynamics of how experiences of maternal failure are generated and lived.

THE BIRTH OF THE MOTHER

It is with an acute awareness of political debates over breastfeeding promotion that I now address the growing body of research on breastfeeding failure and its impacts on maternal identity. I became interested in this area of research following my own physical struggles with breastfeeding and subsequently with postnatal depression. Through framing storied fragments of my own difficult breastfeeding journey in the blurred role and voice of an academic mother, I aim to contribute to the multidisciplinary literature which renders the experience of breastfeeding failure a significant flashpoint for reflection on the ethics of breastfeeding promotion and contemporary frames of maternal identity.

This chapter may be understood as a brief foray into the diverse emotions and practices attached to breastfeeding struggle, as well as a prelude to my current research exploring *other* women's experiences of struggle. In a context in which little work focuses in detail on women's felt experiences of breastfeeding struggle (for exceptional examples although see Kellehear; Palmér et al.; Williamson et al.), this short chapter contributes to the genre of *écriture feminine*, as well as to the larger political project of publicly troubling "personal" breastfeeding experiences (for other examples see Crossley; McCaughey; Shah).

My own difficult breastfeeding journey began in a relatively wealthy part of Sydney in 2008 with the birth of my first child and would continue, albeit for different reasons, with the birth of my second child in 2011. Unlike some other Western nations, it would be safe to observe that Australia has a proudly and overtly pro-breastfeeding culture. Sheehan and Schmied go further to argue that "in Australia there is now a well-constructed cultural imperative to breastfeed" (55). It has a National Breastfeeding Strategy 2010-2015 (Commonwealth of Australia), a government-paid parental leave scheme of eighteen weeks (introduced in 2011), and a National Infant Feeding Survey that shows a low rate of exclusive breastfeeding—15.4 percent of babies are exclusively breastfed until six months (Australian Institute of Health and Welfare 9), which is nonetheless among the very highest rates of OECD nations (Commonwealth of Australia 11). I considered myself extremely fortunate to give birth in a woman-centred hospital that was officially accredited under the UNICEF and World Health Organisation's "Baby-Friendly Health Initiative."

Curiously, it was in this progressive, well-serviced metropolitan environment that I came into new and intense experiences of maternal failure. In my particular case, these were initially framed through the failure to exclusively breastfeed, which is a maternal failure read through the synecdoche of the breastfeeding breast (Nadesan and Sotirin 229). These experiences led me to become particularly interested in how the contemporary mother is born through the breast and to think about what kind of mother is born in the context of the *failure* to successfully establish breastfeeding.

I begin with the core observation that, during my experiences of breastfeeding struggle, the kind of mother I became was shrunken to my questionable production of milk, as well as to the "poor attachment" of my baby to my breast. Although milk was not the only thing I supplied to my baby and breast attachment was not the only physical connection I established with him, it quickly became clear how key these indicators were to mothering success. As I encountered it, breastfeeding was not only critical in sustaining my baby's life but was also a central aspect of reproducing and performing maternal identity and, in particular, a physically attached and bountiful motherhood (see Swanson et al.). Thus the wide reverberations of feeding problems entirely overwhelmed whatever other moments of mothering and motherhood I may also have experienced.

Following what I experienced as a traumatic instrumental delivery, my baby boy was not interested in feeding for about three days, as was recorded in my hospital notes. The so-called "critical" first feed following delivery never happened. My early experiences of breastfeeding on the postnatal ward included two midwives grappling with both my breasts, trying to position them to invite a good latch from the baby that they were simultaneously trying to operate. Failing this, I sat stripped to the waist on a small chair while another midwife squeezed colostrum from my now engorged breasts onto a white plastic spoon. I also recall, after yet more nipple damage, two nightshift midwives stopping to talk to me as I shuffled the ward with my crying baby. They asked if they might look at the shape of my nipples, and I dumbly stood in the hallway and lifted my top so my breasts could be turned up to the fluorescent light. "Oh," said one, "they're not *that* flat." Thus began my nine-month fight to sustain some kind of breastfeeding relationship with my boy.

After giving birth, mothers engage with the overwhelming new form of the just-born baby; however, as breastfeeding mothers, they also encounter and inhabit their *own* newly constituted bodies. This is often a confronting if nonetheless ordinary experience. The materializing of the perinatal breast only through varying elements of its possible dysfunction is thus a raw experience indeed, especially in a context where it has already been made clear that there are "no morally liveable options" by which to nourish a baby outside of breastfeeding (Kukla, "Ethics and Ideology" 177). In this way, the precarious breast puts the *whole* performance of motherhood at risk—a squeezing, shoving, crying mother and an arching, twisting, distressed infant are difficult to witness by intimate others in private, let alone by a public in more accessible spaces such as shopping centres or, worse, mothers' groups.

As I discovered, having a baby in my care was simply not enough to produce the "mother-effect," neither as a public performance nor as a convincingly felt dimension of self- and body-hood. Given the assumption that every mother has enough milk to feed her baby, the first four months of my boy's life were peppered with interactions with a range of acutely puzzled professionals who could not determine what was wrong—first with me and second with my baby. As it turned out, my boy was diagnosed with gas-tro-oesophageal reflux and a suspiciously high palate, and I was diagnosed with nipple vasospasm—but not before I was thoroughly introduced to the astonishing world of breastfeeding struggle. I was stuffed full of medication (Motilium), alternative health reme-dies (breastfeeding teas and herbal milk supply supplements), and homemade milk supply-promoting biscuits. I also began a regimen of breast-pumping and sterilising and was armed with a supply line, cabbage leaves, nipple shields, nipple repair creams, fungal creams, heat packs, two kinds of breastfeeding pillows, and at least three kinds of feeding bottles apparently designed to repli-cate the shape of my nipples. All the while, hidden in my kitchen cupboard—which I privately and only half-jokingly referred to as "the cupboard of shame"—stood an accusatory, gleaming tin of powdered S26 artificial milk.

I engaged in endless note-taking, recording extra amounts of pumped milk and formula milk being given as well as alternatively trying to decipher if my boy's incessant shouting meant that he was starving or simply reacting to the milk he was receiving. I also participated in two early parenting groups, attended a breastfeeding support group, received the close support of child and family nurses at my public early childhood health centre, saw excellent public lactation consultants at a specialist service at my local hospital, and was visited by a private lactation consultant in my home. Our family doctors saw me for multiple considerations of questionable milk supply and breast infection, and they monitored my baby's weight gain and physical distress after feeding. My local pharmacist was kept busy renewing pump-hire tickets and filling scripts for Motilium and antibiotics for mastitis (breast infection), along with medication for my baby's gastro-oesophageal reflux. When I finally decided to invest in my own double-kit breast pump, I was offered an overly generous discount. Although I was sincerely thankful, I never went back there again.

BREASTFEEDING SHAME

These experiences have led me to consider how the physical failure of breastfeeding immediately throws into relief the intricate enmeshment of the physiological and emotional landscape of the body with its broader socio-cultural and geographical one. When the biomedical and socio-cultural message "breast is best" is fiercely and effectively marketed, it should be expected that the physical trauma of breastfeeding difficulty will also be understood and experienced as emotional trauma. However, while breastfeeding is so resolutely understood and promoted as a vitally layered physical, socio-cultural, and emotional practice in the context of *success*, the latter two dimensions seem to remain largely ignored in the context of *unsuccessful* breastfeeding. Thus women are schooled in the hopes and benefits of breastfeeding, such as lasting bonds of infant love, physical prowess, and personal empowerment, yet they are given few tools to negotiate the inverse and devastatingly felt physical, socio-cultural, and emotional impacts of divergent experience. In light of the risks that ambivalent or damaging experiences are assumed to pose for the broader promotion of exclusive breastfeeding (Knaak 414; Maushart 157; Wall 599), women are supported only in their fight for milk, if at all, and are left to make the long and conflicted fight for the crumbs of maternal status and identity on their own. In my breastfeeding journey I was fortunate enough to have comprehensive *lactation* support, but I found myself adrift in managing my crumbling confidence, self-esteem, and self-identity. In fact, I often experienced a sense of my newly dysfunctional breasts as consuming or dwarfing the rest of my body, and this was exacerbated by the numerous breast-focused interactions that had so quickly replaced my previous public embodiment as a non-breastfeeding woman and academic with a busy lecturing schedule.

These experiences have also led me to observe how physiological breastfeeding strife is nonetheless powerfully articulated through reversals of the socio-cultural and emotional hopes for successful breastfeeding. Although the support I received focused on the physiological experience of breastfeeding failure, this failure was also clearly read as a socio-cultural and emotional one. The melding of such dimensions generated the exclamation of a postnatal ward junior midwife who, upon observing my boy screaming and arching away from my breast, said "Oh look, he's rejecting you!" Here the physical failure of nipple attachment and the physiological failure of milk letdown slip so easily into the social and emotional dimensions of failed mother/infant bonding. This is a slip which may confirm a mother's secret fear of inadequacy (see Swanson et al.). The rejection of the second-best breast becomes a rejection of the second-best mother and, perhaps, reflects wider classed and racialized rejections of stigmatized, bottle-feeding mothers in a cultural climate of "total motherhood" with breastfeeding exclusivity at its heart (Wolf, *Is Breast Best?*).

At the time of my struggle, it was assumed by everyone around me that I was understandably sad and anxious, that I would feel like a failure, and that I would blame myself. All the while I was also perpetually—and therefore unconvincingly—reminded that somehow I was still a good mother. I experienced self-torturous sorrow for not delivering the optimal conditions for mother-infant bonding, which put me at enormous risk of transgressing the key exhortation that a "happy mother means a happy baby" (see Williams et al.). Some health professionals thought to cheer me up by shifting blame from my breasts to my baby but, given that I still could not maintain exclusive breastfeeding, this just added a "second-best" baby to my growing list of inadequacies. In this way, I was burdened with the doubled existential expectations of sorrow *and* happiness, and the serious depression and anxiety generated by breastfeeding struggle were not addressed in any depth until several years later.

The breastfeeding breast is thus made readable precisely *through* the powerful alignment of its physiological, socio-cultural, and emotional dimensions and also through its geographic and temporal placement. In the 1960s, for example, the breast was largely rendered unreadable as a breastfeeding breast (and perhaps *more* readable as a sexual breast, as the coincidental emergence of breast-augmentation surgery might suggest) and bottle-feeding was at its height as normative practice (Maclean 8). In contrast, in 2008, in a pro-breastfeeding culture and in a hospital specifically promoting breastfeeding only, my internal and external breastfeeding physiology was graspable in a wholly new way. Prenatally and perinatally, I was instructed only in the mechanics and routines of breastfeeding. While the tiring physical workload of breastfeeding life was made clear, at no point was it ever suggested that breastfeeding could produce shattering and prolonged pain and damage or that it could fail as an exclusive practice; nor was it mentioned that other feeding options even existed. Staggeringly, it also never occurred to me to make such enquiries. Tiredness aside, I was prepared to feel nothing but overwhelming joy, connection, and contentment with my baby at my breast.

BREASTFEEDING PROMOTION AND NEOLIBERAL RISK CULTURE

Whilst historians clearly show that infant feeding has always been at the core of the production and management of maternal feeling—whether this has entailed the promotion and normalization of breastfeeding, bottle-feeding, wet-nursing, or early solids— my specific breasts were born in a feeding moment constructed through the happy alignment of romantic maternalism ("breast") and contemporary medical science ("best") (Nadesan and Sotirin 22). As Wolf argues in *Is Breast Best?*, in neoliberal risk culture, breastfeeding is imagined not just as a practice critical to *motherhood* but also as a broader public health body project that is critical to successful *self*hood and responsible citizenship (66-69). In performing "the natural," and in performing their healthy "choice" of the natural, breastfeeding women access powerfully positive experiences of themselves as disciplined, morally responsible *subjects* (see Murphy) who work to ensure excellent outcomes for their infants and society at large.

However, these experiences rely on the selective naturalization of breastfeeding access and ease. They also produce the figure of the "Other Mother" (Michaels) who is accused of opting for artificially fed "stupid, fat and poisoned" children (Barston 118) because of selfish egoism or uneducated naivety. Rendered in need of state regulation and intervention, the Other Mother, who is presumably as stupid, fat, and poisoned as her children will be, does important work in evidencing the superiority of the slim, white, breastfeeding body and its healthy, adjusted offspring (see Andrews and Knaak 105). As such, it is no longer socially and culturally assumed that resorting to artificial feeding will produce guilt. Instead, in the current climate, the failure to exclusively breastfeed is understood, as research reveals, to cause profound and long-lived *shame* (Labbok; Taylor and Wallace).

Working with a map of subjectivity as dispersed through the body thus enables the clearer appreciation of how negatively charting physiological flaws in powerfully symbolic body parts necessarily entails powerfully symbolic and damaging *self*-transformation (see Palmer et al). In the context of breastfeeding failure, women suddenly find themselves with "second-best" breasts, second-best letdown reflexes, second-best maternal identities, and even second-best babies, whose health and development are already believed to be compromised by questionable breastmilk supply or risky artificial milk. In this context, breastfeeding becomes an *"existential issue"* (Palmér et al. 8, emphasis added) that is burdened with so much expectant joy that its *hurt* remains unspeakable yet totalizing.

TOWARD A WOMEN-FOCUSED, INCLUSIVE BREASTFEEDING DISCOURSE

While I agree with Bernice Hausman that biomedical discourses on breastfeeding remain central in articulating the biological power of women's breastfeeding work ("Mother's Milk" 232), it is also necessary to consider the growing medical evidence about maternal breastfeeding *distress*. This includes the documented connections between breastfeeding struggle and the consequent development of postnatal distress and depression (see Cooke, Schmied and Sheehan; Dennis and McQueen; Shakespeare, Blake and Garcia; Watkins et al.). Given where my own breastfeeding journey eventually led, I do have a particular interest in this literature and especially in recent findings demonstrating increased risks of postnatal depression for mothers who intend to breastfeed but encounter unexpected difficulties in doing so (see Borra, Iacovou and Sevilla).

As discussed at the beginning of this chapter, I also share the feminist perspective that direct political engagement with the social and cultural framing of women's bodies and feelings will most likely provide a solution to these issues. The question then becomes one of how a range of medical evidence can be used to support the development of *complex*, women-focused breastfeeding promotion; just as there is no single moral truth about the "goodness" of breastfeeding there is no single biomedical truth either. An inability to breastfeed need not lead to varying orders of blame, shame, and sadness, unless these are affective forces directly being galvanized in the production and governance of "fetishized" mothering practices (Kukla, "Mass Hysteria" 180). This is where ethical responsibility for breastfeeding promotion becomes a pointed issue and a renewed focus on women's diverse lived realities becomes critical for increasing breastfeeding rates. It is doubtful that exclusivity was ever a part of ancient or early modern breastfeeding cultures, so it would seem a brutal request to insist that women make the attempt to *invent* this practice under the exacting economic, social, and cultural conditions of neoliberal capitalism. Rather, given that women's bodily diversity *has* always existed, it would seem sensible to openly acknowledge and actively account for this diversity through realistic and inclusive breastfeeding promotion.

Australian midwifery academics Atheena Sheehan and Virginia Schmied call for a shift away from infant-focused breastfeeding promotion and towards the provision of individualized care that can account for and respond to women's diverse personal experiences and contexts (70). Whilst this perspective makes sense from a practice perspective, I will add that there is still a significant need to promote breastfeeding in ways that take *social and cultural care* of women. Such promotion would centrally focus on state-sponsored paid maternity leave and publicly sanction complex strategies of feeding that move away from breastfeeding exclusivity and instead focus on supporting the best breastfeeding practice a woman can muster. Such promotion would also give critical consideration to the particularly limiting conditions of physical and emotional struggle, domestic violence, illness, and disability.

Indeed the future of breastfeeding support and increasing stagnant breastfeeding rates may lie in more broadly conceptualised *women's feeding support*. As an alternative to neighbourhood breastfeeding groups, inclusive feeding support groups could generate spaces of physical and emotional safety and access to health education, specialist advice, and peer-exchange respectful of the multiple feeding practices that women engage in, including breastfeeding, supply-line feeding, bottle-feeding, milk-sharing, donor-milk use, hand-and pump-expressing, formula feeding, non-human milk and solids use, and more. Such spaces may enable women to meet in their diversity and to share in the stress, time-consuming labour, knowledges, and pleasure of the embodied commitment that all feeding relationships demand.

WORKS CITED

Andrews, Therese and Stephanie Knaak. "Medicalized Mothering: Experiences with Breastfeeding in Canada and Norway." *The Sociological Review* 61.1 (2013): 88-110. Print.

Australian Institute of Health and Welfare (AIHW). 2010. *Australian National Infant Feeding Survey: Indicator Results*. Canberra: AIHW, 2011. Print.

Bartson, Susan. *Bottled Up: How the Way We Feed Babies Has Come to Define Motherhood, and Why It Shouldn't*. Berkeley: University of California Press, 2012. Print.

Blum, Linda M. *At the Breast: Ideologies of Breastfeeding and Motherhood in the Contemporary United States*. Boston: Beacon Press, 1999: Print.

Borra, Cristina, Maria Iacovou, and Almudena Sevilla. "New Evidence on Breastfeeding and Postpartum Depression: The Importance of Understanding Women's Intentions." *Maternal and Child Health Journal* (2014): n. pag. Web. 30 Aug. 2014.

Commonwealth of Australia. *Australian National Breastfeeding*

Strategy 2010-2015. Canberra: Australian Government Department of Health and Ageing, 2009. Print.

Cooke, Margaret, Virginia Schmied, and Atheena Sheehan. "An Exploration of the Relationship between Postnatal Distress and Maternal Role Attainment, Breastfeeding Problems and Breast Feeding Cessation in Australia." *Midwifery* 23.1 (2007): 66-76. Print.

Crossley, Michelle L. "Breastfeeding as a Moral Imperative: An Autoethnographic Study." *Feminism and Psychology* 19: 1 (2009): 71-87. Print.

Dennis, Cindy-Lee and Karen McQueen. "Does Maternal Postpartum Depressive Symptomatology Influence Infant Feeding Outcomes?" *Acta Paediatrica* 96.4 (2007): 590-594. Print.

Hausman, Bernice L. "Breastfeeding, Rhetoric, and the Politics of Feminism." *Journal of Women, Politics & Policy* 34: 4 (2013): 330-344. Print. [not cited in text]

Hausman, Bernice L. *Mother's Milk: Breastfeeding Controversies in American Culture*. New York: Routledge, 2003. Print.

Hegney, Desley, Tony Fallon, and Maxine O'Brien. "Against All Odds: A Retrospective Case-Controlled Study of Women Who Experienced Extraordinary Breastfeeding Problems." *Journal of Clinical Nursing* 17.9 (2008): 1182-1192. Print.

Kellehear, Christa. "The Physical Challenges of Early Breastfeeding." *Social Science and Medicine* 63.12 (2006): 2727-2738. Print.

Knaak, Stephanie J. "The Problem with Breastfeeding Discourse." *Canadian Journal of Public Health* 97.5 (2006): 412-414. Print.

Kukla, Rebecca. "Ethics and Ideology in Breastfeeding Advocacy Campaigns." *Hypatia* 21: 1 (2006): 157-180. Print

Kukla, Rebecca. *Mass Hysteria: Medicine, Culture and Mothers' Bodies*. Lanham: Rowman & Littlefield, 2005. Print.

Labbok, Miriam. "Exploration of Guilt among Mothers Who Do Not Breastfeed: The Physician's Role." *Journal of Human Lactation* 24.1 (2008): 80-84. Print.

Lee, Elli. "Health, Morality, and Infant Feeding: British Mothers' Experiences of Formula Milk Use in the Early Weeks." *Sociology of Health and Illness* 29.7 (2007): 1075-1090. Print.

Maclean, Helen. *Women's Experience of Breast Feeding*. Toronto: University of Toronto Press, 1990. Print.

Maushart, Susan. *The Mask of Motherhood: How Becoming a Mother Changes Our Lives and Why We Never Talk About It.* New York: Penguin, 2000. Print.

McCaughey, Martha. "Got Milk? Breastfeeding as an 'Incurably Informed' Feminist STS Scholar." *Science as Culture* 19.1 (2010): 79-100. Print.

Michaels, Meredith. "Other Mothers: Toward an Ethic of Post-maternal Practice." *Hypatia* 11.2 (1996): 49-70. Print.

Murphy, Elizabeth. "Risk, Responsibility, and Rhetoric in Infant Feeding." *Journal of Contemporary Ethnography* 29.3 (2000): 291-325. Print.

Nadesan, Majia H. and Patty Sotirin. "The Romance and Science of 'Breast is Best': Discursive Contradictions and Contexts of Breast-Feeding Choices." *Text and Performance Quarterly* 18.3 (1998): 217-232. Print.

Palmér, Lina, Gunilla Carlsson, Margareta Mollberg, and Maria Nyström. "Severe Breastfeeding Difficulties: Existential Lost-ness as a Mother—Women's Lived Experiences of Initiating Breastfeeding under Severe Difficulties." *International Journal of Qualitative Studies on Health and Well-Being* 7 (2012): n.p. Web. 26 Jun. 2014.

Schmied, Virginia, Atheena Sheehan, and Lesley Barclay. "Contemporary Breast-feeding Policy and Practice: Implications for Midwives." *Midwifery* 17.1 (2001): 44-54. Print.

Shah, Divya K. "Is Breast Always Best? A Personal Reflection on the Challenges of Breastfeeding." *Obstetrics and Gynecology* 121.4 (2013): 869-871. Print.

Shakespeare, Judy, Fiona Blake, and Jo Garcia. "Breast-feeding Difficulties Experienced by Women Taking Part in a Qualitative Interview Study of Postnatal Depression." *Midwifery* 20.3 (2004): 251-260. Print.

Sheehan, Atheena, and Virginia Schmied. "The Imperative to Breastfeed: An Australian Perspective." *Infant Feeding Practices: A Cross-Cultural Perspective.* Ed. Pranee Liamputtong. New York: Springer, 2011. 55-76. Print.

Swanson, Vivien, Helen Nicol, Rhona McInnes, Helen Cheyne, Helen Mactier, and Elizabeth Callander. "Developing Maternal Self-Efficacy for Feeding Pre-term Babies in then Neo-natal Unit."

Qualitative Health Research 22.10 (2012): 1369-1382. Print.

Taylor, Erin. "Leaving the Debate Over Science Behind: Questions to Consider." *Journal of Women, Politics & Policy* 34.4 (2013): 384-392. Print.

Taylor, Erin and Lora Wallace. "For Shame: Feminism, Breastfeeding Advocacy, and Maternal Guilt." *Hypatia* 27.1 (2012): 76-98. Print.

Wall, Glenda. "Moral Constructions of Motherhood in Breastfeeding Discourse." *Gender and Society* 15.4 (2001): 592-610. Print.

Watkins, Stephanie, Samantha Meltzer-Brody, Denniz Zolnoun, and Alison Stuebe. "Early Breastfeeding Experiences and Postpartum Depression." *Obstetrics and Gynecology* 118.2 (2011): 214-221. Print.

Williams, Kate, Tim Kurz, Mark Summers, and Shona Crabb. "Discursive Constructions of Infant Feeding: The Dilemma of Mothers' 'Guilt.'" *Feminism & Psychology* 23.3 (2012): 339-358. Print.

Williamson, Iain, Dawn Leeming, Steven Lyttle, and Sally Johnson. "'It Should Be the Most Natural Thing in the World': Exploring First-Time Mothers' Breastfeeding Difficulties in the UK Using Audio-diaries and Interviews." *Maternal and Child Nutrition* 8.4 (2012): 434-447. Print.

Wolf, Joan B. *Is Breast Best? Taking on the Breastfeeding Experts and the New High Stakes of Motherhood.* New York: New York University Press, 2011. Print.

Wolf, Joan B. "The Politics of Dissent." *Journal of Women, Politics & Policy* 34.4 (2013): 306-316. Print.

3.
Unfit Mothers?

Mother-Blame and the Moral Panic over "Obesity"

TRACY ROYCE

AFTER AN ECTOPIC PREGNANCY left Rachel Joint unlikely to ever be able to conceive, the UK resident and her husband Mark turned to adoption in 2004. But the adoption panel perceived one significant obstacle to Rachel becoming an adoptive mother. She recalls, "They hardly aimed any questions at Mark.... They grilled me about my weight. They told me I was obese. They asked if I thought I was physically able to look after children. They were brutal and wanted assurance I was going to do something about my size" (Donnelly).[1]

Perhaps more (in)famously, on the other side of the Atlantic in 2000, Adela Martinez's ninety-pound three-year-old daughter, Anamarie Regino, was forcibly removed from her home and placed in foster care by New Mexico officials (Susman). Anamarie was not returned to her mother until two months later. Not surprisingly, the state-sponsored separation was less effective at producing weight loss than it was at producing familial trauma. Reflecting on the separation more than a decade later, Martinez states, "Literally, it was two months of hell. It seemed like the longest two months of my life.... They say it's for the well-being of the child, but it did more damage than any money or therapy could ever to do to fix it" (Harris and Conley). Incidentally, after Anamarie's return, her weight—the reason for her removal from her mother—was diagnosed as having genetic causes.

Unfortunately, as recent cases have highlighted (see Barnett; Saguy and Gruys 232; Susman), Rachel's and Adela's maternal ordeals are not isolated incidents in their respective countries, nor are they relics of the backwardness of the first few years of the twenty-first century. Mothers of fat[2] children, along with fat mothers and prospective mothers, continue to find themselves the targets of social control and casualties in the so-called war on obesity (Boero, "Fat Kids" 113; Solovay 13-14, 73-74; Susman). The current discourses and policies associated with the "war on obesity" are understood by many scholars and activists involved in fat pride, body diversity, and/or size acceptance movements to be an all-out ideological assault on fat people. When fatness and the family intersect, such policies and discourses contribute to an especially hostile climate for mothers and would-be mothers.

The current era, characterized by what social scientists refer to as a "moral panic" over the size of people's bodies, makes mothers and prospective mothers especially vulnerable to social control and discrimination. Mothers of children deemed "overweight" or "obese" are targeted for sanctions (Boero, "Fat Kids" 113) and in some U.S. states are also at risk for intervention by child protective services agencies or even arrest and prosecution for child abuse or neglect (Barnett; Solovay 13-14, 73-74; Susman). Similarly, fat women are frequently treated as unsuitable candidates for adoption due to their body size (Vireday). In this way, anti-fat discourse has constructed fat mothers and mothers of fat children as categorically unfit.

FATNESS, MORAL PANIC, AND THE CONTEMPORARY CULTURAL CONTEXT OF BLAME

Of course, body size-related and/or weight-related blame is not reserved solely for mothers of fat children and fat mothers. The blaming and shaming of fat people is commonplace across a wide variety of social arenas.[3] In particular, fat people have been blamed as contributors to the high cost of medical care in the US (Landau) and elsewhere, even though data indicate that rising health care costs are attributable to multiple factors unrelated to fatness (Carroll; Saguy 22). Fat people have also been blamed for environmental destruction and climate change; a 2009 study published in the *International Journal of Epidemiology* argues that fat people require excessive amounts of transportation fuel for car travel (which results in greenhouse gas emissions) and food (the agricultural production of which also contributes to greenhouse gas emissions) (Edwards and Roberts 1137). Although Edwards and Roberts's statistical methodology has been questioned (Zeller), their widely publicized article appears to have succeeded in providing those who are already inclined to dislike fat people with an additional rationale for their prejudice. Perhaps even more disturbingly, after a grand jury recently failed to indict New York police officer Daniel Pantaleo for his involvement in the death of forty-three-year-old African American grandfather Eric Garner, Garner's weight became a topic of scrutiny. Republican Representative Peter King, who represents New York's second district, appeared on CNN, where he had the gall to attribute part of the blame for Garner's death not to racism and police brutality but to Garner's weight (Henderson).

The presence and prevalence of such fat-blaming discourse is hardly surprising in an era when mainstream media accounts both in the U.S. and abroad commonly frame fatness as a health crisis (Saguy, Gruys, and Gong 597-598) and ceaselessly circulate stories about the so-called obesity epidemic. Although concern about fatness pre-dates the twentieth century (Farrell 39), the term *obesity epidemic* emerged only recently in the 1990s (Boero, *Killer Fat* 2). At this time, the influential former U.S. Surgeon General C. Everett Koop launched a war against "obesity" in an effort to save the U.S. from itself, an act which he termed "his last crusade" (Loar). Koop stated: "We have to do something, because if you look at the shape of Americans, it's really almost grotesque.... We've been suffering from a new epidemic, an epidemic of disease and disability and death" (qtd. in Loar).

As exemplified here, Koop's rhetoric encapsulates several prominent features of the contemporary media war against fat bodies. First, Koop's use of the term *grotesque* is consistent with the negative reactions many people express when exposed to popular mainstream media images of fat people, who are typically depicted as headless bodies. These anonymous, dehumanized images, which UK scholar and activist Charlotte Cooper refers to as "headless fatties," are ever-present companions to print, video, and electronic media stories on the "obesity crisis" and appear designed to evoke in viewers the kind of disgust that helps fuel negative attitudes about fat people (Vartanian 1302). Perhaps more importantly, former Surgeon General Koop conflates fatness with "disease and disability and death" (Loar), a clumsy, imprecise collapsing of categories that is characteristic of media reports on what Koop labels an "epidemic." In addition to the above, mainstream media accounts of the "obesity crisis" typically attribute fatness to freely chosen behaviour—such as gluttony, sloth, or, at the very least, poor food choices—and assume that lasting weight loss is both desirable and achievable.

Sociologist Abigail Saguy and colleagues' recent research on mainstream media's "obesity crisis" reporting draws attention to how these issues are framed (Saguy and Almeling; Saguy, Frederick, and Gruys). They note that, "News reports on health topics reflect widely-held attitudes and also potentially *shape* attitudes about health risk and health policy" (emphasis mine; Saguy, Frederick, and Gruys 125). This is supported by the fact that, after much repetition by mainstream media outlets, Koop's assertions from two decades ago have now become conventional wisdom. However, researchers have countered that the frequently repeated claims that "obesity is an epidemic; that overweight and obesity are major contributors to mortality; that higher than average adiposity is pathological and a primary direct cause of disease; and that significant long-term weight loss is both medically beneficial and a practical goal" are poorly supported by scientific data (Campos et al. 55, 55-58).[4]

Taken together, the increase in media coverage of fatness (Campos et al. 58), the apocalyptic flavour of the rhetoric surrounding the discussion of fatness (Campos et al. 58; Farrell 9), and the way in which fat people are blamed for social problems suggest that the current media furor over weight and body size constitutes a "moral panic" (Campos et al. 58; Saguy 20). Moral panics occur under conditions of heightened concern about an alleged breakdown of morality, whereby members of a group (typically already margin-alized groups such as immigrants or the poor) are perceived as a threat to social values (Cohen 9; Saguy 20). Such "demon users" or "folk devils" (in this case, fat people) are blamed for society's ills and become targets for displaced anxiety and hostility (Saguy 20), as well as discrimination (Farrell 9). In particular, Campos et al. add that researchers have found that moral panics "displace broader anxieties about changing gender roles" (59). Additionally, Saguy notes that "moral panics identify sympathetic victims" (22) such as fat children, whom the mainstream media often represent as having been abused by overindulgent, smothering, and/or ignorant caregivers (Boero, "Fat Kids" 117). With anti-obesity rhetoric increasingly focusing on the alleged perils associated with "childhood obesity," those who are perceived as creating young, fat bodies have come under heightened scrutiny.[5] This brings us back to the discourse on "unfit" mothers.

"UNFIT" MOTHERS OF FAT CHILDREN AND ADOPTION ORDEALS

The contemporary cultural climate of hostility toward fat people[6] renders mothers and prospective mothers vulnerable to a host of deleterious consequences, including exposure to moralizing public discourses, arrest for child neglect, or even mandated weight loss (Barnett; Viner 34-35). Given that pregnant fat women are warned about how their body weight may negatively impact their children,[7] sociologist Natalie Boero cautions that "mother blame has now made its way into the womb" ("Fat Kids" 117). Nonetheless, due to space constraints, I will focus here on mothers of fat children and fat women applicants for adoption.

As Boero states, "The weight of one's children has increasingly become a litmus test of good mothering" (Boero, "Fat Kids" 113). Given that women are closely associated with cooking, feeding, and other food-related tasks, mothers in particular are routinely held responsible for their children's weight (Boero, "Fat Kids" 113). Mothers are the primary recipients of blame, as they are presumed to be responsible not only for their children's eating habits (Herndon 21) but also their physical activity levels (Boero, *Killer Fat* 19). As such, mothers of fat children are assumed to be overly permissive, neglectful, and/or ignorant of "proper" food choices. Such attributions may be more likely when the mothers in question are poor or racialized (116). Press articles that report on poor people, Latinos, and African Americans are more likely to emphasize sedentary lifestyles, or sedentary lifestyles *and* poor food choices (Campos et al. 58; Saguy and Riley). And since the framing of (perceived) social problems shapes the interventions created to ameliorate such problems, it is hardly surprising that families of colour have become special target populations for campaigners against childhood "obesity." In fact, as of several years ago, the evidence surrounded me every time I got in my car; drivers in Los Angeles would find their urban commutes peppered with PSA billboards featuring stern-faced women of colour and the slogan, "My kitchen, my rules."

Of course, assuming that Black and Brown mothers require reminding that they are the ones responsible for food selection and allocation suggests that without the billboards' intervention mothers of colour would otherwise be too permissive to properly care for their own children. Moreover, both Boero ("Fat Kids" 113) and Campos et al. (58) suggest that this prevailing discursive focus on "obesity" as the product of freely chosen individual behaviour obscures other relevant structural issues such as racism and poverty.

But condescending billboards and blaming rhetoric are not the only obstacles that mothers of fat children face in this age of moral panic. In 2009, African American mother Jerri Gray suffered arrest for child neglect, as well as the removal of her 555-pound son, Alexander Draper, to foster care. The arrest warrant alleged that Gray had placed her son "at an unreasonable risk of harm" (Barnett). Gray's case is not unique; state courts in Pennsylvania, Texas, New Mexico, Indiana, and New York have all "expanded their state's legal definition of medical neglect to include morbid obesity" (Barnett). As if this were not intrusive enough, courts are also empowered to order interventions such as gym workouts, cooking classes, and nutritional counselling (Barnett).

But mothers of fat children are not the only maternal casualties of the "war on obesity." For fat women hoping to adopt, anti-fat bias can stand as a barrier to motherhood altogether, especially for those seeking international adoption from particular Asian countries.[8] As of December 2014, both China and Korea have established upper weight limits for international adoption applicants (Vireday).[9] China bars adoption by applicants with body mass indexes (BMIs) of 40 and above (Katz), whereas Korea "requires that applicants not be more than 30 percent overweight" ("Korea

Weight Guidelines"). Australia and the UK lack codified national policies prohibiting adoption by fat applicants. Nonetheless, as UK resident Rachel Joint discovered, agencies within these countries can still be hostile to adoption by fat applicants (Donnelly).

In fact, as Dawn French can attest, neither career success nor celebrity status guarantees a fat woman an adoption experience free of weight discrimination (Viner). The award-winning English actress and comedian relays her experience of attempting to adopt a child:

> I was told that I had to lose weight—it was non-negotiable. That was hard for me. No one had ever said that to me before, and I had never agreed to do it before. I'm actually the sort of person for whom it's quite a big deal not to [lose weight]. I'm so comfortable after all these years, and I thought, "Who are they to tell me this, unless they can prove to me that I'm going to die?" ...What they were looking at was charts. I had to be in the middle of a chart.... I was told, "These are the rules." I had to lose five stone (31.8 kilograms), and I did. (Viner)

Furthermore, not only did the adoption authorities require French to lose weight prior to adopting her daughter, but they also harangued her about the possibility that she might regain the weight.

Size acceptance activist and childbirth educator Pamela Vireday identifies three rationales that authorities offer for restricting fat people from adopting. Each harkens back to the central claims circulated by proponents of the "war on obesity" (Campos et al. 55-58), stemming from either the conflation of fatness with ill health or the idea that fat parents will contaminate their adopted children, or some combination of these two problematic ideas. According to Vireday, authorities first fear that the fat adoptive parent will not live long enough to raise the child into adulthood. Additionally, adoption panels suspect that prospective parents' fat bodies signal emotional unhealthiness that may portend future unhappiness and emotional instability for the child. And finally, authorities worry that, irrespective of the significant genetic contribution to body shape and size, fat parents will negatively influence their child's weight and health. When agencies use the above tenets to guide adoption policy, they practice size discrimination in the name of child protection. The result is lengthy and taxing ordeals for caring, qualified mothers.

CONCLUSION

Although consternation about fatness is not new, over the last two decades the "war on obesity" has intensified prejudice and discrimination against fat people. For the mainstream media, assigning blame for fatness has taken the place of any serious public examination of the very real prejudice and discrimination that fat people in general, and fat mothers in particular, experience. The discourses circulated in media accounts in turn contribute to an ideological foundation for discriminatory policies, both formal and informal. As April Michelle Herndon states in *Fat Blame: How the War on Obesity Victimizes Women and Children*, "the rhetoric of 'crisis,' 'epidemic,' and 'war' tends to spawn and validate policies and interventions that might otherwise seem extreme" (33). As such, mothers of fat children are increasingly subject to social control. They are not only vulnerable to the removal of beloved children whose weight exceeds the limits of societal tolerance, but they are also at risk for arrest for child neglect. Fat women applying to adopt children may face outright rejection or conditional acceptance provided they submit to intrusive weight loss regimens. In an era of moral panic, such mothers may be designated as the new folk devils, but given the toll the "war on obesity" has claimed on families, surely anti-obesity crusaders are no angels.

ENDNOTES

[1]Although the article describing Rachel Joint's ordeal initially appears to be concerned with weight discrimination in adoption practices (for example, it features passages like, "Rachel found herself under personal attack" [Donnelly]), it is worth noting that the narrative quickly devolves into a weight loss success story. This approach is characteristic of other mainstream media accounts of

size discrimination by adoption authorities.

[2]Here I use *fat* as a value-neutral descriptor of people whose weight and/or body size exceeds their society's tolerance for body diversity. Although *fat* is still frequently used in the pejorative sense, many scholars and activists associated with fat pride, fat liberation, body diversity, and other movements congruent with size acceptance believe that reclaiming the word *fat* is nonetheless preferable to hiding behind euphemisms like *zaftig* or, worse, capitulating to mainstream, anti-fat discourse and adopting more widely accepted yet problematic terms like *overweight* and *obese*. These "O words" perpetuate stigma against fat people as well as the medicalization of fatness. For a more detailed discussion of problems associated with the "O words," see Wann (xii-xiii). Where it has been necessary to use these objectionable terms (i.e. in reference to the so-called obesity epidemic or obesity crisis), I have enclosed them in scare quotes in order to establish some critical distance to terminology that has proven useful mostly in fomenting ill will against fat people. Additionally, although I have previously used the term *fatphobia* (Royce 153) to describe anti-fat attitudes, I now prefer the terms *anti-fat*, *fat hatred*, or *size prejudice*. As Herek has noted with regards to the parallel term *homophobia* (Herek 19-20), the suffix *phobia* carries with it the (potentially) false implication that negative attitudes are motivated by irrational fear. Speculating about the motivation behind negative attitudes is less precise than simply labelling them negative and making explicit their overtly prejudicial nature.

[3]Although the examples of fat blame offered in this paragraph are most closely linked to the U.S. and the UK (Edwards and Roberts are affiliated with the London School of Hygiene and Tropical Medicine), recent trends point towards a globalization of fat stigma. A 2011 cross-cultural anthropological study suggests a "profound global diffusion of negative attitudes about obesity," including to regions that have traditionally held more positive attitudes about larger bodies (Brewis et al. 269). Additionally, Saguy states, "While the United States is on the front lines, nations across the globe are fighting a world war against obesity," (13). For example, in 2008, Japan passed a law setting a maximum waistline size for adults forty years old and older (Saguy 13).

[4]Campos et al. suggest that the recent uptick in governmental and popular concern over weight may have economic (as well as political) roots:

> Many of the leading obesity researchers who have created the official standards for what constitutes "overweight" and "obese" have also received sizable funding from the pharmaceutical and weight-loss industries. These obesity researchers also manage weight loss clinics and have an economic interest in defining unhealthy weight as broadly as possible, by overstating the hazards of obesity, and thus providing justifications for regulatory approvals, as well as for government and insurance industry subsidization of their products. In particular, organizations like the International Obesity Task Force (which has authored many of the WHO reports on obesity) and the American Obesity Association (which has actively campaigned to have obesity officially designated as a "disease") have been largely funded by pharmaceutical and weight-loss companies. Notably, although expert panels on obesity are largely devoted to evaluating epidemiological evidence and claims, qualified epidemiologists are almost never included as members. (58)

[5]Space constraints prohibit a more detailed discussion of the media and policy maelstrom over "childhood obesity." See Herndon.

[6]Particularly, but certainly not exclusively, in the U.S, as Korean and Chinese adoption policies and adoptive mother Dawn French's cases illustrate.

[7]Including the possibility that their child might be fat him/herself.

[8]To be fair, both fat women *and* fat men are subject to additional hurdles or outright rejection when they attempt to adopt, particularly from China or Korea. However, there are multiple cases of otherwise qualified prospective mothers being barred from adoption because of their weight or, alternately, cases where they are permitted to adopt only upon the condition that they commit to following a weight loss regimen.

[9]As of October 2015, I would fail to meet Korea's weight criteria for adoption.

WORKS CITED

Barnett, Ron. "S.C. Case Looks on Child Obesity as Child Abuse. But Is It?" *USA Today*. 23 July 2009. Web. 8 Dec. 2014.

Boero, Natalie. "Fat Kids, Working Moms, and the 'Epidemic of Obesity': Race, Class, and Mother Blame." *The Fat Studies Reader*. Ed. Esther Rothblum and Sondra Solovay. New York: New York University Press, 2009. 113-119. Print.

Boero, Natalie. *Killer Fat: Media, Medicine and Morals in the American "Obesity Epidemic."* New Brunswick, NJ: Rutgers University Press, 2012. Print.

Brewis, Alexandra A., Amber Wutich, Ashlan Faletta-Cowden, and Isa Rodriguez-Soto. "Body Norms and Fat Stigma in Global Perspective." *Current Anthropology* 52.2: 269-276 (2011). Web. 11 August 2015.

Campos, Paul, Abigail Saguy, Paul Ernsberger, Eric Oliver, and Glenn Gaesser. "The Epidemiology of Overweight and Obesity: Public Health Crisis or Moral Panic?" *International Journal of Epidemiology* 35 (2006): 55-65. Print.

Carroll, Aaron. "The Blame Du Jour." *The Incidental Economist*. 10 Sept. 2010. Web. 10 Dec. 2014.

Cohen, Stanley. *Folk Devils and Moral Panics: The Creation of the Mods and Rockers*. 3rd ed. New York: Routledge, 2002. Print.

Cooper, Charlotte. "Headless Fatties." *Dr. Charlotte Cooper*. Jan. 2007. Web. 14 Nov. 2014.

Donnelly, Sophie. "Told I Was Too Fat to Adopt." *Express*. 24 Mar. 2011. Web. 11 June 2014.

Edwards, Phil and Ian Roberts. "Population Adiposity and Climate Change." *International Journal of Epidemiology* 38.4 (2009): 1137-1140. Print.

Farrell, Amy Erdman. *Fat Shame: Stigma and the Fat Body in American Culture*. New York: New York University Press, 2011. Print.

Harris, Dan and Mikaela Conley. "Childhood Obesity: A Call for Parents to Lose Custody." *ABC News*. 14 July 2011. Web. 14 Dec. 2014.

Henderson, Nia-Malika. "Peter King Blames Asthma and Obesity for Eric Garner's Death. That's a Problem for the GOP." *The*

Washington Post. 4 Dec. 2014. Web. 13 Dec. 2014.

Herek, Gregory M. "The Psychology of Sexual Prejudice." *Current Directions in Psychological Science* 9 (2000): 19-22. Print.

Herndon, April Michelle. *Fat Blame: How the War on Obesity Victimizes Women and Children.* Lawrence, Kansas: University Press of Kansas, 2014. Print.

Katz, David. "China Restricts Adoption Policies." *ABC News.* 21 Dec. 2006. Web. 14 Dec 2014.

"Korea Weight Guidelines." *Dillon Adopt.* n.d. Web. 14 Dec 2014.

Landau, Elizabeth. "Health Care Costs to Bulge Along With U.S. Waistlines." *CNN.* 18 Sept. 2012. Web. 12 Dec. 2014.

Loar, Russ. "Doctor's Orders: Ex-Surgeon General Koop Calls for War against Obesity." *Los Angeles Times.* 18 Mar. 1995. Web. 13 Dec. 2014.

Royce, Tracy. "The Shape of Abuse: Fat Oppression as a Form of Violence against Women." *The Fat Studies Reader.* Ed. Esther Rothblum and Sondra Solovay. New York: New York University Press, 2009. 151-157. Print.

Saguy, Abigail. C. *What's Wrong With Fat?* New York: Oxford University Press, 2013. Print.

Saguy, Abigail C. and Rene Almeling. "Fat in the Fire? Science, the News Media, and the 'Obesity Epidemic.'" *Sociological Forum* 23.1 (2008): 53-83. Print.

Saguy, Abigail C., David Frederick, and Kjersten Gruys. "Reporting Risk, Producing Prejudice: How News Reporting on Obesity Shapes Attitudes About Health Risk, Policy, and Prejudice." *Social Science and Medicine* 111 (2014): 125-133. Print.

Saguy, Abigail C. and Kjersten Gruys. "Morality and Health: News Media Constructions of Overweight and Eating Disorders." *Social Problems* 57.2 (2010): 231-250. Print.

Saguy, Abigail C., Kjersten Gruys, and Shanna Gong. "Social Problem Construction and National Context: News Reporting on 'Overweight' and 'Obesity' in the United States and France." *Social Problems* 57.4 (2010): 586-610. Print.

Saguy, Abigail C. and Kevin W. Riley. "Weighing Both Sides: Morality, Mortality and Framing Contests Over Obesity." *Journal of Health Politics, Policy, and Law* 30.5 (2005): 869–921. Print.

Solovay, Sondra. *Tipping the Scales of Justice: Fighting Weight-*

based Discrimination. New York: Prometheus Books, 2000. Print.

Susman, Tina. "200-Pound Boy Taken from Mother; She Says Weight Not Her Fault." *Los Angeles Times* Blogs. 29 Nov. 2011. Web. 1 Dec. 2014.

Vartanian, Lenny R. "Disgust and Perceived Control in Attitudes towards Obese People." *International Journal of Obesity* 34 (2010): 1302-1307. Print.

Viner, Brian. "The Dawn French Revolution." *The New Zealand Herald*. 13 Apr. 2002. Web. 15 Dec. 2014.

Vireday, Pamela. "Adoption and People of Size." *The Well Rounded Mama*. 19 Jan. 2009. Web. 13 Dec. 2014.

Wann, Marilyn. "Foreword: Fat Studies: An Invitation to Revolution." *The Fat Studies Reader*. Ed. Esther Rothblum and Sondra Solovay. New York: New York University Press, 2009. ix-xxv. Print.

Zeller, Tom. "Climate Research That Might Not Help." *The New York Times* 27 Apr. 2009. Web. 13 Dec. 2014.

II.
Blaming "Othered" Mothers

4.
Fated Fate?

Patriarchal Ethics and Reproductive Politics
in Southwest China

FANG-TZU YEN

T HIS CHAPTER UTILIZES feminist ethnography to explore
how ethnic minority Kam women in rural Southwest China
are blamed for high infant mortality rates—not only by the
patriarchal concept of "fated fate," which holds mothers responsible when they experience infertility or the loss of a child, but
also by China's medical modernization programs that stigmatize
Kam women's traditional mothering practices. Here I draw from
observations and interviews with Kam women and doctors in Shan
and Wang villages to contextualize how the Chinese government
marginalizes ethnic minorities through its implementation of modernization programs. The chapter further explores how minority
women are implicated in the clash between local and state powers
in China's contemporary reproductive politics.[1]

CHINA'S HIGH INFANT MORTALITY RATES
AND MEDICAL MODERNIZATION

The Chinese government has encountered difficulties implementing family planning policies and decreasing infant mortality rates
in rural areas. In this regard, the Kam people of Shan village in
Guizhou have been lauded for their zero population growth rate,
as well as for the villagers' seeming ability to manage birth control
by traditional medicine and cultural means, whereby 98 percent
of households produce exactly one son and one daughter (Shi 33,
42-43; Zhou 16-17). However, Kam women's voices debunk this
reproductive myth; their narratives reveal the loss of children in

their reproductive histories and expose harmful practices such as sex-selective infanticide and abortion in their pursuit of this idealized family structure (Yen, A. 20). Since these issues have been largely concealed, village women have suffered in silence while the myths of China's successful family planning strategies remain prevalent.

In contrast to Shan village, high infant mortality rates among the Kam people in Wang village have not been successfully hidden. To address this issue, China has implemented a series of maternal and infantile health programs for nearly two decades, but according to reports by health workers in Congjiang County, rates among the Kam people have only slowly decreased. Indeed, Wang village's birth and death registration collected by the township family planning station reveals high infant mortality rates: 562.5 per thousand in 2000 and 605.3 per thousand in 2001 (Li 1). The government has since adopted a series of modernization programs, ostensibly for the purpose of combating poverty, illness, and perceived civilian ignorance, to tackle these alarming figures.

In contrast to the pervasive belief that Kam women's inadequate mothering is to blame for high infant mortality rates, Kam traditions see mothers dedicate much time and energy to caring for their children. Before the birth of a child, for instance, rituals are held to drive ghosts away and pray for healthy descendants. After giving birth, Kam mothers carry their children on their backs and every child wears a beautiful hat to protect its soul. All the embroidery worn by Kam children shows that their mothers dote on them, yet due to intersecting systems of oppression, mothers cannot guarantee that their children will live. This chapter accordingly addresses why Kam women in China's Shan and Wang villages face high infant mortality rates, as well as why they are subject to blame for their children's deaths.

FEMINIST STANDPOINT AND ETHNOGRAPHY

In their pursuit of modernization, both the Chinese government and the local cultures have blamed Kam women for their reproductive failures; the former attributes high infant mortality rates to mothers' perceived negligence and ignorance, while the latter blame women's "bad fate" for curtailing their husbands' family continuity. This chapter employs feminist standpoint theory (Haraway 576; Harding 119-137) to debunk these dominant myths about the causes of high infant mortality rates among Kam people. As women are agents of pregnancy, reproduction, and wellbeing for themselves and their children, women's narratives can provide critical information that challenges patriarchal rhetoric (Petchesky and Judd 21).

For this research I performed interviews with Kam women in the Kam language. During this process I was mindful that these women's stories have long been suppressed by local village cadres, Chinese government elites and policy-makers, and pervasive patriarchal ideologies. In this way, the ethnic minority Kam women are situated in intersecting gender, ethnicity, and economic class oppressions (Zinn and Dill 321-331). To date, no researchers have lived in the mountainous Kam villages for extensive periods of time to conduct in-depth studies about the relationship between women's health and high infant mortality rates. I gained access to my participants by identifying my status as a researcher from Taiwan, a Kam daughter-in-law, and a mother; still, the results of my fieldwork are likely limited by my Taiwanese, Han, and woman-researcher identities. In my interviews, I asked women to share the experiences and reproductive stories they were most familiar with. The insights provided in this chapter are thus gleaned from face-to-face interviews I conducted with 106 Kam women and doctors in Shan and Wang villages, as well as workers at Maternal and Child Health Centers in Congjiang and Liping Counties, Guizhou Province.

PATRIARCHAL ETHICS AND THE CONCEPT OF "FATE"

Kam traditions are largely shaped by patriarchal ethics, which allow a patrilineal society to maintain male privilege and power relations. In this cultural framework, women are valued if they achieve the "fate" prescribed for them in accordance with traditional gender roles. As such, if a woman produces a healthy child of both genders, it is presumed that she has "good fate"; however, if she experiences reproductive failure, she is likely to bear the consequences alone, including experiences of distress, grief, and social stigma.

In cases where it is determined that a woman cannot bear children, it is believed that she poses a threat to her husband's health. In such cases, the couple's "fates" are deemed incompatible, and they are required to separate. This may result in the woman being accused of attracting an aggressive or "bad" fate to her husband's family. This belief system favours the continuity of the patrilineal family and thereby prioritizes the well-being of the husband and his descendants. The husband's family uses the notion of mutual restriction in the couple's fate to divorce a wife who cannot provide healthy children, as well as to justify remarriage in the hope of producing offspring. In this way, patriarchal ethics unequivocally reinforce unequal gender power relations among the Kam people.

The concept of fate is thus a prevalent one in Kam people's attempts to understand and mitigate reproductive failure. According to informants over eighty years old, Wang village was once attacked by measles over a long period of time,[2] and many children died during the subsequent period of confinement. In light of these experiences, villagers have developed a series of beliefs and rituals to manage maternal and infantile health during periods of vulnerability. For instance, the village shamans contend that the number of flowers[3] a woman has in her fate will determine the number of children she has. According to this belief system, when these children are waiting in hell for the bridge that will allow them to access this world, some babies do not survive due to a ghost's attack. Similarly, the ritual *Weex Jiuc* is usually carried out by couples who fail to have a living child after the first few years of marriage due to miscarriage, stillbirth, premature birth, or premature death. Despite these beliefs and practices, village women believe that their birth number is doomed to fail people's expectations, since many children die before the age of five.

Mother So,[4] one of my informants in Shan village, engaged in such rituals so that she and her husband could have a son. She explained how the previous loss of three children urged them to expel the ghosts responsible for the children's deaths and to build a bridge to receive a child from the underworld. My fieldwork in Shan village reveals that, if all these efforts and rites of passage prove to be in vain and reproductive failure occurs, village women like Mother So will continue to seek help from female herbalists who provide herbs for abortion, illness, and confinement; they may also seek medication from pharmacies but will only visit hospitals as a last resort. Traditional shamans are also frequently consulted in an effort to prevent miscarriage and identify causes of reproductive failure. In these instances, the male shaman will take note of the couple's birthdates to ascertain whether their combined fates represent harmony or conflict according to the ancient Kam Book. If he determines that the couple's fate is harmonious, the shaman will identify ways to remove barriers to reproduction that cause miscarriage, stillbirth, or premature death.

When taken together, these beliefs and practices reflect a patriarchal ideological framework that ultimately blames women for reproductive failure. This cultural logic holds mothers responsible for causing the loss of a child as well as poisoning her husband and his family with her "bad fate." The villagers believe that the fault lies with the child only when the mother dies from difficult labour. While the notion of fate allows women to emotionally navigate and process their children's premature deaths, women are consistently threatened with social condemnation, which focuses specifically on their gender roles in reproduction and nurturing. Inhorn maintains that such condemnation results in "gendered suffering," (185) which manifests here as "fated fate." In this capacity, Kam women bear the emotional burden of responsibility and social stigma for high child mortality rates, while their husbands are relinquished from any stake or responsibility in reproductive failure. This notion of fate prescribed by village leaders perpetuates patriarchal ethics, and while this notion provides a conceptual framework for understanding reproductive failure, it does nothing to improve maternal and infantile health in Kam society.

THE SOCIAL ORIGINS OF KAM WOMEN'S SUFFERING

This study adopts the perspective of social suffering in its critical examination of the relations between health conditions, cultural representations, and social structures for Kam women. Kleinman, Das, and Lock argue that political, economic, and institutional forces collectively perpetuate social suffering, just as they influence responses to social problems (ix). This approach contextualizes experiences of trauma, pain, and disorders within the larger realm of cultural politics, and it elucidates the social origins and consequences of collective suffering. To that end, research on infant mortality rates reveals how people address and cope with the issue through communal and ritual practices (Gammeltoft 37). For example, poor northeastern Brazilian mothers lose many children due to hunger, and their collective suffering is reflective of how colonial structural violence and agricultural transformation impacts women's everyday experiences (Scheper-Hughes). Along this trajectory, Riessman's research in South India reveals how upper-caste women who own more political and economic resources have been able to lessen their suffering by instigating socioeconomic change (112-135). However, such possibilities are constrained for Kam women who are marginalized by intersecting gender, race, and class identities. This social suffering perspective thus contextualizes high infant mortality not only as an issue related to maternal and infantile health, but also reflective of broader political and social systems.

By unpacking Kam women's personal narratives, it becomes clear how their suffering derives from discriminatory reproductive politics, as well as the sex/gender system (Rubin 159, 204) that dominates the Kam people's reproductive decisions and influences maternal and infantile health. The ideal time for Kam villagers to marry is before the age of twenty, so that the next generation will be produced when the parents are around forty years old. Wealthy families who have advantageous marriages can be confident that this pattern will occur uninterrupted in every generation; they often become grandparents in their forties, which is also viewed as "good fate." To produce another generation takes longer for families of the lower caste; they have fewer children, their children are more vulnerable to illness and premature death, and they are more likely to commit infanticide or abortion to limit births.

To that end, Kam villagers must maintain good health and work hard to achieve a good harvest in the mountainous areas. To meet subsistence production, both men and women engage in agricultural work. Reproduction in this living environment is a burden for village women, and pregnant women often do not stop working until they enter labour. I was informed that some women work during the daytime and give birth to their baby at night, or even go into labour on the slope. Pregnant women walk on the ridge with their swollen bellies obscuring the way, which sometimes causes them to fall. Women who lack childcare support have to carry their children on their backs, and they must walk a long way on the ridge to work in the fields. In addition, the previous two decades of economic reform have required men and young women to leave home to work on the east coast of China, thus causing married women to become the principal labourers in both Shan and Wang villages. With this development of socialist modernization, agricultural feminization has exacerbated women's reproductive health challenges, just as it deepens women's secondary status in the sex/gender hierarchy.

Heavy labour, minimal rest, and subsistence diets lead to women's exhaustion and render them susceptible to reproductive illness. They frequently experience headaches, backaches, anemia, arthritis, malnutrition, miscarriage, and abnormal menstruation, all of which reduce women's abilities to have healthy pregnancies. Furthermore, Kam society makes reproductive decisions by considering factors such as class status and the availability of childcare assistance. According to my informants in Shan village, Kam women of lower castes may practice infanticide when they lack supportive parents or parents-in-law to look after young children as they work. They may also resort to abortion or infanticide to limit family sizes when they feel they cannot support additional children, and they do not consider infanticide to be a sin. Mother Nei, a research participant from a lower-caste family in Shan village, shared, "As a mother, I had to abandon [my child] because I would have had bad fate…. If I had wanted it, others would have criticized me for having excess births." She believed that if the baby had lived, they both would have suffered.

In this sense, the need to limit births is caused by economically disadvantaged women's necessary participation in agricultural production, as well as the social stigma that accompanies excess births. In contrast, I found that in at least ten cases, the upper-caste families had more than three sons. After 1950, many upper-caste families—especially party cadre families—had two sons and two daughters. However, low-caste families normally had two to three children of both sexes. The plight of Kam women's suffering is thus shaped by social inequality derived from interlocking oppressions, and it is further exacerbated by Chinese reproductive politics.

BLAMING KAM WOMEN FOR HIGH INFANT MORTALITY RATES

China has implemented a series of maternal and infantile health programs to reduce high infant mortality rates. The Kam infant mortality rate was 63.43 per thousand in 2000—nearly three times higher than that of the Han people (Chen, Zhang and Zhang 2231). The rates among mountainous Kam villages were even worse than the total Kam infant mortality rate. According to reports by health workers in Congjiang County, Wang village's birth and death registration reveals high infant mortality rates: 562.5 per thousand in 2000, 605.3 per thousand in 2001, and 406 per thousand in 2003 (Li 1). When Li's report, *The Health Dilemma of High Infant Mortality*, gained attention online and in other mass media, public opinion pressured Chinese authorities to remove such shameful information from the public record.

Investigations of the Maternal and Child Health Center reveal that the local government spent one million RMB (161,830 USD) to launch a series of civilization programs that aimed to combat Wang village's high instances of poverty, illness, and lack of education. The local government reproached the pre-industry minority society for following old cultural practices—such as birthing at home, early marriage and early birth, praying to gods, and feeding infants with chewed rice—rather than adopting modern medical knowledge or cultivating new hygienic practices—such as giving birth in hospitals and employing professional midwives. The official reports of the Maternal and Child Health Center largely blamed Kam mothers' perceived cultural backwardness for high infant mortality rates (Li 3-4).

In their quest for modernization, the government has regulated minority women's bodies through eugenics programs and mandatory birthing at hospitals. Due to Wang village's inconvenient location and chronic poverty, a director and two doctors of the Maternal and Child Health Center were stationed there in rotation. Along with the village doctor, these officials ensured that pregnant villagers consulted professional midwives at the village health center. If they did not, the authorities disallowed the child's household registration and the family was consequently denied access to medical resources. In order to avoid this punishment, Wang villagers no longer give birth at home. In this way, birth has come under the control of state surveillance.[5]

To pursue the course of integration and socialist modernization, China's nationalism has accentuated the distinctions between Han Chinese and minority ethnic groups, just as it has been used to justify discriminatory reforms in minority areas. It is noted that China's socialist reforms and modernization efforts benefit only a fraction of its people who reside in coastal provinces while those in western provinces remain impoverished, with restricted access to education and minimal prospects for upward mobility (Mackerras 66-70). Owing to these circumstances, mountainous Kam villagers continue to experience high infant mortality.

THE CONSEQUENCES OF CHINA'S REPRODUCTIVE POLITICS

As The People's Republic of China began implementing family planning initiatives in the late 1970s, resistance to sterilization came from both men and women in Shan village. Mother Hu, who belongs to an upper-caste family, recounted villagers' experience of birth control practices to me. At first, three males of excess-birth households were asked to have a vasectomy; they found that their backs ached and they could not work as much following the operation. Thereafter, the village men managed to avoid sterilization. Kam men have the responsibility for planting staple foods, and sterilization is believed to interfere with their procreative role in agricultural production. Women were thus more likely to undergo forced sterilization, and this provoked village women's collective fear and anxiety. In one interview, a retired family planning worker described how women who were taken away to be sterilized would cry all the way from the mountainous village to the family planning station in the county center.

Greenhalgh ("Peasantization" 220, "Controlling Births" 13) notes the pivotal role that village cadres play in manipulating the local politics of reproduction in rural China. What we have known about Shan and Wang villages largely comes from male Kam elites, village leaders, and cadres. They have constructed a myth of the Kam people's population control, which echoes the family planning propaganda that was written into China's constitution in the 1980s.[6] They claim that the villagers consciously practice birth control by employing ethnomedicine and their customary law, such as administering the ancestor oath about birth control during a specific festival and driving away families who have excess births (Cue 36-37; Shi 78-80). The township government that was once located in Shan village exempted the villagers from sterilization in 1989 based on their outstanding achievement of zero population growth during the forty-year period between 1950 and 1990. Since then, the villagers have not been sterilized, even after having two children. However, villagers are still expected to conform to state-initiated and nationally recognized methods of birth control, so the village women have intrauterine devices (IUDs) inserted.

To that end, research on reproductive politics reveals how state regulation of motherhood and the pursuit of modernity have transformed female bodies (Anagnost 22-41; Jolly 148-177). Since China began building a modern socialist state, it has promoted the modernization of women's identities, adherence to monogamous marriage patterns, a compliance with delayed marriage and childbearing, and a eugenic model of motherhood. In practice, the Chinese government utilizes its bio-power to control births (Greenhalgh, "Planned Births" 197), such as by mandating sterilization for couples who have excess births. In other words, family planning has been used to produce a regulated population in modern China, and nationalist discourses are used to justify medical intervention and the regulation of women's bodies.

At the same time, local village leaders' deceptive tactics highlight the clash of interests between the state and the upper-caste Shan villagers, as well as the conflict between family planning policies and family continuity. In some respects, the myth of Shan village's zero population growth, as devised by the upper-caste Shan village leaders, has enabled a decrease in state surveillance and regulation. It also allows upper-caste families to continue their practices of early marriage, early births, and higher birth rates. Moreover, this patrilineal society has always practiced bilateral inheritance, which influences the villagers' preferences to have one son and one daughter, and many villagers practice sex-selected infanticide to achieve this.[7] On the whole, it is evident that such family planning policies increase instances of infanticide and abandonment, which deepen women's social suffering. The government implements family planning to limit and space births, but it provides no appropriate socioeconomic resources for doing so.

CONCLUSION

This chapter has explored the structural dilemmas and social suffering that Kam women face in the context of China's contemporary reproductive politics, as well as the patriarchal ethics that shape their local moral world. These women's experiences challenge hegemonic political and medical discourses regarding high infant mortality rates, just as they reveal how patrilineal traditions maintain and perpetuate unequal gender power relations. Such interlocking oppressions subject Kam women to mother-blame and social stigma when they experience reproductive failure. In this regard, cultural beliefs regarding women's "fate" are socially constructed to uphold patriarchal ethics, and they further work to constrain women's reproductive agency while disregarding their health and well-being.

Rather than blame individual women for reproductive failure, it is critical to name and dismantle the intersecting sex, race, and class hierarchies that cause high infant mortality rates among villagers. While Kam women are largely constrained by the oppressive notion of "fate" as it is embedded in their sex/gender system, improved access to knowledge and resources has the potential to improve their health and reproductive agency. To that end, it is necessary to challenge government policies that blame minority village women's "traditional" and "primitive" maternal practices as the cause of premature deaths. It is also prudent to understand how the clash between local power and state surveillance leads to reproductive practices that harm maternal and infantile health. Although family planning and medical modernization programs

77

might lessen women's reproductive responsibilities and burdens to a degree, they do not address the myriad oppressions that constrain women's reproductive agency, and in this sense they are severely limited. Transformative political and economic change, greater equality in gender, race, and class relations, and increased decisional power are thereby needed to empower Kam women to fight for improved maternal and infantile health.

ENDNOTES

[1] This chapter expands upon my doctoral research in Shan village by including fieldwork that was done eleven kilometers away in Wang village. While the former is lauded as a model village for family planning, the latter is infamous for its high infant mortality rates. Both villages are located at the junction between Congjiang and Liping Counties in the mountainous areas of China's Guizhou Province. For further reading, see F. Yen.

[2] The World Health Organization (WHO) points out that measles had killed 3-4 million children a year in the People's Republic of China (PRC) by the 1970s. In the absence of a vaccine, almost everyone was infected with measles. Under the WHO's support, Guizhou province carried out a measles immunization program in 2004. Since then, the prevalence of measles has remained low.

[3] In accordance with the Taoist worldview, one's life is just like a tree blooming with flowers, which symbolize the health of a woman and how many children she will give birth to.

[4] Pseudonyms are used in this chapter to guarantee anonymity.

[5] At first glance, it seemed that all the efforts put forth by the Department of Public Health did decrease Wang village's infant mortality rates—according to the official statistics of the township family planning station, the IMR was 250 per thousand in 2008 and decreased to 86.96 per thousand in 2009. However, this statistical decrease was likely skewed by underreported cases of infant mortality, since the village doctors were responsible for maintaining and submitting records to the family planning station.

[6] In addition to the Kam people, reproductive myths have been constructed by a number of ethnic minorities. The local ethnic

subjects—including party cadres and other elites—intentionally promote their unique cultural practices in order to appear germane to the project of socialist modernization in reform-era China. This strategy enables these ethnic subjects to appear advanced in development and to have transcended the troublesome history of Maoist socialist reforms (Litzinger 219).

[7] A great deal of research demonstrates that Chinese women in rural areas are more likely to commit infanticide when the child is a girl. Such a situation arises from the conflict between Han people's patriarchal clan system and China's one-child policy. However, my fieldwork with Kam women contradicts this commonly held assumption.

WORKS CITED

Anagnost, Ann. "A Surfeit of Bodies: Population and the Rationality of the State in Post-Mao China." *Conceiving the New World Order: The Global Politics of Reproduction*. Ed. Faye Ginsburg and Rayna Rapp. Los Angeles: University of California Press, 1995. 22-41. Print.

Chen, Xiaofang, Juying Zhang, and Qiang Zhang. "An Analysis on the Trend of Infant Mortality Rate of Chinese Minorities." *Modern Preventive Medicine* 33.12 (2006): 2231. Print.

Cue, Haiyang. *Human and Paddyland: A Research on Traditional Livelihood of Dong Ethnic Group in Huang Gang Village, Liping County, Guizhou Province, China*. Kunming: Yunnan Renmin, 2009. Print.

Gammeltoft, Tine M. "Between Remembering and Forgetting: Maintaining Moral Motherhood after Late-term Abortion." *Abortion in Asia*. Ed. Andrea Whittaker. New York: Berghahn Books, 2010. 56-77. Print.

Greenhalgh, Susan. "Controlling Births and Bodies in Village China." *American Ethnologist* 221.1 (1994): 3-30. Print.

Greenhalgh, Susan. "The Peasantization of the One-child Policy in Shaanxi." *Chinese Families in the Post-Mao Era*. Ed. Deborah Davis and Stevan Harrell. Berkeley: University of California Pres, 1993. 219-250. Print.

Greenhalgh, Susan. "Planned Births, Unplanned Persons: 'Population' in the Making of Chinese Modernity." *Signs* 30.2 (2003): 196-215. Print.

Haraway, Donna. "Situated Knowledges: The Science Question in Feminism and the Privilege of Partial Perspective." *Feminist Studies* 14.3 (1988): 575–599. Print.

Harding, Sandra. *Whose Science? Whose Knowledge? Thinking from Women's Lives*. New York: Cornell University Press, 1991. Print.

Inhorn, Marcia. *Reproductive Disruptions: Gender, Technology, and Biopolitics in the New Millennium*. New York: Berghahn Books, 2008. Print.

Jolly, Margret. "From Darkness to Light? Epidemiologies and Ethnographies of Motherhood." *Birthing in the Pacific: Beyond Tradition and Modernity?* Ed. Vicki Lukere and Margaret Jolly. Honolulu: University of Hawaii Press, 2002. 148-177. Print.

Kleinman, Arthur, Veena Das, and Margaret Lock, eds. *Social Suffering*. Berkeley, California: University of California Press, 1997. Print.

Li, Guangshou. *Huanggangcun: Yiner Gaosiwang Beihou de Yiliao Zhi Kun (Huanggan Village: The Health Dilemma of High Infant Mortality)*. 11 May 2005. Web. 12 March 2006.

Litzinger, Ralph. *Other Chinas: The Yao and the Politics of National Belonging*. London: Duke University Press, 2000. Print.

Mackerras, Colin. *China's Ethnic Minorities and Globalization*. New York: Routledge, 2003. Print.

Mohanty, Chandra Talpade. "Under Western Eyes: Feminist Scholarship and Colonial Discourses." *Third World Women and the Politics of Feminism*. Ed. Chandra Talpade Mohanty, Ann Russo and Lourdes Torres. Bloomington: Indiana University Press, 1991. 51-80. Print.

Petchesky, Rosalind and Karen Judd. Introduction. *Negotiating Reproductive Rights: Women's Perspectives across Countries and Cultures*. Ed. Rosalind Petchesky and Karen Judd. London: Zed Books, 1998. 1-30. Print.

Riessman, Catherine Kohler. "Stigma and Everyday Resistance Practices: Childless Women in South India." *Gender and Society* 14.1 (2000): 111-135. Print.

Rubin, Gayle. "The Traffic in Women: Notes on the 'Political

Economy' of Sex." *Toward an Anthropology of Women.* Ed. Rayna Reiter. New York: Monthly Review, 1975. 157-210. Print.

Schepher-Hughes, Nancy. *Death without Weeping: The Violence of Everyday Life in Brazil.* Berkley: University of California Press, 1992. Print.

Shi, Kaizhong. *Jiancun De Dongzu Jihua Shengyu De Shehui Jizhi Ji Fangfa (The Social Organism and Methods of Kam Family Planning in Jien Village).* Guiyang: Huaxiao Wenhua, 2001. Print.

Whittaker, Andrea. *Intimate Knowledge: Women and Their Health in North-East Thailand.* St Leonards, N.S.W.: Allen & Unwin, 2000. Print. [not cited in text]

Wu, Quanxin. "Zhanli-Wo De Jiaxing (Zhanli-My Homeland)." *Echo* 32 (1991): 12-30. Print.

Yen, Aura. "Reproductive Politics in Southwest China: Deconstructing a Minority Male Perspective on Reproduction." *Reconceiving the Second Sex in Reproduction: Men, Masculinity, and Reproduction.* Ed. Marcia C. Inhorn, Tine Tjørnhøj-Thomsen, Helene Goldberg, and Maruska La Cour Mosegaard. New York: Berghahn Books, 2009. 217-244. Print.

Yen, Fang-tzu. *The Politics of Women's Reproductive Health in Shan Village, Guizhou, Southwest China.* Diss. Queensland, Australia: Griffith University School of Nursing, 2006. Print.

Zhou, Xiaozheng. "Renko Lingchengzhang Shi Ruhe Shixian De? (How Could Zero-Population-Growth-Rate Be Realised?)." *Echo* 32 (1991): 16-17. Print.

Zinn, Maxine Baca and Bonnie Thornton Dill. "Theorizing Difference from Multiracial Feminism." *Feminist Studies* 22 (1996): 321-331. Print.

5.

"I Was the One Who Opened My Legs"

The Tropes and Consequences of
Blaming Pregnant and Mothering Teens

JENNA VINSON AND SALLY STEVENS

SINCE THE 1970S, politicians, journalists, researchers, and lobbyists have placed the blame for many societal ills—such as poverty, educational failure, and men in the prison system—squarely on "teenage pregnancy." More specifically, this stigmatizing discourse is focused on young mothers and often neglects biological fathers who, quite often, are not teens (Males 21; Kelly 127). Many researchers have long refuted the statistics used to associate negative outcomes with the age of a woman's first birth and demonstrate how the so-called consequences of teenage pregnancy and motherhood are actually the lived realities of poverty—an economic condition that cannot be solved by controlling when women give birth (Furstenberg 5; Kearny and Levine 2; Luker 39; SmithBattle 417).[1]

Looking at contemporary representations of teenage pregnancy and motherhood in popular culture, pregnancy prevention campaigns, and sex education initiatives in the United States, it is clear that the widespread shaming and blaming of pregnant and mothering young women continues. It remains rhetorically commonplace to position teenage pregnancy and teen mothers in lists of issues plaguing society. This is because, as historian Rickie Solinger suggests, throughout U.S. history "the fertility of different groups of women" has proved a useful target of blame for politicians and other authorized experts seeking to claim that they have a solution for major social issues (4; Chase 47). Stereotypes of "bad" mothers—such as unfit mothers, teen mothers, welfare mothers, and drug-addicted mothers—help to simplify complicated socioeconomic problems while at the same time supporting patriarchal, racialized gender ideologies. These ideologies position women—and specifically women's sexual and reproductive decisions—as responsible for their life outcomes, their children's life outcomes, and the socioeconomic health of the U.S. Widespread public discourse about a teenage pregnancy problem implicitly teaches us that women are solely responsible for sexual activity, reproductive outcomes, and childrearing.

In this chapter, we share stories from focus groups with twenty-seven young pregnant and/or mothering women to explore the impact of teen-mother blaming, specifically in regard to what it teaches young women (and others) about dual standards for sexuality and the obligations of "good" motherhood.[2] The idea for this chapter came from three separate instances wherein focus group participants explained a life experience or dismissed a personal feeling by using the phrase "I was the one who opened my legs." "Opened my legs" is a metonymic reference to sexual intercourse. As it is used in everyday discourse, a woman may agree to have sex by "opening her legs," thereby opening herself, at one and the same moment, to accusations of being promiscuous ("easy"), as well as to blame for any deleterious outcomes. Or, she may "keep her legs closed" to ensure a good reputation and bright future for herself and her future children. This binary is constructed by multiple assumptions about gendered roles in heterosexual relationships. First, in forwarding the idea that women open or close their legs to agree to a sexual act with a man, this trope renders invisible the body and actions of the man, therein suggesting his actions are normal and inevitable. Second, the trope obfuscates a more complicated understanding of sexual consent, making it difficult to discuss issues such as sexual desire, social pressure, sexual abuse, and rape.[3]

It is important to note that the open/closed legs binary also relates to Western norms of gendered embodiment that signify an unequal power structure. Men are often raised to take up more space and stand or sit with legs wide apart (Cashdan 211). In contrast, women are encouraged to take up less space, crossing their legs at the thigh or ankle (Martin 494; Young 145). A woman who "opens her legs" may be seen as violating a normative script. Thus, the open/closed legs binary signifies a gendered power structure that positions women as bearing full responsibility for anything that contacts, penetrates, or emanates from their bodies.

Focusing on moments when a participant used this trope, we identify themes of responsibility that surfaced across participants' voiced experiences. We argue that the U.S. discourses that blame teenage mothers encourage pregnant and/or mothering young women to accept gendered discrimination and the primary burden of raising the child in order to perform "good" motherhood. In addition, we present data that suggest fathers do not assume such responsibility, and that it is socially acceptable for them to play a minimal role in supporting pregnancies and childrearing.

RESEARCH METHODOLOGY

The analysis in this chapter stems from the "My Pregnancy Story Project" (MPSP)—a research project we conducted with pregnant and mothering women in Arizona to learn about the support systems available or unavailable to them. Given the troubling tendency of the media and associated literature to homogenize teen pregnancy—therein erasing young women's identities and lived experiences other than being a "teen mom"—we intentionally selected four research sites that offered us the opportunity to meet with participants who are diverse with regard to race, ethnicity, economic class, region (e.g., rural/urban), and mothering context. Two of the sites were traditional public high schools with teenage parent programs (TAPP), one of which is located in an urban area and the other in a rural area. The third site was an Arizona Department of Juvenile Correction's (ADJC) "safe school" or correctional facility, and the fourth site was a community-based, non-profit organization designed to support pregnant and parenting teens. Over a four month period, from October 2011 to January 2012, 27 young pregnant and mothering women between the ages of fifteen and twenty participated in the study. Six participants were pregnant with their first child and two participants were pregnant with their second child. Nineteen participants were not pregnant but were mothers—17 were raising one child and two were raising more than one child.

As expected, the demographic profile of the participants differed by site (see Vinson and Stevens 326).

As feminist researchers, we recognize that young pregnant and mothering women are often shamed for their pregnancy and/or decision to give birth. If they are invited to speak publicly, it is often to share their story of failure so that others can learn how to avoid that fate. These messages come from multiple people and venues, thus influencing young women's perceptions of their place in society and often silencing alternative perspectives about teen pregnancy. To counter this, we intentionally framed the MPSP as a positive opportunity for young pregnant and mothering women to tell us (and each other) their pregnancy story and to honour their pregnancy, birthing, and child-raising experiences. The title of the project and our recruitment flyer requested their voices: "What's Your Story? Come share the trials & triumphs, struggles and successes of being a pregnant or parenting teen...." In accordance with feminist research methods (Fonow and Cook 8), we also attempted to minimize the hierarchical division between the researchers and participants: "Come join us at [location] for a lively discussion...."

Our mixed-method research design included a brief questionnaire and focus group discussion. The questionnaire was administered prior to the start of the focus groups and asked participants about their background demographic, family and educational profile, support systems, and pregnancy. The focus groups immediately followed the administration of the questionnaire. We asked nine questions during each group session, but the conversation often shifted as new topics were introduced by participants. Through attentive listening practices and informal commentary between participants and facilitators, we aimed to create an open conversation during which the authors and participants could learn from each other. Throughout the study, we strove for a collaborative process that engaged the participants. For example, we facilitated group sessions after the data were analyzed so that participants could provide feedback on our interpretations of the data.

We used a grounded theory approach for data analysis (Pope, Ziebland, and Mays 114) to identify common responses to the planned focus group questions, as well as other themes not specifically related to these questions. First, the focus groups were audiotaped and transcribed. All identifying information was deleted to guarantee participant anonymity and their names were replaced with pseudonyms. Then, we independently reviewed the transcriptions to document emerging themes along with supporting narrative (see Vinson and Stevens 326). Several themes emerged from this process, including the blaming of teen mothers and the positioning of responsibility for pregnancy and childrearing on the young pregnant and mothering woman. For the purposes of this chapter, we focus on the themes that relate to the prevalence and potential impact of teen mother-blaming. First, we examine themes of responsibility illuminated through an analysis of the "opened my legs" trope, including women as (a) solely responsible for sex and any outcome of sex, (b) entirely responsible for childrearing tasks, and (c) totally deserving of public judgment. Then, we discuss findings related to help and support with pregnancy and parenting, including participants' varied sources of support and their disappointment with the father of the baby, along with a critique of dual standards for sex, pregnancy, and childrearing.

ANALYSIS OF THE "OPENED MY LEGS" TROPE

In this section, we closely analyze three instances wherein participants used the phrase "I was the one who opened my legs" as part of their story of teenage pregnancy and motherhood. We connect each specific instance to a particular theme of responsibility that surfaced across focus groups and point to connections to broader US discourses about teenage pregnancy and motherhood.

Instance 1: Woman as Solely Responsible for Sex and Any Outcomes

One theme that emerged was the unique responsibility women have to deal with the consequences of their decision to have sex. For example, one instance of the "open my legs" trope occurred during a focus group session at the rural TAPP school when Sandra explained how she felt when she learned she was pregnant:

Honestly, the pregnancy, it wasn't planned, but I love kids so I was kinda scared, happy, and like mad—not mad—but like disappointed at the same time... So it was like weird. I knew I was gonna probably end up following in my mom's footsteps. Except, the good thing is, I waited two more years than she did. So, I'm happy about that part!

Here Sandra expresses mixed feelings about the pregnancy. On the one hand, she wanted to be pregnant at some time in her life and she believed that, since she was born to a teen mother, she was likely to have kids early too. On the other hand, Sandra felt afraid and later explained how she did not like that the news of her pregnancy disappointed her family. Sandra continued, "Yeah, I just think it was a little too early, but I was the one who opened my legs so [she trails off and laughs]." Sandra quickly dismisses any negative feelings about the timing of her pregnancy. Using the "I was the one who opened my legs" trope, Sandra articulates her pregnancy as the consequence of her decision to have sexual intercourse with her boyfriend.

Not only are young women often assigned sole responsibility for the sex act, but they are also assigned the responsibility of dealing with any consequences that ensue from the sexual act. For example, Miranda emphasized the importance of giving birth to the child and caring for him as the responsible way to accept the consequences of her sexual activity: "So, yeah, me and my mom found out at the exact same time. So I was scared, didn't wanna believe it, and [pauses] nervous, but I decided to keep him because I made the responsibility to do what I did so, it was my responsibility to take care of him." Miranda's statement is admittedly cryptic, but it seems that she correlates her sole responsibility for the sexual act (i.e., "doing what I did") with her responsibility to raise the child, not noting responsibilities of the partner in the sexual act.

The "opened my legs" trope, as it is used to explain sexual and reproductive outcomes, conflates the participants' sexual activity with carrying a pregnancy to term, giving birth, and long-term childrearing, thereby limiting an understanding of options and influences shaping young pregnant and mothering women's experiences. Although sexual partners have multiple points of decision-making along the way (e.g., Plan B contraception, abortion, adoption), discussion of these decisions did not often surface in the focus groups and were not the focus of the study. There are powerful ideological rationales for a worldview that sees women's participation in heterosexual intercourse as tacit agreement to carry any potential pregnancies to term: some see sex as first and foremost a procreative act and abortion as an unacceptable, and potentially dangerous, option. In a later point of the discussion, Sandra said she does "not believe in abortion, at all. I just think it is wrong." Miranda never explicitly referenced her beliefs about other options for dealing with an unexpected or unwanted pregnancy. Beyond their personal views on abortion, it is important to note that Sandra and Miranda's explanations of their sexual and reproductive outcomes reflect a pattern in U.S. media and prevention campaign representations of teenage pregnancy. Such representations often simplify the complicated politics of the "choices" women have in terms of sexual and reproductive outcomes (Kelly 51; Murphy 9; Nathanson 50).

In addition, Miranda's comment that "it was my responsibility to take care of him" presents the inequitably gendered task of childrearing as a consequence of her sexual activity. Research suggests that women of all ages are more likely than men to do the labour of childrearing, whether they are the biological parent or not (Collins 192; Crittenden 25; O'Reilly 17). Reality-based television and teenage pregnancy prevention campaign representations of the life of the teen mom de-politicize this gendered reality by positioning women's primary role in childrearing as a natural consequence of becoming pregnant and raising a child in their teenage years. As we learn from campaigns like the National Campaign to Prevent Teen and Unplanned Pregnancy's 2001 "Sex Has Consequences" series, and from the MTV reality series *Teen Mom*, young mothers are supposed to be at home changing diapers and missing out on opportunities for friendships and dating.[4] Rather than presenting this as an unfair lived outcome of the patriarchal, neoliberal construction of childrearing as a private, individualized task for which women have exclusive responsibility, these events are constructed as obvious and inevitable outcomes of sexual relations. Young mothers, their partners, parents, and friends may thereby internalize this message and, in turn, participate in the construction of this lived experience. Specifically, young mothers may face hostility and rejection from people who think they have made "bad choices" and should, thus, pay for the consequences by doing the labour of pregnancy and childrearing on their own (Kaplan 73). Furthermore, as we will discuss in the following section, young mothers may be persuaded by these messages to believe that being a responsible mother means refusing breaks from mothering or opportunities for relaxation or socialization.

Instance 2: Woman as Entirely Responsible for Childrearing Tasks

Indeed, another theme that emerged around "responsibility" and motherhood was the obligation that many participants felt to stay at home with their children at all times. During a focus group session in the juvenile correctional facility, the "open my legs" trope surfaced as the discussion turned to the need to stop "going out" when one has a child. For example, Belinda explained, "Yeah, and you want to go out. And you can't. You don't have anyone to watch your baby so it's like, 'Really?'" Pregnancy and motherhood are often represented as a time when women need to sacrifice friendships or any other type of fun that is not related to childrearing. Connie related to Belinda's feelings as she pointed out, "Then like, if you do [go out], you'll feel like, I'd feel guilty, like I was all having fun while someone else is taking care of my kid." Belinda then responded:

> That's how I felt. Now I still feel like that, because my mom is taking care of my kids so it's like, I know she is tired. So, that's why I need to go home. To help my mom. Do my responsibility—what I am 'posed to be doing. But it is hard. [She laughs]. It is hard. You know, friends be coming over, you be like "Oh, I can't come out, I am watching my baby right now." And usually they are going to a party and you hear it was good, and it is like "Really? He was there? What? Oh, I wanted to see!" You know? It's like, that's why we want to have fun. My mom says, "That's what you do when you open your legs! You got to take responsibility" [laughter from the group].

Belinda learns that "opening your legs" demands responsibility. Her mother's metonymic reference to Belinda's body brings attention to Belinda's need to stay at home with the child. Good mothers are supposed to stay home with their children and miss out on fun and socializing. Another participant, Beatrice, explained:

Even though you have friends and everything and you feel like, "Oh, I wanna go out with them too." But you have a baby, so you got to take care of the baby instead of having your mother, like, taking care of it. Or, I, you could just take care of your baby and be a good mother. I don't know because, I used to go out too ... and my mom [would] take care of the baby while I was out and I [would] feel guilty about that.

Beatrice understands the dominant cultural narrative that a good mother abstains from social activities so she can always act as the sole and primary caregiver for her child.

This construction of good motherhood ultimately devalues extended kin support, and it also conflicts with advice that is often given to older women who have children, such as "take a night off" or "take time for yourself."[5] In fact, scholars of white, middle-class motherhood often critique the guilt women are made to feel as part of the "institution of motherhood" that positions women as uniquely responsible for all aspects of caregiving (O'Reilly 20). The rhetoric of good motherhood is largely defined by a mother's ability to stay with her child at all times and to sacrifice her own self-development for the child. These expectations invariably shape the experiences of women who mother. As Molly explained, "My parents don't [babysit]. I don't go out. Ever." In fact, the idea that young mothers should never go out, that they should sacrifice their education, and that they should focus their entire attention on their child is typically used as a persuasive tactic to convince others to avoid pregnancy and childrearing during their teen years (see Stay Teen; "You're Supposed to Be Out").[6] This rhetoric of what it takes to be a good mother stifles young mothers' opportunities for personal achievement and contributes to a self-perception of personal unworthiness, both of which may propel an acceptance of undue responsibility for negative public judgment, as we will discuss in the following section.

Instance 3: Woman as Deserving of Public Judgment

Perhaps the most disconcerting use of the trope was when a participant used it to explain who was responsible for the hostile stares and comments she received as a teenage mother. Belinda, again, referenced the effects of opening her legs when she explained how she dealt with "enemies" or "people that just be hating you, that say something about you.... That's what I had in school. People just looking at me while I am in there." Belinda explained that these scrutinizing stares and comments, particularly directed at her growing mid-section, did not really bother her because she understood, "Like, it's me that opened my legs and got pregnant. It's not them.... It's not them that having a baby, it's me. So I really don't care [about their opinions]." Belinda further explains that, while she may be deserving of this negative attention, she is too busy with the responsibility of her actions to care or worry about it. Her comment suggests that she understands the cause of these judgments to be her visible pregnancy, rather than a culture that continually legitimates the public scrutiny and disciplining of specific types of pregnant and mothering women in the name of social progress (Roberts 8-10, 295; Solinger 4, 21). Belinda's conception reflects common discourses perpetuated by teen pregnancy prevention campaigns that construct pregnant teenagers as abnormal and deserving of scrutiny. For example, in 2007, One Milwaukee launched a prevention campaign featuring "Pregnant Boys"—young men photo-shopped to appear pregnant—with the tagline "It Shouldn't Be Any Less Disturbing When It's a Girl" ("Pregnant Boys"). These ads prompt Milwaukeeans to see young women's pregnancies as "disturbing" and, presumably, to judge them accordingly.[7]

Such representations encourage and legitimize public scrutiny of young pregnant and mothering women. At a focus group session with students at the rural TAPP program, we discussed whether there should be a school or city-based campaign that encourages people to be more respectful of young pregnant and mothering women—an idea that surfaced in our previous three focus groups at other sites. Participants dismissed this idea by explaining that hostile stares and commentary from strangers are expected consequences of teenage pregnancy and motherhood. Mia explained, "We might of not all been like 'hey let's get pregnant,' but we chose to have a child." Mia suggests that when young women decide to raise a child during their teens, they should expect to experience open hostility. Miranda then responded to Mia's comment, explaining, "We did what we did and put ourselves in that situation." It is unclear whether the "situation" Miranda is referring to is the sex act (recall her earlier comment about childrearing as the responsible course of action) or carrying the pregnancy to term and raising the child. Mia thought there was no point to a public awareness campaign because she did not think it mattered—"rude people" are going to make comments to young pregnant and mothering women because that is the consequence of teenage pregnancy. In this sense, judgment and disrespectful treatment is regarded as an inevitable consequence of young motherhood.

WHAT ABOUT FATHERS?

In the previous section, we explored how participants' use of the trope "I was the one who opened my legs," and other comments about the responsibilities of sex, good motherhood, and public scrutiny, reflect common themes in media representations and teenage pregnancy prevention campaigns. These tropes prompt women to accept patriarchal gender binaries that position them as solely responsible for any consequences of sexual acts and deserving of any hostile reactions to their pregnancies or motherhood. In this section, we share who our participants identified as helpful with their pregnancies and raising their child. Specifically, we discuss the apparent disparity between the support offered by mothers and fathers, the (often undervalued) assistance from other relatives, and the ways in which the participants' experiences and stories disrupt the poignant gender binary for sex, pregnancy, and parenthood.

Our questionnaire included two questions about help with pregnancy and childrearing. Specifically, we asked if anyone was 1) helping them through their pregnancy and 2) helping them raise their child. We provided a list of possible people, such as friends, their own mothers and fathers, the baby's father, grandparents, and other relatives, and prompted them to circle all that applied to their experience. We did not specify what "help" meant, so as participants circled items they could have been thinking of financial, emotional, or labour-related support. During the focus groups, participants shared stories that often clarified what types of help were offered by different supportive figures in their life.

Mothers Provide More Support than Fathers

Mothers were reported to be the most supportive group for participants with 77 percent reporting that their mother helped them during pregnancy and 81 percent helped with raising their child. This was confirmed during the focus groups when participants often mentioned their mothers in stories about going to health clinics and managing childcare. Friends were also a strong of source of support during the pregnancy (67 percent); however, after the birth of the child, support from friends decreased (26 percent). During our focus group discussions of the participants' experiences with mothering a baby, there were few mentions of friends. As previously discussed, some participants explained that they no longer "went out" to socialize after having their baby, which may explain why friends are less present as sources of support when raising children.

In comparison to mothers, fathers (both of the participant and of her baby) appear to be less helpful. Overall, we learned many participants' fathers played a limited role in supporting the pregnancy and caring for the child. Less than half of participants reported their fathers as a source of support during the pregnancy (41 percent) or with raising the child (48 percent). If their fathers were present in their life, most participants explained that their dads were simply angry with them for being pregnant, or they were quiet about the matter.

During some focus groups, it was difficult to broach the subject of the baby's father given that some of the participants did not have any contact with them. Less than half of participants reported the child's father as a source of support during the pregnancy (48 percent), although support from the child's father marginally increased after birth (59 percent). At least three participants reported a marked decrease in contributions from the child's father once he started dating a different woman. Usually, if the baby's father was distant, the family of the father was too.

For many participants who remained in contact with the baby's father, comments often centered on disappointment about the father's lack of responsibility or questionable presence. For example, some participants explained how their babies' fathers did not make plans or change their behaviours to support the pregnant mother or the child after learning of the pregnancy. Some participants were upset that having the baby meant continued contact with the father of the child. Sara, a participant at the urban TAPP program, explained that her baby's father "loves the baby, but I think it's more that he just wants to have me here." Her peer, Sasha, agreed: "Same here. I think my baby's dad uses it as like 'oh well I'll have this baby with her.' But a lot of times it's just like, 'Well, how are you doing?' or 'What are you doing?' ...He uses the baby as an excuse to check up on me and see what I am doing and like keep me around." At the community-based site, Tabitha shared her story of coming to the realization that, although she loved the father of her two children, she needed to leave him because of his controlling behaviours, which included calling her thirty times when she left the house and demanding that she not wear dresses or makeup. She feared his behaviour would be a bad example for her daughters. For Tabitha, Sara, and Sasha, the continued presence of the father was a problem—or at least not very helpful for raising their children. Instead, the help of their mothers or other family members was key. The diversity of these participants' stories demonstrates that the presence or absence of help from the father of the child cannot be simply labelled "bad" or "good."

Valuing "Other" Support and Disrupting the Gender Binary

Focusing solely on the biological mother and father of a child often obscures how others may support pregnancy and childrearing.[8] This does not honour the enhanced role of extended families and communities that many cultures embrace—or would like to embrace—in the raising of children. In fact, our data suggests that "others" are as supportive if not more supportive than fathers; 56 percent of our participants identified other relatives as helpful with pregnancy and 59 percent identified other relatives as helpful with childrearing. Popular representations of teenage pregnancy and motherhood in pregnancy prevention campaigns typically do not highlight the supportive role of "others" in parenting. Rather, they emphasize the likely absence of the father and use this as a persuasive tactic to 1) convince the public that teenage childrearing is a problem and 2) encourage young women to avoid sex and pregnancy. For example, a 2008 Candie's Foundation public service announcement video featuring Jenny McCarthy ends with a young man symbolically abandoning a young woman with a baby and McCarthy telling the young woman, "Welcome to reality" ("Jenny McCarthy"). As another example, in 2013, the New York City Human Resources Administration's teenage pregnancy prevention campaign included a poster featuring a small child adjacent to the statement: "Honestly, mom, chances are he won't stay with you. What happens to me?" Through this line of reasoning, young women are encouraged to see a man's absence and lack of help as always detrimental to their future. In addition, these representations suggest that a man's conscious decision to leave his pregnant partner and/or his child is an expected consequence of the pregnancy because she is the one who "opened her legs."

At the urban TAPP school focus group session, a lively discussion erupted when participants critiqued the dual standards for mothers and fathers of teen pregnancies. Frieda explained that the obligation to care for the pregnancy and child is "not on the guy. It's like, if they want, they can walk out whenever they want and we can't." Sara agreed, pointing out, "It's assumed that the mom is there for the baby, and that if the mom's not there it's like really bad. But the guys—it's like something that is normal." Frieda responded, "The pressure's not on them!" At the community-based focus group, Courtney suggested that:

> People are more accepting if [fathers of teen pregnancies] decide not to do something. Not enough people are standing up and saying, "Hey, you're in this too. Just because you are not the one who is physically attached to it." I think people are just letting them off really easy…. I mean if he does decide to stick around people really don't do anything. I don't think he gets judged; he gets congratulated.

The gender binaries are poignant—the pregnant or mothering young woman is judged harshly while the father is not expected to be supportive.

Courtney's observation about the differences in public reactions to pregnancies and parenthood, particularly that fathers are "congratulated" if they participate in childrearing in any way, is echoed by feminist writers and researchers studying the gender dynamics of childrearing. For example, in her article "The Single Parent Double Standard," Ellen Friedrichs draws on recent research from the *Journal of Feminist Family Therapy* to demonstrate that people demonize single mothers as women who made poor choices while martyring single fathers as honourable victims of circumstance. In other words, the gendered expectations communicated in representations of the "problem" of teenage pregnancy and critiqued by young mothers do not just affect the lives of teen mothers and their children. They also contribute to and reflect our understanding and practices of fatherhood in general. As previously discussed, our data indicate less involvement on the part of the fathers of participants as well as the fathers of the pregnancies, which suggests men, too, learn the lesson of who is responsible for supporting pregnancy and childrearing and may act accordingly. Drawing on her interviews with twenty-six teenage fathers, sociologist Jennifer Beggs Weber demonstrates how the young men in her study blamed their teen female partners for failing to prevent the pregnancy and/or deciding to keep the child (also see Paschal 62). Weber explains that her participants relied on "norms of masculinity—specifically that sexuality is an essential and natural part of masculinity, but family planning (and all things family-related) is the domain of women" to suggest that they are not responsible for pregnancy or childrearing (911). Indeed, messages in dominant teen pregnancy discourses often naturalize the disproportionate labour of women in childrearing by positioning this labour as a premise in a claim about the importance of preventing teen pregnancy. Yet, we should also be skeptical of representations that persuade us to believe that the fathers of teen pregnancies are always absent because of a selfish desire to leave. For example, there are multiple factors—including but not limited to racism, economic disparity, and immigration policies—that contribute to the absence of men in low-income communities of colour.

CONCLUSION

The teen "mother-blame game" is continually supported by popular media and pregnancy prevention campaign representations that naturalize the cultural belief that women have sole responsibility for pregnancies and any other consequences that arise from sex acts. The instances in our focus groups when participants explained life circumstances with the phrase "I opened my legs" demonstrate that young women may internalize the beliefs that they are responsible for pregnancy and childrearing and that they are deserving of any disrespect and hostility they experience. Furthermore, in accordance with societal norms and the media messages that perpetuate them, less than half of our participants reported that their own fathers provided support and only about half of the babies' fathers provided help. Although researchers, activists, and young mothers have been speaking out against these issues for several decades, our data and analysis suggest that these gendered realities remain prevalent.

So where do we go from here? In considering which steps to take, we approach this problem from our different disciplinary lenses. Jenna is a trained scholar of rhetoric—attentive to the ways in which symbolic representations produce (and are produced by) lived, material realities. From this perspective, it is important to deconstruct and problematize teenage pregnancy prevention campaigns. Recently, young mothers and reproductive justice advocates Natasha Vianna, Gloria Malone, Jasmin Colon, Consuela Greene, Lisette Orellana, Christina Martinez, and Marylouise Kuti-Schubert have taken great strides to intervene in negative teen pregnancy prevention campaigns—such as the ones forwarded by Candie's Foundation and the New York Human Resources Administration—through their #NoTeenShame campaign. These activists call for the end of representations that shame and stigmatize young parents because these tactics 1) make life harder for young parents and 2) do not actually help to prevent pregnancies. Malone explains, "Overall, as a society, we need to realize there's no need to mention young parents and their families when we're talking about prevention" (qtd. in Culp-Ressler).

We support these activists' efforts and, based on our findings, we add that negative representations of teen parents in pregnancy prevention initiatives also encourage ready acceptance of heterosexist beliefs that affect women of all ages. Public service announcements often suggest that men are inevitably hypersexual and less responsible for pregnancy prevention and childrearing, that motherhood means the end of a socially/politically active life, and that childrearing is naturally a woman's prerogative. Family-planning advocates must address how these representations encourage mother-blaming and naturalize inequitable childrearing practices. Renewed focus on these issues is especially important given that 82 percent of all custodial parents are mothers and only 38 percent of custodial parents receive the full amount of child support they are entitled to (Solomon-Fears 2). Women may be more likely to raise children on their own, but involuntary single motherhood should not be represented as a woman's fault, and voluntary single motherhood should not be pathologized as always detrimental to the future of the woman and child. The lack of structural and social support that is available to mothers is not a reason to campaign against pregnancy; rather, it should give reason to address the socioeconomic issues that cause this lack of support.

Sally is a trained social scientist—attentive to the ways in which data are collected, analyzed, and utilized. From a feminist research perspective, the subjective nature of "objective data" must be acknowledged. Findings can be impacted by who is (and is not) included in the research, what questions are asked, how the questions are framed, and how the data are analyzed. Thus, research can be construed to fit a particular agenda. For example, teen pregnancy can be made to look more problematic if data are summarized for all teen pregnancies, yet the vast majority of teen pregnancies are among older teens, aged eighteen and nineteen years. Moreover, as noted earlier [and below], the age of the father is rarely reported or included in data analysis. Researchers, educators, medical providers, family-planning personnel, and pregnant and parenting teens should be educated on how data can be manipulated to represent experiences of teen pregnancy and parenting as singularly problematic. It is thus important to critique how data are employed in teenage pregnancy prevention campaigns and to understand how such campaigns perpetuate narrow and harmful ideologies—namely the belief that young pregnant and mothering women must withdraw from their education and social lives to care for their children, thus increasing the likelihood that they will experience long-term poverty and isolation.

In concluding, it is important to highlight some limitations of our analysis. Our data on fatherhood are limited by the fact that we did not speak to the fathers of participants' pregnancies. Some qualitative research does suggest that teen fathers similarly believe that their female teen partners are to blame for unexpected pregnancies and should assume the primary role in childrearing (Paschal 62, 78-87; Weber 910). These studies focused specifically on teen fathers as a way to respond to the stereotypes and stigmas of teen fatherhood. Yet, as sociologist Mike Males points out, six out of ten fathers of "teen pregnancies" are not teens, and we do not count the pregnancies that male teens father with non-teen women as "teen pregnancies" (21). Future research could consider the perspectives and practices of responsibility for sex, pregnancy, and childrearing by non-teen men, not only because it is more likely that a non-teen man will father the pregnancy of a female teen, but also because our data demonstrate a lack of support from both the participants' fathers and the fathers of the participants' pregnancies. Mother-blaming discourses often obscure how men assume and shirk responsibility in matters of sex, pregnancy, and childrearing as well as the social structures that shape men's actions.

In advocating for renewed attention to this discourse, we do not mean to suggest that young women do not already negotiate and contest these messages. As illustrated by participants' comments about dual standards for mothers and fathers of teen pregnancies, many participants demonstrated a critical awareness of these injustices as they explicitly critiqued sexist worldviews. Due to limited time and resources, we did not fully explore these differences in participants' perspectives, nor did we investigate how these outlooks shifted across research sites and participant demographics. Future research could explore the differences that shape whether young women accept or reject these worldviews. Our objective in this chapter was to highlight how the cultural beliefs about responsibility and good motherhood that surfaced in the focus groups reflect and reproduce sexist tropes and themes in popular discourses about teenage pregnancy. The teen mother-blame game continues the troubling tradition of positioning women's fertility as a public target of blame that interferes with the liberty, respect, and equity of all women, regardless of age and mothering status.

ENDNOTES

[1]In fact, some researchers demonstrate that poor women who give birth earlier in life help to ensure better social support and physical health for themselves and their children (Geronimus 883; Males 22).
[2]We are extremely grateful to the participants of this study. This research was made possible by funding from the Crossroads Collaborative and the Southwest Institute for Research on Women.
[3]The focus on women's bodies as a source of blame for men's sexual and/or abusive acts has been explored by feminist theorists studying rape culture. For one example, Cahill.
[4]For further discussion of these themes in the National Campaign's ad see Vinson; for analysis of the MTV reality television series see Todd.
[5]Of course, even the advice to "take a night off" reinforces the assumption that mothers should be otherwise child-focused 24/7. Here is a prime example of the conflicting perspectives on good mothers needing a break: The website of the U.S. psychologist/celebrity "Dr. Phil" McGraw includes an article titled "Four-Step Priority Plan for Mothers" that aims to help mothers change their perception of what a "good mother is" so that mothers "don't feel guilty for taking time for yourself. It's not selfish to make yourself a priority." On the same website, the article "Teen Pregnancy: Adoption or Motherhood?" is designed to help pregnant teenagers decide between motherhood and adoption (the only two options

provided). This article asks pregnant teens considering motherhood whether they are "prepared to end their adolescence" and "make sacrifices over the next 20 years." While this article prompts pregnant teens to think of motherhood as a twenty-year period of sacrifice that curtails self-development, the article aimed at seemingly married, older mothers explicitly challenges the assumption that good mothers always sacrifice themselves for their children.

[6]For example, the National Campaign to Prevent Teen and Unplanned Pregnancy's website StayTeen.org, designed as a means of providing pregnancy prevention messages and contraception information to teenagers, includes a series of public service announcements that represent adolescence as an always active, social, happy, and carefree period of life in order to encourage viewers to "stay teen." This implies that once a teen becomes pregnant or a parent, s/he cannot be active, social, or happy. Other PSAs on this site, such as the "Stay Joven" series aimed at Latina/o youth, feature a friend of a teen mother who talks about how she never sees her friend anymore because "she had to take care of her baby." In much the same way, the public service announcement featured on the home page of the Candie's Foundation website exclaims, "You're supposed to be out changing the world ... not changing diapers" (ellipses in original). This claim is built on the premise that parents are never "out" doing things publically/civically/socially. They supposedly are (and, it is implied, should be) "in" changing diapers.

[7]In 2013, the Chicago Department of Public Health re-purposed these images in their own teenage pregnancy prevention campaign titled "Unexpected." For further analysis of these ad campaigns and their potentially harmful effects for transgendered people see "Pregnant Boys and a Counter Ad" and Beauchamp.

[8]Patricia Hill Collins' observations on the importance and value of "women-centered family networks" in African-American communities speak to this point. Collins brings attention to the role of "othermothers" or women in the community who help to raise the child but are not the biological mother. Collins writes that "women's centrality" to childrearing "is characterized less by the absence of husbands and fathers than by the significance of women" (192, emphasis in original). Representations of family

that idealize childrearing in a privatized, heterosexual, two-parent family structure overlook (or even pathologize) communal childrearing practices.

WORKS CITED

Beauchamp, Toby. "Expectations: Trans Youth and Reproductive Politics in Public Space." *Media Fields Journal* 7 (2013): n.pag. Web. 6 May 2014.

Cahill, Ann J. "Foucault, Rape, and the Construction of the Feminine Body." *Hypatia* 15.1 (2000): 43-63. Web. 6 May 2014.

Cashdan, Elizabeth. "Smiles, Speeches, and Body Posture: How Women and Men Display. Sociometric Status and Power." *Journal of Nonverbal Behaviour* 22.4 (1998): 209-28. Web. 6 May 2014.

Chase, Susan E. "'Good' Mothers and 'Bad' Mothers." *Mothers and Children: Feminist Analyses and Personal Narratives.* Ed. Susan Chase and Mary Rogers. New Jersey: Rutgers University Press, 2001. 30-59. Print.

Collins, Patricia Hill. *Black Feminist Thought: Knowledge, Consciousness, and the Politics of Empowerment.* New York: Routledge, 2009. Print.

Crittenden, Ann. *The Price of Motherhood: Why the Most Important Job in the World is Still the Least Valued.* 10th ed. New York: Picador, 2010. Print.

Culp-Ressler, Tara. "How to Help Prevent Teen Pregnancies without Shaming Young Women." Think Progress. Center for American Progress. 1 May 2014. Web. 8 Oct. 2014.

Fonow, Mary Margaret and Judith Cook. *Beyond Methodology: Feminist Scholarship as Lived Research.* Indianapolis: Indiana University Press, 1991. Print.

"Four-Step Priority Plan for Mothers." Dr. Phil. n.d. Web. 8 Oct. 2014.

Friedrichs, Ellen. "The Single Parent Double Standard: Demonizing the Moms and Martyrizing the Dads." *Everyday Feminism* 20 Apr. 2014. Web. 8 Oct. 2015.

Furstenberg, Frank F. *Destinies of the Disadvantaged: The Politics of Teen Childbearing.* New York: Russell Sage Foundation, 2007. Print.

Geronimus, Arline T. "Damned If You Do: Culture, Identity, Privilege, and Teenage Childbearing in the United States." *Social Science & Medicine* 57 (2003): 881-93. Web. 31 Jan 2010.

"Jenny McCarthy PSA." The Candie's Foundation. 2011. Web. 3 Sept. 2012.

Kaplan, Elaine Bell. *Not Our Kind of Girl: Unraveling the Myths of Black Teenage Motherhood.* Berkeley: University of California Press, 1997. Print.

Kearney, Melissa Schettini and Phillip B. Levine. "Why is the Teen Birth Rate in the United States So High and Why Does it Matter?" Working Paper 17965. Cambridge: National Bureau of Economic Research, 2012. Web. 4 Apr 2014.

Kelly, Deirdre M. *Pregnant with Meaning: Teen Mothers and the Politics of Inclusive Schooling.* New York: Peter Lang, 2000. Print.

Luker, Kristin. *Dubious Conceptions: The Politics of Teenage Pregnancy.* Cambridge: Harvard University Press, 1996. Print.

Males, Mike. *Teenage Sex and Pregnancy: Modern Myths, Unsexy Realities.* Santa Barbara: Praeger, 2010. Print.

Martin, Karin. "Becoming a Gendered Body: Practices of Pre-schools." *American Sociological Review* 63 (1998): 494-511. Print.

Murphy, Caryn. "Teen Momism on MTV: Postfeminist Subjectivities in 16 and Pregnant." *MTV and Teen Pregnancy: Critical Essays on 16 and Pregnant and Teen Mom.* Ed. Letizia Guglielmo. Lanham: Scarecrow Press, 2013. 3-18. Print.

Nathanson, Constance. *Dangerous Passage: The Social Control of Sexuality in Women's Adolescence.* Philadelphia: Temple University Press, 1991. Print.

O'Reilly, Andrea. "Outlaw(ing) Motherhood: A Theory and Politic of Maternal Empowerment for the Twenty-first Century." *Hecate* 36.1-2 (2010): 17-29. Web. 11 June 2014.

Paschal, Angelia M. *Voices of African-American Teen Fathers: "I'm Doing What I Got to Do."* New York: The Hawthorth Press, 2006. Print.

Pope, Catherine, Sue Ziebland, and Nicholas Mays. "Qualitative Data in Health Care: Analyzing Qualitative Data." *British Journal of Medicine* 320 (2000): 114-16. Print.

"Pregnant Boys." United Way of Greater Milwaukee and SERVE

Marketing, 2007. Web. 1 July 2015.

"Pregnant Boys and a Counter Ad." Media Literacy Project. Albuquerque Academy. n.d. Web. 6 May 2014.

Roberts, Dorothy. Killing the Black Body: Race, Reproduction, and the Meaning of Liberty. New York: Pantheon Books, 1997. Print.

SmithBattle, Lee. "Legacies of Advantage and Disadvantage: The Case of Teen Mothers." *Public Health Nursing* 24.5 (2007): 409-20. Web. 21 Jan. 2011.

Solinger, Rickie. *Pregnancy and Power: A Short History of Reproductive Politics in America.* New York: New York University Press, 2005. Print.

Solomon-Fears, Carmen. *Child Support: An Overview of Census Bureau Data on Recipients.* U.S. Congressional Research Service. 13 Dec. 2013. Web. 8 Oct. 2014.

Stay Teen. The National Campaign to Prevent Teen Pregnancy. 2014. Web. 6 May 2014.

"Teen Pregnancy: Adoption or Motherhood?" *Dr. Phil.* n.d. Web. 8 Oct. 2014.

Todd, Anastasia. "Teen Moms Negotiate Desire: The (Re)Production of Patriarchal Motherhood, Morality, and the Myth of Choice." MTV *and Teen Pregnancy: Critical Essays on 16 and Pregnant and Teen Mom.* Ed. Letizia Guglielmo. Lanham: Scarecrow Press, 2013. 35-48. Print.

Vinson, Jenna. *Teenage Mothers as Rhetors and Rhetoric: An Analysis of Embodied Exigence and Constrained Agency.* Diss. University of Arizona, 2013. Print.

Vinson, Jenna, and Sally Stevens. "Preventing Pregnancy OR Supporting Students? Learning from the Stories of Young Mothers." *Sexuality Research and Social Policy* 11.4 (2014): 322-36. Web. 1 July 2015.

Weber, Jennifer Beggs. "Becoming Teen Fathers: Stories of Teen Pregnancy, Responsibility, and Masculinity." *Gender & Society* 26.6 (2012): 900-21. Web. 16 Sept. 2014.

Young, Iris. *Throwing Like a Girl and Other Essays in Feminist Philosophy and Social Theory.* Bloomington: Indiana University Press, 1984. Print.

"You're Supposed to Be Out Changing the World." The Candie's Foundation. 2013. Web. 6 May 2014.

6.
"Because You Had Me as a Teen"

Neoliberalism and the "Problem" of Teen Pregnancy

VANESSA REIMER

I'm twice as likely not to graduate high school because you had me as a teen.
—New York City's 2013
"The Real Cost of Teen Pregnancy" campaign

You're supposed to be changing the world ... not changing diapers.
—2013 teen pregnancy prevention campaign
by the Candie's Foundation

I N HIS 2013 STATE OF THE union address, U.S. President Barack Obama listed teen pregnancy directly after violent crime as a social ill that is threatening young citizens' quality of life. Later that year, May 1 was declared the National Day to Prevent Teen Pregnancy. Both of these instances illustrate the pervasive belief that young motherhood is fundamentally and unequivocally deleterious to the well-being of individual women and children—so much so that it requires its own designated periods of prevention and awareness, much like breast cancer and heart disease. In a similar vein, common sense rhetoric in North America constructs "teen pregnancy" rates as so integral to societal well-being that their growth or decline provokes numerous media headlines and government-funded reports which speculate about their broader impacts. This chapter accordingly employs an intersectional (Crenshaw) feminist materialist framework to examine how two 2013 US teen pregnancy prevention campaigns operationalize neoliberal discourses of individual risk management and, in so doing, construct young mothers as the individual causes and perpetuators of poverty in their communities and society at large. Importantly, it also considers how young mothers and their allies work to resist the hegemonic "good mothering" ideologies that pathologize and devalue their maternal practice.

THE MATERIAL FOUNDATIONS
OF "GOOD MOTHERING" IDEOLOGIES

This analysis begins with the premise that women's particular ways of knowing and experiencing the world are rooted in the material conditions of their lives (Hartsock 218-219), and these conditions further intersect with identity markers such as race and ethnicity, sexual orientation, gender identity, age, and bodily ability (Collins 311). Furthermore, women's lived experiences are intrinsically shaped by a sexual division of labour that is predicated on their mythical-universal potential to conceive, bear, and raise children (Hartsock 223). For this reason women are held collectively responsible for performing social reproductive work, such as providing physical and emotional care for those who cannot care for themselves (Abramovitz 15-16). This work most often—and most visibly—involves the physical and pedagogical reproduction of children. However, even though social reproductive work such as childcare is integral to the functioning of any nation's socio-economic order, it is ultimately devalued by the prevalent belief that women are "naturally" suited to provide such care, as well as the belief that such work is a "private" enterprise that should be unwaged and confined to the domestic sphere. In this regard, women's social reproductive work, and particularly childcare, is constructed as a "labour of love" with little or no market value in the public sphere.

These beliefs about the nature and value of women's social reproductive work play a critical role in determining ideologies of "good" mothering, and women's abilities to fulfill such expectations are invariably constrained by the material conditions of their lives. In a contemporary North American socioeconomic context, such expectations are largely contingent upon a middle-class lifestyle, while the mothering performed by poor and working-class mothers is consequently pathologized. In this sense, "good" mothering ideologies first and foremost necessitate an economically self-sufficient family unit comprised of a male breadwinner and full-time female caregiver (Walkerdine and Lucey 227, 233). They are further informed by ideologies of white supremacy that have been enacted and sustained through systems of economic exploitation, all of which work to devalue the mothering performed by racialized women (hooks 60). Ideologies that identify, blame, and shame "bad mothers" are thereby aptly contextualized within the material conditions and intersecting identity markers that constrain women's lived experiences. As such, the dominant discourses which construct and perpetuate the "problem" of teen pregnancy should be specifically contextualized within the neoliberal socioeconomic and ideological frameworks that currently enjoy dominant status within North American industrial capitalism.

INTENSIVE MOTHERING AND NEOLIBERAL RISK MANAGEMENT

North America's neoliberal turn has manifested through numerous interconnecting material and ideological shifts. Neoliberal socioeconomic restructuring was enabled in the 1970s as Western governments began dismantling social safety nets and opening their borders to international competition, thus effecting market inflation and increased costs of living (Abramovitz 20-21). These structural transformations materialized most vividly throughout the 1980s and 1990s as social spending shifted significantly from service provisions to private investments (Wall 163). The neoliberal turn has since been solidified through continued market deregulation and decentralization, the diminished production of social goods, and the upsurge in precarious labour conditions wherein employees work temporary, part-time, flexible positions for more hours and less pay in order to achieve economic self-sufficiency (England 136; Madsen 25; Smith 830; Tomlinson 401, 407; Wall 162).

Ideologically, the neoliberal turn has materialized through shifting beliefs about citizenship rights and responsibilities. In this sense, "good citizens" are primarily demarcated by their economic self-sufficiency, and the material benefits that one may expect to receive from the State—such as unemployment insurance and subsidized childcare—have been severely limited by ideologies of personal responsibility and self-reliance (Madsen 26-28, 32; Wall 162). Along this trajectory, discourses of individual risk management have been integral to perpetuating and naturalizing the neoliberal turn (Wall 162-163). As Glenda Wall argues, "Inherent in neoliberal risk discourse is the assumption of individual responsibility for risk mitigation, and the assumption that individuals, if they educate themselves and plan accordingly, can anticipate and control situations, and influence outcomes" (167). Within this discursive framework, unemployment and poverty are conceptualized as individual failures, rather than being symptomatic of broader socioeconomic structures and cycles (England 136).

Neoliberal risk discourses have also been instrumental in forging ideologies of "proper" family structures and "good mothering" ideologies. Neoliberal policies and ideologies necessitate that "the family" operates as a site of individual responsibility and economic self-sufficiency, which in turn justifies the State's retreat from social welfare governance and economic regulation (England 132; Madsen 29). Neoliberalism accordingly necessitates a sharp demarcation between "public" market productivity and "private" domestic life, thereby absolving the State from any stake or responsibility in social reproduction. To that end, voices from the "New Right" that gained momentum throughout the 1980s and 1990s constructed a political platform which fused neoliberal economics with socially conservative political ideologies, therein constructing economic privatization and "traditional family values" as inextricably linked—even though this "traditional" family structure has never been accessible to many poor, working-class, or racialized populations in North America, and it has also become increasingly inaccessible to white, middle-class families today (hooks 134; Ruether 84). Nonetheless, neoliberal "common sense" rhetoric maintains that this privatized family structure is universally attainable through individualized planning and risk management (Cady 367; Vavrus 49), and socially conservative political ideologies naturalize the belief that the "private" work of social reproduction should be exclusively performed "in the home" by women who are biologically suited to provide such care (England 138; Wall 162).

It is within this discursive framework that neoliberal policies intersect with and reproduce intensive mothering ideologies. Andrea O'Reilly explains how cultural conceptions of "good" mothering require women to invest lavish amounts of time, money, and energy in providing care for their children (38-39). It is pertinent to note that these intensive standards reached fruition throughout the 1980s in conjunction with renewed glorification of the "traditional" nuclear family, and that these ideological shifts further coincided with increased costs of living that propelled unprecedented numbers of women into the workforce (Campbell 185; Wall 162). Sharon Hays accordingly argues that women's commitment to intensive mothering serves the demands of free market enterprise since they are overrepresented in temporary, part-time, low-paying positions while being simultaneously compelled to purchase a vast array of goods to ensure their children's future successes (162). The neoliberal rhetoric of individual choice further justifies women's precarious employment by maintaining that they prefer to engage in "flexible" paid work that allows them more time to perform their "natural" duties as caregivers in the domestic sphere (Vavrus 51).

On the whole, neoliberal policies glorify the mythical "traditional" family structure wherein social reproductive work remains an intensive and unwaged enterprise, while simultaneously undermining this structure by compelling men and women to enter the paid workforce in equal numbers to achieve economic self-sufficiency. This socioeconomic paradox has critical implications for women's lived realities; even though the majority of mothers engage in paid labour out of economic necessity, employment and childcare policies in industrialized countries are informed by intensive mothering ideologies which presume that women can and should provide full-time, unwaged care for their children at home (Campbell 193; Tomlinson 214; Wall 162-163). Furthermore, rather than acknowledge how market inflation and deregulation have compelled increasing numbers of women to enter the paid workforce while childcare benefits have been simultaneously slashed (England 136; Michalopoulos and Robins 466), neoliberal discourses contend that "good" mothering ideals can be achieved through individual risk management. Such discourses are vividly apparent in commonsense rhetoric concerning the "problems" of teen pregnancy and single motherhood.

NEOLIBERALISM AND THE "PROBLEM" OF SINGLE MOTHERHOOD

The threshold of "acceptable" risk regarding parental competence has decreased dramatically as neoliberal economics and intensive mothering ideologies demand ever-increasing material resources for "proper" childrearing (Wall 162-163). Since "good" mothers must foremost maintain social reproductive work as a privatized and unwaged enterprise, it is not surprising that single mothers are incriminated for the challenges they present to the neoliberal socioeconomic order. Even though poverty programs have never represented more than a small fraction of social spending—and even though transnational corporations have greatly benefited from State subsidies under neoliberal policies—single mothers who collect benefits have long borne the brunt of public back-lash in North American neoliberal discourse (Smith 831). Such backlash has also been highly racialized; even though women of colour were largely excluded from the post-war welfare benefits that allowed many middle-class white women to care for their children at home into the 1960s (Abramovitz 19-20; hooks 134; Ruether 93), black single mothers have been particularly demonized through a controlling "welfare queen" discourse that gained prevalence throughout the 1980s (Monahan, Shtrulis and Givens 204; Ruether 93). The neoliberal state thereby seeks to manage the "risk" posed by the reproductive potentials of so-cially undesirable women, and the collective "problem" of single motherhood is ultimately loaded with cultural assumptions about race and economic class.

It is within this neoliberal discursive framework that national imperatives to prevent "teen pregnancy" are critical to consider. Indeed, it would seem that alarmist rhetoric regarding the socio-economic threats posed by single motherhood has shifted from an overtly racialized "welfare queen" discourse to one that focuses on age, even though teen pregnancy rates have been steadily declining in most industrialized nations, including the U.S. (Adams et al. 45; McKay and Barrett 49). However, while the societal "problems" posed by teen pregnancy stem from the economic vulnerability that is structured into young women's lives, neoliberal common-sense rhetoric constructs young motherhood as an unequivocally deleterious social phenomenon in its own right. The neoliberal imperative to mitigate the risk posed by young motherhood is op-erationalized in such state-mandated initiatives as abstinence-only sex education and teen pregnancy prevention campaigns. These examples illustrate the hegemonic presumption that there is a causal relationship between young motherhood and poverty, even though most socioeconomically disadvantaged young mothers do not fare worse than child-free women from the same age demographic and socioeconomic background (Shanok and Miller 252). As Arielle Shanok and Lisa Miller contend:

> According to the prevailing assumptions, teens should not become pregnant because they have not finished school, achieved financial security, and established steady roman-tic relationships. In a neighborhood where over half the population does not finish high school, a large percentage lives below the poverty line, and only a quarter of adult women are married, regardless of age, women may never achieve the conditions deemed necessary for child rearing by these predominantly upper/middle class Caucasian perspectives. (259)

As such, rather than problematize the socioeconomic structures that enforce and naturalize young women's economic vulnerabil-ity, neoliberal discourses take for granted that teenaged mothers function as a societal "risk group." In doing so, they devalue and pathologize the social reproductive work that young mothers per-form, just as they blame and shame teenaged mothers for being the individual causes and perpetuators of poverty in their communities and society at large. I will now explore how a selection of 2013 U.S. teen pregnancy prevention campaigns operationalizes these neoliberal discourses of individual risk management.

TEEN PREGNANCY PREVENTION AS
NEOLIBERAL RISK MANAGEMENT

Several now-infamous teen pregnancy prevention campaigns have garnered heated public discussion in recent years. These include the U.S. National Campaign to Prevent Teen Pregnancy's 2008 print campaign that imposed terms such as "Dirty" and "Reject" over the bodies of racialized teenaged girls,[1] as well as the "Pregnant Boys" campaign launched by the city of Chicago in 2013 (see: "Provocative New Ad Campaign"). The Candie's Foundation, a non-profit organization that seeks to educate and motivate young people to prevent teen pregnancy, has gained particular notoriety for its print and video campaigns, including two 2009 video ads featuring Bristol Palin. The organization contends that its campaigns "use celebrities that teens can relate to, in a style that speaks to teens on their own terms. We go beyond raising awareness; our goal is to influence teen culture" ("Celebrity PSAs").

The Candie's Foundation continued to generate discussion in 2013. In support of the National Day to Prevent Teen Pregnancy, it released a print campaign in May featuring Canadian pop singer Carly Rae Jepsen. "You're supposed to be changing the world ... not changing diapers," reads the ad, which features an immaculately styled Jepsen staring coyly into the camera as an empty crib stands in the background (see "Celebrity PSAs"). This campaign vividly illustrates the neoliberal ideologies which naturalize the privatization of social reproductive work and construct it as inimical to market productivity. Within this discursive framework, a young woman who performs childcare at home cannot "change the world" since "real" productivity only occurs through garnering wages and consuming goods. Such discourses ultimately devalue childrearing and unpaid social reproductive work more generally, just as they naturalize and reinforce the neoliberal socioeconomic structures that render young mothers economically vulnerable.

Similar discourses are employed in a series of teen pregnancy prevention ads that were released by the New York Human Resources Administration in March 2013.[2] This print campaign forges an inextricable causal link between teen motherhood and poverty in New York, even though the city has seen a twenty-seven percent decrease in teen pregnancies throughout the past decade ("Mayor Bloomberg"). Nevertheless, Mayor Michael Bloomberg's office released a press statement promoting the campaign, contending that:

> We aim to build on our success by asking teens to take an honest look at some of the realities of parenthood they may not have considered. By focusing on responsibility and the importance of education, employment, and family in providing children with the emotional and financial support they need, we'll let thousands of young New Yorkers know that waiting to becoming a parent could be the best decision they ever make. ("Mayor Bloomberg")

This statement encapsulates the campaign's larger neoliberal presumption that individual risk management is key to overcoming and avoiding poverty. This initiative accordingly urges young people to purposefully delay pregnancy, even though very few teens engage in sex for the purpose of becoming pregnant or impregnating someone else (Hacker et al. 247). It also fails to address the significant correlation between high teen birth rates and a lack of access to comprehensive sex education and affordable contraception (McKay and Barrett 43; Secura et al. 437).

Nevertheless, these ads construct a causal relationship between teen pregnancy and poverty, just as they place the onus on individual young people to break deeply entrenched cycles of socioeconomic inequality. For example, one of the ads features four visibly distraught infants, next to which the text reads, "If you finish high school, get a job, and get married before having children, you have a 98% chance of not being in poverty." Such a broad claim overlooks the socioeconomic structures that create and perpetuate cycles of poverty, many of which are exacerbated by the neoliberal "free market." In arguing that graduating high school and acquiring "a job" are key to avoiding poverty, this campaign blatantly discounts how neoliberal restructuring has resulted in an upsurge of temporary, part-time, low-paying work without health benefits, sick days, or pensions. It also negates the growing rates of unemployment and underemployment faced by young adults with post-secondary and professional degrees as market deregulation continues (Silva 4-10). In this sense, the experiences of the working poor are rendered invisible, even though roughly one-quarter of those who experience poverty in the U.S. are active in the labour force ("A Profile of the Working Poor"), and most welfare recipients cycle back and forth between paid market labour and state benefits due to increasingly low wages and insecure employment conditions (Smith 831).

Another ad similarly depicts a black infant girl; the text next to her reads, "Honestly Mom ... chances are he won't stay with you. What happens to me?" In accordance with right-wing "traditional family values" rhetoric, this statement insinuates that having children after marriage is key to achieving familial stability and economic self-sufficiency, and it stigmatizes any family unit that lacks a patriarchal "breadwinner." It is also not insignificant that the infant featured here is of colour, as the ad connotes racialized stereotypes regarding the "welfare queens" and "deadbeat dads" who are believed to proliferate among African American communities. Not only does this ad overlook how many women become single mothers as a result of divorce, at which point they become increasingly vulnerable to experiencing poverty (Mather), it also ignores how heterosexual marriage may make women vulnerable to experiences of spousal abuse and further economic hardship. Nevertheless, the neoliberal socioeconomic order cannot tolerate the risk posed by single-mother-headed families, since market deregulation and privatization undermine their capacities to achieve economic self-sufficiency while maintaining childcare as an intensive, privatized enterprise.

This campaign accordingly perpetuates neoliberal ideologies by constructing young, single mothers as unequivocally deficient in their capacities to care for their children. In doing so, it disregards how single and partnered mothers who work for pay have long subverted "traditional" familial norms, such as the othermothering and community mothering practices utilized by black mothers in North America (hooks 145; O'Reilly 110). In a similar vein, this campaign overlooks the many single mothers who experience poverty despite working multiple jobs (Tomlinson 409, 412), as well as the numerous dual-income families that straddle the poverty line (Roberts, Povich and Mather). However, rather than address the neoliberal economic restructuring that continues to slash un-employment benefits, state-funded healthcare, public housing, and other social welfare programs that assist economically vulnerable mothers and children (Smith 830), as well as the systemic discrimination that many young mothers experience based on their sex, race, and economic class (Shanok and Miller 252), this campaign blames and shames young mothers by constructing them as the individual causes and perpetuators of poverty.

Pervasive beliefs about the "problem" of teen pregnancy are thus aptly contextualized within a neoliberal discursive framework. These teen pregnancy prevention campaigns operationalize neo-liberal risk management discourses which devalue young mothers' social reproductive work by constructing childrearing as inimical to "real" productivity in the market. It is thereby evident that teenaged mothers pose an incontrovertible threat to a neoliberal socioeconomic order which demands that social reproductive work be maintained as an intensive and privatized enterprise within economically self-sufficient family units.

CONCLUSION: YOUNG MOTHERS PUSH BACK

It is readily apparent that teen pregnancy prevention campaigns which construct young motherhood as a social ill do not recog-nize young women's abilities to function as empowered mothers (O'Reilly 45). Similarly, by constructing childrearing as inimical to "real" market productivity, they fail to acknowledge mother-work as a valuable site wherein women may effect social change. These ideologies stand in stark contrast to the lived experiences of young mothers and their children. As Shanok and Miller contend, dis-cussions about teen mothering place a disproportionate emphasis on pathology rather than resilience (259); their research reveals that most teenaged mothers actually view their pregnancies as a source of enrichment in their lives, as well as motivation to progress in their education, procure employment, and establish valuable social support networks (253, 260).

To that end, it is critical to acknowledge how young mothers and their allies have challenged the neoliberal "common sense" rhetoric that informs teen pregnancy prevention initiatives (see

"Fuck Yeah Teen Moms"; "Take Action"; Vianna). For instance, young mothers' online activism garnered significant credence in various mainstream news media throughout 2013 as they spoke out against the selected campaigns (see Bielski; O'Neil; Szalavitz). Such efforts demonstrate how economically vulnerable mothers—who may or may not be young or single—do in fact engage in empowered maternal practice, and in doing so challenge the neoliberal discourses that stigmatize and dismiss their social reproductive work. In this regard, the care that young mothers provide for their children cannot be duly validated until care more generally is acknowledged as *work* that requires particular skills, time, and material resources. As bell hooks argues, it is essential to rethink the nature of work and evaluate women's work beyond the narrow framework of market exchange value (105). Similarly, the voices and experiences of young mothers and single mothers must be sought out and affirmed in public discussions about the very real challenges they face; however, such challenges must be appropriately contextualized within broader socioeconomic systems that reproduce cycles of poverty. In this sense, only when women's social reproductive work is validated as "real" work that is fundamentally necessary to societal well-being—and this resolution is tangibly supported by and reflected in economic policies—can the work of "changing diapers" be duly recognized as an act with the potential to "change the world."

ENDNOTES

[1]This campaign is now defunct, however the original images can still be viewed online. See "The National Campaign to Prevent Teen Pregnancy Ads and Commercial Archive."
[2]This campaign is now defunct, however the original images can still be viewed online. See Durkin).

WORKS CITED

"A Profile of the Working Poor, 2012." *U.S. Bureau of Labour Statistics*. BLS Reports 1047. March 2014. Web. 22 April 2015.

Abramovitz, Mimi. "Women, Social Reproduction, and the Neo-Liberal Assault on the U.S. Welfare State." *Legal Tender of Gender: Law, Welfare, and the Regulation of Women's Poverty*. Ed. Shelley Gavigan and Dorothy Chunn. Oxford: Hart Publishing, 2010. 15-46. Print.

Adams, E. Kathleen, Norma I. Gavin, Ayadi M. Femi, John Santelli, and Cheryl Raskind-Hood. "The Costs of Public Services for Teenage Mothers Post-Welfare Reform: A Ten State Study." *Journal of Health Care Finance* 35.3 (2009): 44-58. Print.

Basch, Charles E. "Teen Pregnancy and the Achievement Gap Among Urban Minority Youth." *Journal of School Health* 81.10 (2011): 614-620. Print.

Bielski, Zosia. "New York Latest Strategy to Fight Teen Pregnancy? Shaming." *Globe and Mail Official Website*. 8 March 2013. Web. 14 March 2013.

Cady, Kathryn A. "Labour and Women's Liberation: Popular Readings of *The Feminine Mystique*." *Women's Studies in Communication* 32.3 (2009): 348-379. Print.

Campbell, Angela. "Proceeding With 'Care': Lessons to be Learned from the Canadian Parental Leave and Quebec Daycare Initiatives in Developing a National Childcare Policy." *Canadian Journal of Family Law* 22 (2006): 171-222. Print.

"Celebrity PSAs." *The Candie's Foundation Official Website*. 1 May 2013. Web. 25 May 2013.

Collins, Patricia H. *Black Feminist Thought: Knowledge, Consciousness, and the Politics of Empowerment*. 2nd ed. New York: Routledge, 2000. Print.

Crenshaw, Kimberlé. "Demarginalizing the Intersection of Race and Sex: A Black Feminist Critique of Antidiscrimination Doctrine, Feminist Theory and Antiracist Politics." *University of Chicago Legal Forum* (1989): 139-168. Print.

Durkin, Erin. "Shame Campaign: NYC Ad Campaign on Teen Pregnancy Marshals Crying Babies." *New York Daily News*. 4 March 2013. Web. 8 March 2013.

England, Kim. "Home, Work and the Shifting Geographies of Care." *Ethics, Place and Environment* 13.2 (2010): 131-150. Print.

"Fuck Yeah Teen Moms." *Tumblr*. n.d. Web. 24 Feb 2015.

Hacker, Karen A., Yared Amare, Nancy Strunk, and Leslie Horst.

"Listening to Youth: Teen Perspectives on Pregnancy Prevention." *Journal of Adolescent Health* 26.4 (2000): 279-288. Print.

Hartsock, Nancy C. M. 1983. "The Feminist Standpoint: Developing the Ground for a Specifically Feminist Historical Materialism." *The Second Wave: A Reader in Feminist Theory* Ed. Linda Nicholson. New York: Routledge, 1997. 216-240. Print.

Hays, Sharon. *The Cultural Contradictions of Motherhood.* New Haven: Yale University Press, 1998. Print.

hooks, bell. *Feminist Theory: From Margin to Centre.* 2nd ed. Cambridge: South End Press, 2000. Print.

Madsen, Lene. "Citizen, Worker, Mother: Canadian Women's Claims to Parental Leave and Childcare." *Canadian Journal of Family Law* 19 (2002): 12-74. Print.

Mather, Mark. "U.S. Children in Single-Mother Families." *Population Reference Bureau.* PRBorg. May 2010. Web. 18 March 2014.

"Mayor Bloomberg, Deputy Mayor Gibbs and Human Resources Administration Commissioner Doar Announce New Campaign to Further Reduce Teen Pregnancy." *The Official Website of the City of New York.* 3 March 2013. Web. 14 March 2013.

McKay, Alexander and Michael Barrett. "Trends in Teen Pregnancy Rates from 1996-2006: A Comparison of Canada, Sweden, U.S.A., and England/Wales." *Canadian Journal of Human Sexuality* 19 (2010): 43-53. Print.

Michalopoulos, Charles and Philip K. Robins. "Employment and Child-Care Choices of Single Parent Families in Canada and the United States." *Journal of Population Economics* 15 (2002): 465-493. Print.

Monahan, Jennifer L., Irene Shtrulis, and Sonja Brown Givens. *"Priming Welfare Queens and Other Stereotypes: The Transference of Media Images into Interpersonal Contexts. Communication Research Reports* 22 *(*2005): 199-205. Print.

O'Neil, Lauren. "Teen Pregnancy 'Shaming' Campaign Slammed by Young Parents." *CBC News Community Blog.* 7 March 2013. Web. 22 March 2013.

O'Reilly, Andrea. *Rocking the Cradle: Thoughts on Motherhood, Feminism and the Possibility of Empowered Mothering.* Toronto: Demeter Press, 2006. Print.

"Provocative New Ad Campaign Sparks Citywide Conversations

About Teen Parenthood." *City of Chicago Official Website*. 14 May 2013. Web. 20 May 2013.

Roberts, Brandon, Deborah Povich and Mark Mather. *The Working Poor Families Project*. Policy Brief. Winter 2012-2013. Web. 18 March 2014.

Ruether, Rosemary Radford. "Christianity in the Family: Ancient Challenge, Modern Crisis." *Conrad Grebel Review* 19.2 (2001): 83-95. Print.

Sawhill, Isabel V. "Welfare Reform and Reducing Teen Pregnancy." *Public Interest* 138 (2000): 40-52. Print.

Secura, G., T. Madden, J. Mullersman, C. Buckel, Q. Zhao, and J. Peipert. "No-Cost Contraception Results in Substantial Reductions In Teen Pregnancy, Birth and Abortion." *Contraception* 88.3 (2013): 437. Print.

Shanok, Arielle F. and Lisa Miller. "Stepping Up to Motherhood Among Inner-City Teens." *Psychology of Women Quarterly* 31.3 (2007): 252-262. Print.

Silva, Jennifer M. *Coming Up Short: Working-Class Adulthood in An Age of Uncertainty*. New York: Oxford University Press, 2013. Print.

Smith, Anna Marie. "Reproductive Technology, Family Law, and the Postwelfare State: The California Same-Sex Parent's Rights 'Victories' of 2005." *Signs: Journal of Women in Culture & Society* 34.4 (2009): 827-850. Print.

Szalavitz, Maia. "Why New York's Latest Campaign to Lower Teen Pregnancy Could Backfire." *Time Official Website*. Time Inc. 23 March 2013. Web. 26 March 2013.

"Take Action to Support the Young Parents' Dignity Agenda." *Strong Families Movement Official Website*. N.pub. n.d. Web. 22 Aug 2014.

"The National Campaign to Prevent Teen Pregnancy Ads and Commercial Archive." *Coloribus*. N. pub. n.d. Web. 18 February 2015.

Tomlinson, Jennifer. "Employment Regulation, Welfare and Gender Regimes: A Comparative Analysis of Women's Working-time Patterns and Work-life Balance in the UK and the U.S." *International Journal of Human Resource Management* 18.3 (2007): 401-415. Print.

Vavrus, Mary Douglas. "Opting Out Moms in the News: Selling New Traditionalism in the New Millennium." *Feminist Media Studies* 7.1 (2007): 47-63. Print.

Vianna, Natasha. "Candie's Foundation: Stop Shaming Young Parents." *Change.org Petition.* n.d. Web. 13 April 2013.

Walkerdine, Valerie and Helen Lucey. "It's Only Natural." *Maternal Theory: Essential Readings.* Ed. Andrea O'Reilly. Toronto: Demeter Press, 2007. 224-236. Print.

Wall, Glenda. "'Putting Family First': Shifting Discourses of Motherhood and Childhood in Representations of Mothers' Employment and Child Care." *Women's Studies International Forum* 40 (2013): 162-171. Print.

7.

From the Court of Law to the Court of Public Opinion

The Role of Mother-Blame in Canadian Infanticide Cases

KALEY M. AMES

KATRINA EFFERT WAS BORN into a lower-middle-class family in the small town of Wetaskiwin, Alberta. As she grew into a teen, Effert was by all accounts a "good" daughter. She sang in her church choir and assisted her mother by working in the family hair salon. Sometimes, Effert went out drinking and smoking marijuana with her friends, as many teens do. At the age of nineteen, Effert found herself unexpectedly pregnant. The paternity of her child has never been uncovered in all the subsequent investigations, court documents, or newspaper articles documenting her case. Perhaps paternity was never known, even by Effert herself.

Effert went through her pregnancy alone, without a partner and without divulging her condition to her parents. On Thursday April 14, 2005, Katrina gave birth to her son in the basement of her parents' home. Katrina cradled her son in her arms for a number of hours before strangling him to death with her underwear. The new mom wrapped her son's body in a sheet and disposed of him behind her neighbours' shed. When the bundle was later discovered and authorities began their investigation, Effert was petrified. Lying to the RCMP officer who canvassed the neighbourhood, Effert claimed she was a virgin and could not possibly be the boy's mother. Opposing stories from neighbours stirred inconsistencies in this interview, and eventually she was considered a suspect. Under the mounting pressure, Effert cracked, confessing everything to her father. Mr. Effert, in turn, notified the RCMP of the truth, which led to his daughter being charged in the death of her son (*R. v. Effert*; Staples).

Not quite three years later, on March 27, 2008, Katrina Effert's lawyers stood in front of the Alberta Court of Appeal to ask that her trial be moved from small town Wetaskiwin to a larger city where they could gain access to an unbiased jury pool. After much protestation from the Crown, the judge granted the request. This was an extraordinary measure taken by Effert and her legal team to secure an unbiased jury. The publicity surrounding Effert's first trial was so widespread and poisonous to her reputation, she could not find an unbiased jury in her town. To be sure, the reaction from the public was to be expected: Katrina Effert was on trial for strangling her newborn son.

The trial that ensued followed the historical legal tradition regarding Canadian infanticide cases. Ultimately, the court was sympathetic towards Katrina's case, and she served little time for killing her infant son. The public, however, deemed the young mother a monster, and it is unlikely her reputation will ever recover. Effert's case demonstrates the power of mother-blame as well as the pervasiveness of certain myths about motherhood that perpetuate and sustain the oppression of mothers and mask the struggles they face within patriarchal societal structures that shape experiences of mothering to this day.

The culture of mother-blame is so dominant that it is taken for granted; it goes unchallenged and has seeped into the pores of our culture's narrative. One way mother-blame presents itself is through public reactions to infanticide. Infanticide, which occurs when a mother kills her own child, is a federal crime taken so seriously that it has its own separate and distinct category within the homicide section of the criminal code and is an act so reviled by society that mothers who commit it are forever deemed monsters. Therefore, infanticide is both one of the most complicated and compelling examples of mother-blame in a contemporary Canadian context.

How can we untangle the various social factors surrounding infanticide in order to understand what drives mother-blame? Framing is crucial for illustrating how infanticide law is part of a larger social condition in Canadian society. The question is, What can we learn about mother-blame from infanticide cases? Certainly, the first question that comes to mind is, What *mother* kills her own child? This question places the sole responsibility on the mother, and I believe it is the wrong question—or perhaps it is the right question with the wrong emphasis. The question I seek to ask instead is, *What* mother kills her own child? The shift in emphasis takes the blame away from mothers themselves and instead focuses on the context that has shaped them *into* infanticidal mothers. By asking, *What* mother, we apply a question mark to her other circumstances, whether social, economic, romantic, or health—all of the factors that determine a person's ability to function within society to the best of their ability.

Mother-blame pervades our culture so deeply that it is often difficult to recognize. Paula J. Caplan sought to illuminate the understudied topic of mother-blame in her book *Don't Blame Mother: Mending the Mother-Daughter Relationship*. Here she focuses on the dynamic between mothers and their daughters and the role that mother-blame plays in that relationship dynamic. Caplan cites ten myths as being the particular locus of tension between mothers and daughters, myths that are socially constructed and socially reified. Therefore, it is particularly useful to examine how these myths appear outside the mother-daughter relationship and the broader family dynamic, as well as how they appear in society as a whole. For the purposes of this paper, I will examine Caplan's analysis of four such myths surrounding the "good" and "bad" mother constructs.

MOTHER-BLAME

The myths that surround mother-blame, writes Caplan, are curious, given their binary oppositional nature. All "good" mothers must rely on expert advice, which contradicts the notion that all women are born with the natural and innate ability to mother. Caplan writes, "These conflicting myths serve an important function: they are ways to justify demeaning and mistreating mothers" (60). These contradictions serve the purpose of applying social confusion to mothers, and where there is confusion and chaos, there is misunderstanding and mistreatment. That which is less understood is apt to be less valued. The more we lower mothers' value within society, the more blame we can assign them. When it comes to children with eating disorders, those who bully other children, and even children who are the victims of sexual or physical abuse, blaming the mother is the easiest explanation, for the mother has no real power and is therefore an easy target for blame and judgment. Caplan contends, "By keeping women down, ashamed, frightened; we are the judged, not the judges" (60). By scapegoating mothers as the root of normative child aberration, or for any ills their children suffer, we keep mothers oppressed. When we make mothers the sole bearers of responsibility for their child's issues, we do not seek other causes of the problems that may plague their children.

If mother-blame is a means of oppression, then the web of sometimes conflicting binary social expectations on women and mothers creates the space for it through fear and envy. One fear surrounding mothers is that if women were freed from the shackles of male oppression, women would become *too* powerful. Caplan states, "Men are afraid that if women were freed from shame, anxiety, and fear, they could wield enormous power" (61). Caplan locates this fear of power in the fact that women are socialized to stay in touch with their full range of emotions, whereas men are taught to keep their emotions at bay and have shame surrounding their expression. Therefore: "Many men, having learned to be uninterested in or uncomfortable about emotions, fear this unfamiliar strength. Their fear is of the unknown" (Caplan 61). Fearing women's potential power allows men to oppress women and keep them from fulfilling their greater potential.

Motherhood as a source of envy, writes Caplan, is akin to the Freudian notion of penis envy. The envy surrounds the access to emotions afforded to mothers: "Womb envy is not just literal, not just a wish to be able to become pregnant and nurse an infant; it also symbolizes men's envy of women's freedom to be nurturant and to express a range of feelings" (Caplan 62). Denied from expressing emotions, men envy what has often been called the "source" of women's emotions, their womb. Men often make a mockery of a woman's outward display of emotions, which undermines her true experience, turning it into a source of derision. As a result, the patriarchal notions surrounding gender expression dictate that a mother's positive actions get subverted into negative ones.

Subsequently, these notions act as a source of oppression out of a misplaced sense of envy. For example, a mother who comforts her child after they fall at the playground may be scoffed at for coddling, whereas a father may tell his child to "buck up" and have "no tears," even if he would like to give his child a hug. Men take their source of envy and turn women's emotional and nurturing capabilities into a source of ridicule. In this way, patriarchy has managed to maintain its control over women.

GOOD/BAD MOTHER MYTHS

Building on the binary and oppositional conditions for mother-blame, we can continue to see how specific myths operate in practice. Remembering that mother-blame myths are sustained by fear and envy of women's power and emotional work in society, Caplan details ten myths, although she recognizes that there are many more. For the purposes of this paper, I have chosen to focus on four myths, two of the "good mother" myths and two of the "bad mother" myths that specifically apply to mothers who kill their children.

Myth 1: "Mothers are Endless Fountains of Nurturance"

This myth relies on the requirement that mothers not simply be nurturing, but that their nurturing must be constant and unconditional. Caplan identifies the "endlessness" of the nurturing expected from mothers as a particularly troubling "perfect mother myth." Caplan writes that "being a warm, generous person is not a bad thing; the 'endless' part is what causes trouble" (77). Again, Caplan is writing this in relation to the mother-daughter relationship dynamic, saying that when daughters come to realize their mothers are not endless fountains of nurturing, but real people with limitations, daughters come to resent their mothers and their inability to fulfill their every need. Conversely, we are more forgiving of fathers because of the double standard that takes it for granted that fathers should not have the "endless nurturance" mothers are expected to embody. Indeed, when fathers are nurturing, it is seen as a welcome anomaly for which they are usually given undue praise.

The "endless nurturer" mother myth can also be applied outside of the mother-daughter relationship. When mothers are seen not to embody that nurturing spirit, they are labelled as bad mothers and cast aside. This is especially true for mothers of colour, for they are held to different standards than white mothers. For example, if a mother is seen to be ignoring her crying baby while talking to her friend, or if she scolds her child in the grocery store or on the playground, she is seen as a harsh disciplinarian. The consequences for a mother being seen in this light are enormous and can result in her being ostracized or even reported to authorities.

In the case of Katrina Effert, the killing of her own child only leaves room for Katrina to be seen as an aberrant mother. Having committed infanticide, Katrina violated the "endless nurturance" myth to the extreme. That said, few commentators mention how Katrina cradled her son in her arms for hours before she made her final decision. It is difficult to grasp the duality of this image of Effert as a mother. On the one side, Effert was an affectionate mother who spent a vast period of time cuddling her son, yet she also disposed of his body behind her neighbours' backyard shed. But this is the difficult thing about mother-blame: we are unsure which picture is more important, and so we choose the one that is traditionally easier to explain.

The "endless nurturer" myth leads to the next "perfect mother" myth. If mothers are supposed to be bottomless fountains of nurturing spirit, then, too, they are not supposed to get angry. This leads to our second mother myth that especially applies to mothers who kill their children.

Myth 2: "Mothers ... Don't Get Angry"

Social norms dictate that there is no room for anger in mothering. Women are socialized from a very young age to believe their purpose is to nurture, give, and be supportive. Anger does not factor into the emotional equation of traditional femininity. Paula Caplan writes, "Anger is a natural part of any close relationship, but anger is considered unfeminine ... in contrast, showing anger is consistent with the male image, even enhancing it" (88). The display of anger on the part of mothers is taboo because it opposes the image of traditional femininity set out by society.

For many, anger is a natural response to many of life's frustrations and can be either expressive or non-expressive. It has often been said that women control their anger by turning it inward into a non-expressive and depressive state. Conversely, men express their anger in the form of verbalization or violent action. In this way, anger as an emotion becomes gendered. Catherine E. Ross and Marieke Van Willigen, in their article titled "Gender, Parenthood, and Anger," report on conducting a sociological study that tests for maternal anger, not depression, resulting from inequality in the household. This research indicates that rather than turning to an inward depression as a result of their anger, mothers are actually more expressive than their male counterparts when it comes to anger.

The results of the above study, however, are quite shocking when we take into consideration our societal myths and stereotypes about mothers. The results are literally the opposite of what we as a society pretend to be true. Mothers, such as Katrina Effert, are not immune to the aggression that can express itself in dangerous ways. Of course, there is no justification for Katrina's actions, but this does not preclude us from understanding and sympathizing with her situation. If we were to allow mothers to remove the mask of perfect nurturance they are expected to wear, and allowed them to express their anger and frustration in smaller, everyday ways without deeming them failures, perhaps the results of Ross and Van Willigen's study would not be so surprising. Not only this, but if maternal anger were less taboo, perhaps Katrina would have been able to reach out for help before reaching the point of killing her son. Perhaps someone would have noticed her emotional struggle and given her the necessary care.

Myth Three: "Mothers Are Inferior to Fathers"

This myth of maternal inferiority, writes Caplan, is "the most pervasive mother myth" (96). The belief that mothers are bottomless wells of nurturance contributes to this myth, as "we are quick to criticize our mothers for not being perfect but appreciate our fathers for merely trying" (96). But this myth pervades family households in more insidious ways as well. Given that fathers are more likely to be the primary income earners for their households, their "work" is seen as legitimate because of its economic value. In contrast, mother-work, or the work associated with running a household and childrearing, remains invisible and less valued. Therefore, fathers are valued for their income earning potential and mothers are hardly valued at all. That is not to say this myth has no negative effects on fathers. For men to be considered valuable only in relation to their earning potential also negatively impacts them. However, for mothers not to be valued at all for the household and childrearing work they perform is far more damaging.

Given that mothers are generally seen as inferior in relation to their children's fathers, they are apt to be treated as such. Mothers are often the targets of verbal abuse from their children, who may view their mothers as easy targets because of their perceived lower status. Mothers are also frequently the victims of spousal abuse by their husbands.[1] While domestic violence is a complex and multifaceted issue, there is an undeniable correlation between mothers being perceived as inferior to fathers and their being subjected to violence from their husbands.

Regarding Katrina Effert's story, it might seem less obvious that she is a victim of the dichotomy between superior fathers and inferior mothers. The baby's father is completely absent from the picture. However, it is precisely due to the fact that the father is never mentioned in the court proceedings that he is in the superior position. Every ounce of responsibility for prenatal care and parenthood was thrust onto Effert when she became pregnant as a teenager. The counter-argument can be made, however, that perhaps the father of the child was not notified of the pregnancy. The key, however, does not lie in whether or not the father was aware of Katrina's pregnancy; rather, this father's male privilege lies in not having the responsibility of pregnancy placed solely on his shoulders, as well as having the ability to flee a sexual encounter where conception occurred. At first glance, we may see Katrina holding the superior position here since she seemingly holds all the power and control. Yet, if we shift our focus to consider that Katrina's position as a single mother was the product of biological processes that allowed her to conceive with another person but to be the only one who became pregnant, we rediscover the true meaning of superiority versus inferiority. The father of Effert's baby has the privilege of not going through gestation or childbirth, of not being a single parent, and of going unnamed.

The above three myths leads to the last myth that particularly applies to mothers who kill their children. Given the myths that mothers should be endless fountains of nurturing, that mothers cannot or should not get angry, and that mothers are naturally inferior to their husbands, we are led to the logical assumption that mothers should be powerless.

Myth Four: "Mothers Are Dangerous When They Are Powerful"

The myth that maternal power is threatening is curious, as it is challenging to identify what power looks like in a maternal context. Caplan's theory regarding the negative aspect of maternal power is slightly limited in that she does not explicitly define her understanding of "power." Caplan contends that male power is "channeled for their benefit into power lunches, corporate politics, war games, and violence against women" (119). In other words, male power is something that is wielded over others. Inversely, we can deduce maternal power is wielded over the people with whom mothers work—their children.

Adrienne Rich examines the dichotomy of power and powerlessness in the third chapter of her ovarian work *Of Woman Born*. She writes, "Power is a both a primal word and a primal relationship under patriarchy" (64). This power flourishes under patriarchy because men's very identities are rooted in wielding power over others:

> Through control of the mother, the man assures himself of possession of his children; through control of his children he insures the disposition of his patrimony and the safe passage of his soul after death. It would seem therefore that from very ancient times the identity, the very personality of the man depends on power, and on power in a certain, specific sense: that of *power over others*, beginning with a woman and her children. (64, original emphasis)

Men are meant to have power, and their possession of it is never called into question. This type of power, the kind that is wielded over others, is dangerous no matter who has it. So if we are to understand female power in a patriarchal structure to mean that they command control *over* others, we can see how motherhood could be easily manipulated to fill a woman's power vacuum.

Rich elaborates on how patriarchy confuses women in their expression of power and how it manifests within the family structure. She writes, "The one aspect in which most women have felt their own power in the patriarchal sense—authority over and control of another—has been motherhood" (67). Women may express this patriarchal power through motherhood by enforcing excessive rules, such as restrictive diets, on their children or forcing them to join a team they have no interest in. But this power can take on more insidious forms; as Rich explains, mothers literally hold the power of life and death over their children. It is a fact that largely goes unnoticed: "The helplessness of the child confers a certain narrow kind of power on the mother everywhere—a power she may not desire, but also often a power which may compensate to her for her powerlessness everywhere else" (Rich 67).

Let us consider Rich's statement closely. The "helplessness of the child" can trigger latent feelings of power within a mother, which she then lords over her child. A mother may or may not actually *want* this power beforehand, but there is something undeniable about the power a mother has over her child: "The power of the mother is, first of all, to give or withhold nourishment and warmth, to give or withhold survival itself" (Rich 67). In order to experience and express power, a mother may wield it over her child in the only way she knows: by refusing or awarding nourishment or, in the most extreme cases, by giving or taking away life.

The myth that mothers are dangerous when they are powerful takes on new meaning when we consider the expression of maternal power under patriarchy. While it is prudent to fear what a mother may do when she is pushed to the brink, especially in relation to infanticide, this is a largely misplaced fear. Rather than fear mothers, we should redirect our fear towards the culture of mother-blame. For a mother directing her perceived sense of power towards her powerless child is really and truly a symptom of the larger problem: that women are disempowered in patriarchal motherhood. When we understand how and why, we may be able to begin to repair the damage.

MOTHER-BLAME IN LAW

When Katrina Effert stood on trial for murdering her hours-old son, the question was not whether she committed infanticide but how she should be charged. The Canadian Criminal Code classifies infanticide as a separate and lesser charge than that of murder and manslaughter. The Canadian criminal system developed the infanticide clause within the Criminal Code as a legal response to managing the all-too-common occurrence of infanticide in the late nineteenth century. While the particulars of the infanticide law are beyond the scope of this paper,[2] the historical and patriarchal climate under which it was created is important to understand the current legal and social response towards mothers who commit infanticide. While the law was created in sympathy towards infanticidal mothers, albeit a misplaced patriarchal sense of it, the trends in charging mothers who have killed their children have shifted towards harsher charges and sentences. This directly corresponds to the rising social trend of mother-blame within society.

In her book *Petticoats and Prejudice: Women and Law in Nineteenth-Century Canada*, Constance Backhouse cites three particular reasons why judges and juries were largely compassionate towards infanticidal mothers. Backhouse begins by locating a curious paradox within the judicial system. The all-male judicial system of judges, juries, and lawyers may have actually been impressed with the resiliency these women displayed in killing their children. Writes Backhouse, "It was almost as if the male lawyers believed that these women were acting out a sense of honour ... they may have been impressed by the courage and resourcefulness that the women exhibited as they struggled to hold their lives together" (136). Given that prostitution was often an inevitable fate for women who bore children out of wedlock, Backhouse writes, male legislatures were "very sympathetic to the motives that forced women to take the lives of their own offspring" (136). Allowing their minds to be clouded by the possible fates of these women had they not killed their children, the all-male justice system allowed these women to receive a lesser punishment than other murderers. The fates of these women, however, were shaped by the men handing down this more lenient sentence. Therein lies the paradox.

It is commonly believed that because of greater access to contraception, abortions, adoption agencies, and newborn drop-off centers[3] that there is no excuse for the infanticide such as the one Katrina Effert committed. Indeed, in the past, women had few other options (Backhouse, "Desperate Women"), and infanticide was seen as a normal and horrific but understandable response to the shocking lack of social and government infrastructure to help women. Yet, even though there are more options for opting out of motherhood available to contemporary women, it is important to note how there remains a stigma surrounding many of these avenues, abortion and adoption in particular. It is this stigma that results in mothers eschewing these options as possibilities, only to become overcome by frustration and desperation at a later point.

Even today, the enduring existence of infanticide is testament to women's circumstances and our placement within the patriarchal structure of society. The societal phenomenon of infanticide is multifaceted: it cannot be fixed with a round of contraception or by giving a struggling mother the number for an adoption agency. However, all of that is not to say a woman has no agency when it comes to killing her child. No amount of research into social dynamics and factors can deny the fact that a woman has taken the life of a human being. However, this fact should be tempered by the knowledge that many women before her, and many women after her, will have the same murderous thoughts toward their children. We have to admit that when a mother kills her child, society is complicit in setting up those barriers and stigmas so that mothers in dire distress cannot meaningfully access the means to escape their oppression. In the same way that the all-male judges and juries of the 1800s admitted their own hand in creating women's oppression by establishing a lesser charge for infanticidal mothers, so too must contemporary Canadian society admit that we give far too little help to mothers. In a minority of cases, infanticide can sometimes be the consequence of this lack of support for mothers. The difference between us and the all-male juries is that they sought a way to repair, albeit in a backwards way, the damage they had caused. We, however, make infanticide trials so unbearable that women like Katrina Effert cannot even find an untainted jury pool in her own town. While she was still handed down our Criminal Code's lesser charge associated with killing one's baby, there was no attendant sympathy from her community.

This brings us back to mother-blame. As discussed previously, Paula Caplan writes that when a group is undervalued, it is easier to make an example of them. Mothers are scapegoats in the twenty-first century. Of course, murder is always tragic. Yes, mothers who kill their own children should have to answer to the criminal justice system in some capacity. But we too must answer for not providing mothers with the tools they need to seek out meaningful help during times of crises. The law has created a mechanism for mothers to serve their time and the law largely forgives them, while we as a society do not. We must begin the painful process of understanding how a mother could arrive at the point where she kills her own child, forgiving her for her actions and forgiving society for allowing it to happen at all. Only then we can begin to repair the damage of mother-blame both in our courts of law and the court of public opinion.

ENDNOTES

[1]"In 2010, there were over 102,500 victims of intimate partner violence, including spousal and dating violence. This translates into a rate of 363 per 100,000 population aged 15 years and older and was almost 2.5 times higher than the rate recorded for family violence against a child, parent or other family member (150 victims per 100,000).... Police-reported rates of intimate partner violence tended to be highest among female victims and among those aged 25 to 34 years" (Sinha 5).

[2]For more on the history of the infanticide law in Canada and the issues surrounding the law, please see: Cunliffe; Davies; Grant; Hoffer; Kramar and Watson; Walker.

[3]Some hospitals, like St. Vincent's in Vancouver, BC, have set up

safe and anonymous drop-off centers for new mothers to drop off their infants into government care. To read more about the program at St. Vincent's, see "Angels' Cradle."

WORKS CITED

"Angels' Cradle." *Providence Health Care.* Providence Health Care. 2013. Print.

Backhouse, Constance B. "Desperate Women and Compassionate Courts: Infanticide in Nineteenth-Century Canada." *The University of Toronto Law Journal.* 34.4 (1984): 447-478. Print.

Backhouse, Constance B. *Petticoats and Prejudice: Women and Law in Nineteenth-Century Canada.* Toronto: Osgoode Society by Women's Press, 1991. Print.

Caplan, Paula J. *The New Don't Blame Mother: Mending the Mother-Daughter Relationship.* New York: Routledge, 2000. Print.

Cunliffe, Emma. "Infanticide: Legislative History and Current Questions." *Crim. LQ* 55 (2009): 94-119. Print.

Davies, D. Seaborne. "Child-Killing in English Law." *The Modern Law Review* 1.4 (1938): 269-287. Print.

Grant, Isabel. "Desperate Measures: Rationalizing the Crime of Infanticide." *CCLR* (2010): 253-271. Print.

Hoffer, Peter Charles, and N. E. H Hull. *Murdering Mothers: Infanticide in England and New England 1558-1803.* 1st ed. New York: New York University Press, 1981. Print.

Kramar, Kristin Johnson, and William D Watson. "Canadian Infanticide Legislation, 1948-1955: Reflections on the Medicalization/Autopoiesis Debate." *Canadian Journal of Sociology* 33.2 (2008): 237-263. Print.

R. v. Effert. Alberta Court of Appeal. 2009. Alberta Court of Appeal. Web. March 2014.

Rich, Adrienne. *Of Woman Born: Motherhood as Experience and Institution.* New York: W. W. Norton & Company, 1986. Print.

Ross, Catherine E., and Marieke Van Willigen. "Gender, Parenthood, and Anger." *Journal of Marriage and Family* 58.3 (1996): 572-584. Print.

Sinha, Maire. *Family Violence in Canada: A Statistical Profile, 2010.* Ottawa: Ministry of Industry, 2010. Print.

Staples, David. "The Verdict on Katrina Effert." Canadian Children
Rights Council, 28 June 2010. Web.

Walker, Nigel. *Crime and Insanity in England*. 1st ed. Edinburgh:
University Press, 1968. Print.

8.
"*We* Want to Consistently Address *Their* Needs"

Explorations of the Perceptions, Experiences and Challgenges of Parenting Interventions for Incarcerated Mothers

TALIA ESNARD

INCARCERATED MOTHERS ARE uniquely disadvantaged within the broader discourse on mothering (Enos; Hagen and Myers). Specifically, they are labelled as "unfit" or "bad" mothers based on the shame, blame, and stigmatization associated with their incarceration (Allen, Flaherty and Ely; Ferraro and Moe; Gabel and Johnston; Hagen and Myers; Myers et al.; Schram). In many cases, mothers' feelings of disgrace and culpability are compounded by strained relationships with their children during and after incarceration (Loper and Tuerk), by societal debates about the relevance of sustaining ties between mothers and children during incarceration (Hairston; Gabel; Johnston; Miller), as well as broader concerns over children's welfare during periods of incarceration (Esnard and Okpala; Johnston and Gabel).

It is evident that incarcerated mothers' identities emerge from the complex effects of their incarceration, including separation, social labelling, secrecy, stigmatization, loss, guilt, as well a sense of maternal failure (Gabel; Miller; Myers et al.; Sandifer; Seymour; Snowden and Kotze; Thompson and Harm). As a result, their maternal identities are often displaced by their criminalized status (Enos), they experience a painful scrutiny of the self as a whole (Jackson et al.), and they have to prove their worth as "good" mothers in order to negotiate access to their children (Enos; McKim). In their recent study *Mothering at the Margins: the Case of Poverty Stricken Women in Trinidad and Tobago,* Esnard and Okpala argue that, in addition to experiencing ongoing feelings of despair, humiliation, and disappointment, incarcerated mothers also grapple with a lack of self-confidence as it relates to their maternal skills, a denial of their maternal self, and in some cases a deliberate withdrawal from their children and family members where it is perceived as beneficial for the children. While the gains and strains of parent-child relationships during incarceration remain a contentious issue in the literature, such cases underscore the need for effective programs that can provide strategic assistance to incarcerated mothers and their children.

In assessing the degree to which incarcerated mothers can alter their maternal subjectivities during incarceration, other researchers call attention to the near-impossible odds that mothers face in the process (Allen, Flaherty and Ely). Among these are the institutional and familial positionalities that further confound incarcerated mothers' marginalizing circumstances. Scobie and Gazso note the complex means through which "their relationships with social and criminal justice policies and programs, before, during and after incarceration ... [further fracture] their mothering identities" (157). While it is possible for incarcerated mothers who face such social stigmatization to reassert their maternal identities and sense of attachment with their children through ongoing maternal visits and written communication (Esnard and Okpala), these efforts are often curtailed by the weight of strained relationships between mothers, children, and their caregivers during incarceration (Clark). Ultimately, incarcerated mothers are left frustrated and powerless in such circumstances (Allen, Flaherty and Ely).

To that end, it is also important to identify the ways in which such ideological, institutional, and societal marginalizations motivate others to intervene. Even though parent intervention programs are being offered to incarcerated women in growing numbers throughout the Caribbean, there has been little empirical research on the nature and outcomes of these programs. We also know very little about intervention programs that specifically address the concerns of incarcerated mothers (as in the case of the English-speaking or Commonwealth Caribbean), or about the roles, experiences, and challenges of external facilitators who intervene on their behalf. Rather, what exists is a handful of research projects and reported consultancies that address: (i) the invisibility of children of incarcerated parents in Spanish-

and French-speaking Latin American and Caribbean countries (Saavedra et al.), (ii) the need for prison and judicial reforms in the Caribbean (GOTT *Cabinet Appointed*), and (iii) broader studies on drugs and criminal activities that highlight the vulnerability of women and young persons (Harriott et al.; Klein, Day and Harriott; Inter-American Commission of Women).

This chapter accordingly addresses this knowledge deficit by providing some insight into the experiences of external facilitators who work with incarcerated mothers in Trinidad and Tobago. My main objectives here are to: (i) understand the extent to which facilitators identify with the effects of mother-child separation on the emotions of incarcerated mothers, (ii) gain greater insights into the multiple ways in which these programs attempt to reposition the relationships between incarcerated women and their children, and (iii) explore the challenges that shape these relationships and circumstances. It is my hope that this chapter will not only heighten awareness of how separation and social stressors affect mother-child relationships post incarceration, but also communicate the need for structured and coordinated intervention programs that are capable of empowering incarcerated mothers, both before and after release.

This chapter begins by describing the socioeconomic and historical facets of criminalized mothers' backgrounds and experiences in the Caribbean. These represent assessments of the structural, relational, judicial, and historical spheres of Caribbean life that affect the marginalization and criminalization of women. Given the absence of any empirically based Caribbean literature on intervention programs specifically for mothers in prison, I subsequently refer to international research in my discussion of the rationale, potential utility, and challenges of parenting interventions for incarcerated mothers. While the applicability of these international studies may come into question, I contend that these contributions remain useful insofar as they highlight salient issues that underpin the experiences of incarcerated mothers and outline useful strategies for those who intervene on their behalf. More localized or contextual issues and the utility of such findings can be unearthed and advanced through specific research agendas. I then outline the methodological framework, procedures, data collection methods, and sample used in the research. Thematic findings as they relate to the perceptions, practices, experiences, and challenges of parenting intervention agents, as well as their implications for policy frameworks, institutional practice, and future research on the same, are also discussed.

INCARCERATED WOMEN IN THE CARIBBEAN

"There is a spiraling number of women in prison in the Commonwealth Caribbean. Most of them are poor; often they are single heads of households or victims of physical abuse; and many of them have been charged and convicted after they have been caught with trafficable quantities of illegal drugs" (Klein, Day and Harriott 109). The most recent available data for Trinidad and Tobago show that the major offenses of 1,709 women arrested between 2007 and 2012 included: possession of narcotics (605 or 35.4 percent), other serious crimes (203 or 11.8 percent), larceny (200 or 11.7 percent), burglaries and breakings (168 or 9.8 percent), fraud (164 or 9.5 percent), and robberies (123 or 7.1 percent) (GOTT *Data on Women*).

Collectively, these social statistics point to the many ways in which incarcerated women are often already disadvantaged in the social structures of the Caribbean. While the need for greater research on these issues remains pertinent, such limited data also direct attention to deeper social and economic processes that affect the criminalization of women in the Caribbean. These include structural poverty and high rates of unemployment in some countries (Singh), the weight of women's primary roles as caregivers for their children (Mohammed and Perkins), the historical regulation and criminalization of women who find alternative sources of income in situations of economic marginalization (Pemberton), the persistence of genderless and gender-insensitive socioeconomic policies (GOTT "Women in Prison"), and the entrenched culture of violence in the Caribbean region (Harriott et al.). How these factors intersect to create complex contexts in which women become victims of these social structures and processes, as well as inmates within the prison system of the region, remains unexplored. While these burning issues are beyond the scope of this chapter, they pose a critical area for future research in the Caribbean.

PARENTING INTERVENTIONS

Custodian detention provides an opportunity to provide some parenting education and support programs that can promote healthier child-mother relationships during incarceration (Newman, Fowler and Cashin; Purvis). From this standpoint, some researchers posit that parenting interventions can serve as an important catalyst for enhancing the maternal practices and experiences of incarcerated women, as well as their commitment and sensitivity to the wellbeing of their children (Kennon, Macintosh and Myers; Makariev and Shaver). Specifically, Makariev and Shaver assert that parenting interventions can aid "in breaking the cycle of crime and incarceration ... [which can improve] parents' mental health [and] relationships with their children" during and post incarceration (312). For Kennon, McKintosh and Myers, "these skills are essential for maintaining the parent-child relationship during the separation as well as for when [the mother] returns home and resumes the hands-on parenting role" (14). Others have proposed that these interventions could reduce parental stress, strengthen alliances with their children's caregivers, and foster general contact with their children (Abidin and Brunner; Gonzalez, Romero and Cerbana). They could also provide adaptable skills that promote positive parenting behaviour (Purvis), particularly by increasing visits over a period of time (Johnston).

However, other researchers and evaluators of prison parenting programs call this rationale, in addition to the quality and outcomes of such programs, into question. As a starting point, these scholars call attention to the nature of parent-child visits in jail, for instance, the frequently poor visiting conditions that are not conducive to meeting children's needs (Bloom and Steinhart; Johnston; Mumola), as well as caregivers' unwillingness to bring these children to visit their mothers during the period of incarceration (Esnard and Okpala; Hairston; Saavedra et al.). Creasie Hairston accordingly suggests that, while maintaining family and community ties during incarceration may reduce the possibility of recidivism, it is often challenged by the family dynamics of the mother before and during incarceration. The nature and perception of parent-child relationships prior to incarceration, as well as the correlational policies of the prison system, also present critical barriers that should be considered.

Given the above, other researchers point to the need for ongoing research that assesses the outcomes of maternal visits for mothers, children, and their families during incarceration (Mumola). They call for the development of new programs that offer effective coping strategies for mothers and children during these visits, as well as throughout the broader period of the incarceration (Bloom and Steinhart; Hagen and Myers). Given such concerns and related skepticism about mother-child relationships during incarceration, it remains imperative for researchers, particularly in regions like the Caribbean where empirical research on prison parenting programs remains non-existent, to engage in further research that underscores the social dynamics and processes that influence the outcomes of these programs. This chapter begins to address this gap.

RESEARCH DESIGN: CASE STUDY APPROACH

Case study research presents an "extensive analysis and description of a single unit or system bounded by space and time" (Hancock and Algozzine 10-11). Through such analysis, researchers attempt to gain deeper insights into the broader circumstances that affect particular events, programs, or individuals, as well as the embedded meanings for those involved.

In the case of this study, the primary aim was to understand and underscore the dynamics and processes that shape the outcomes of prison parenting programs designed for incarcerated mothers. This focus was informed by the need for greater research that probes the underlying yet often neglected factors which curtail the outcomes of these programs. Thus, while this study provides a rich description of existing prison parenting programs for incarcerated mothers in Trinidad and Tobago that is grounded in the narratives of the facilitators, it also offers layers of analysis that cut across contextual and perceptual facets of their experiences.

SAMPLE: FACILITATORS

To capture the processes and dynamics underlying the outcomes of prison parenting programs for incarcerated mothers, I used a purposive snowballing sampling technique to access those who are involved in the implementation of such intervention programs. Two individual facilitators (one male and one female) and one group (an organization called Hope) were willing to participate in this study. The female facilitator, a former high school teacher named Mrs. Ramjattan, operated as a sole agent in the delivery of continuous academic classes and empowerment seminars two days per week for the past six years. Mr. Stayer, a former male inmate, offered spiritual and academic classes to both male and female offenders and also served as an advocate for continuous visitation by their children during court trials. Hope, a non-governmental organization (NGO), is comprised of professional women who work across various fields and hold different levels of experience. Through their prison project, Hope professionals volunteer their time to extend courses, workshops, advice, counselling, and practical hands-on sessions in cooking, sewing, and arts and crafts to incarcerated mothers.

TARGET GROUP: INCARCERATED MOTHERS

Given the restrictions on the release of data on inmates and the need to protect the identities and backgrounds of incarcerated mothers, access to the specificities of maternal incarceration has been limited for researchers. In their interviews, facilitators revealed that these incarcerated mothers were victims of gender-based violence, economic dependency, low educational achievement, labour market segregation, and limited avenues for economic survival or mobility. Socio-demographic statistics indicate that the majority of female inmates in Trinidad and Tobago are nationals (69.1 percent), of African descent (31 percent), less than thirty years old (43 percent), single parents (41.7 percent), unemployed (27.6 percent), semi-skilled (hairdresser, seamstress, or electrician; 19.5 percent), and hold only high school education (44.3 percent) (GOTT "Women in Prison"). Facilitators expressed a shared desire for prison intervention programs that focus less on the individual circumstances in which women become inmates and more on their broader social and economic needs.

METHODS

This study used semi-structured interviews to capture the dynamics underlying prison parenting programs in Trinidad and Tobago. Interviews sought to address the nature, objectives, frequency, structure, experiences, and challenges of these programs. Interviewees were also asked to provide feedback from program participants. Interviews lasted between one and two hours and were conducted at the facilitators' personal residences. Pseudonyms are used to maintain the anonymity of facilitators. Four Hope members took part in the focus group interview: Mary (a counsellor), Jennifer (a lawyer), Judith (a musician), and Emmy (a university professor and educator). This group interview was conducted in founding member Jennifer's home. Interviews were transcribed, manually coded, thematically analyzed (Creswell), and organized around the general characteristics underlying the intervention processes. In this case, narratives were used to make visible the social circumstances that shape facilitators' subjective positionalities (Reissman), as well as address how these circumstances impact the effectiveness of intervention programs offered to incarcerated mothers in Trinidad and Tobago.

FINDINGS

Several themes emerged from the interviews with these facilitators. However, two main themes were drawn around the related objectives of the study: the strong sense of maternal powerlessness felt by incarcerated mothers and the complex, socially constrained nature of parent intervention programs.

MATERNAL POWERLESSNESS

Allen, Flaherty and Ely note how the "one thing that incarcerated women share is their invisibility" (162). In this way, incarcerated mothers are viewed as "throwaway moms" in the eyes of society due to their criminal status as well as their inability to demonstrate that they are "good" mothers. This study's findings provide compelling evidence to support the above assertion; for instance, the facilitators related many conversations with incarcerated mothers in which the latter expressed a communication breakdown with their children's caregivers, as well as deliberate attempts by some caregivers to keep children away from them. These experiences initiated a resultant worrying process that curtailed their abilities to practice mothering during incarceration. Mary, a Hope facilitator, shared the case of one mother whose knowledge, fondness, and desire to reconnect with her child remains trapped within a distant frame of reference that was created more than nine years ago. Mary communicated:

> One woman was making a craft or stuffed doll for her daughter. She has been in prison for more than six years and is so excited to give her daughter this stuffed doll. When I asked her how old this child is, she said 12 years. It hurts to see that [the mother] can't see the child really is 12. Her only memory of that child is at three years old and [the mother] is still stuck with the child's interest in dolls at that time. As far as she is concerned, the stuffed doll is what [her daughter] would like.

In this case, Mary drew on and was moved by the mother's inability to shift her standpoint and makes sense of a developmental process in which her growing daughter's previous interest in dolls could be replaced by other interests. For Mary, these idealized memories and "knowledge breakdown, [rather than] a failure as can be perceived by the untrained person," are a direct consequence of the "lack of communication with the child" and the mother's related need for more "current knowledge of the changes taking place in the life of that child and the unspoken pain that comes along with these." Mary also hinted that, while the mother's incarceration may be the main source of her distress and sense of powerlessness, the broader experiences of social scrutiny and their collective effects on her maternal self create confounding feelings of self-blame. As Mary opined, "It becomes a triple jeopardy where these mothers have to deal with the guilt of what they have done, how it affects their children and conversation with family and prison folks who think that they should not be allowed to have more continuous or frequent visits with their children." This triple jeopardy became the major source of the mother's guilt and internalized defamation.

Emmy, another Hope facilitator, revealed a similar instance where "a woman expressed much excitement as it relates to tucking in her son's shirt for him." She stated that "when I asked [the mother] how old is the child and she said 14, I am thinking what 14-year-old would want a mother to tuck in his shirt?" For Emmy, it is as if "their minds come to an end and they imagine [their children] as they saw them the last time." This scrutiny of the images and associations that the mothers hold in relation to their children is not out of disdain on the part of the facilitators, but an attempt to (i) process their understandings of how these women see themselves as mothers, (ii) use these understandings in shaping relevant intervention strategies, (iii) bring to the centre the personal stories and struggles of incarcerated mothers, and (iv) sensitize others to the crippling effect that separation has on these mothers and their children.

Incarcerated mothers feel stressed about their children's well-being, as well their own parenting skills and capacities during incarceration (Enos; Esnard and Okpala; Kennon, Mackintosh and Myers; Saavedra et al.). This was clearly articulated in the facilitators' interviews. For instance, Mr. Stayer expressed how incarcerated mothers are hindered by their lack of knowledge of their children's day-to-day lives and experiences: "They fear how their children will be 'mined' [taken care of]." He further highlighted the tendency for mothers to ask questions related to the well being of their children, experiences with other peers at school, and with caregivers. From Mr. Stayer's perspective, these questions emerge from the mothers' lack of confidence in their children's caregivers, as well as their own inabilities to influence the process by which their children are placed in the care of relatives. While he did not mention it specifically in his narrative, these questions also reflect the lack of communication between incarcerated mothers and caregivers, as well as the mothers' awareness that their incarceration may negatively impact their children's experiences and behaviours. It is in such cases of helplessness and insecurity about the welfare of their children that incarcerated mothers evaluate their maternal performance as good or bad mothers (Snowden and Kotze).

In *Children of Incarcerated Parents: Latin America and the Caribbean*, Saavedra et al. draw on the "testimonies of relatives, caretakers and children included in the study [that] clearly show the stigmatization that all of them face, and how this stigmatization affects their dignity and self-esteem" (5). Mr. Stayer expressed similar concerns over the mental state of incarcerated mothers. He related that mothers frequently ask questions about their legal claim to their children post-release and whether they, that is, the children, will have any respect for their parents given their recent incarceration. These questions reflect a deep sense of insecurity, fear, and worry over the multiple negativities associated with the separation, the shame of that experience, the deterioration in their relationships with their children, and the burden of these social experiences. Thus, Mrs. Ramjattan similarly expressed that these "women are depressed, hurting, sad, talk about their children and the mess they made, about missing them and sometimes they give the names of their children for me to pray for them. They have regrets and they can't wait to reconcile with their families. They want a forum to talk about the accomplishments of their children."

Jennifer, a Hope facilitator and lawyer, also reflected on the mothers' pain and anxieties. She expressed the need to develop prison parenting programs and relevant legislation that allow mothers to bond with their children, as well as remove the stigmatization and blame associated with mothering while incarcerated. She stated:

> Some of them suffer from anxieties—they worry about their children—particularly with capital charges where they do not know when their case will be called. Some of them see the doctor; they are depressed. We need to get their families to understand what they are going through and beg them to visit. Those who get bail have reason to be excited, but for those who don't, the only thing we can do for them is to give them updates.

In this narrative, two salient issues related to effective prison programs for incarcerated mothers must be further interrogated. First, Jennifer argues for the need to consider and appreciate the role of mothers' criminalized status (based on the type of offense committed), as well as their experiences of anxiety and depressive symptomatologies. Second, she calls for greater sensitivity to the social burdens, pain, and marginalization experienced by incarcerated mothers and their families. The consequences of these experiences are deep, untold, and far-reaching. At times, this lack of contact with children can result in mothers' lowered self-esteem and withdrawal (Gonzalez, Romero and Cerbana; Thompson and Harm). However, broader concerns about the emotional and behavioural welfare of children who visit their incarcerated mothers complicate decisions about moving forward (Enos; King). Thus, while prison parenting programs must be perceived as indispensable and responsive to the due process that affects mothers' experiences while incarcerated, many questions remain as to the implications of such maternal access for their children's welfare, in addition to the relative power of legislative reforms to address the effects of the stigmatization and possible discrimination experienced by all involved. In such cases of conflicting interests, intervention programs must find innovative and creative ways to cross the widening social cul-de-sac in this blame game.

PRISON PARENTING PROGRAMS AS COMPLEX AND SOCIALLY CONSTRAINED

Kennon, Mackintosh and Myers remind us that parenting education programs provide some "skills [that] are essential for maintaining the parent-child relationship during separation as well as for when she returns home and resumes the hands-on parenting role" (14). They further elucidate that "these features enable parents to regain control, reduce feelings of guilt and isolation, increase empathy with their children, and feel confidence in helping their children." Thus, where personal development programs can also alter and reconstruct maternal thinking and practice (Esnard and Okpala), designing intervention programs for incarcerated mothers as a corrective treatment would require preparation "that is based on exploration of past behaviours, skill development, and enhancement of the iof the individual's self-confidence and self-efficacy to the meet the demands of the future" (Gilham 100). These narratives suggest that such wide-ranging effects require a holistic and dynamic approach to prison parenting programs.

COUNSELLING SESSIONS

Loper and Tuerk contend that "given the challenges that inmates experience when attempting to parent from prison, both children and incarcerated mothers may be best served by parent education that addresses ways of coping with stressful separation" (90). Thus, parenting programs are needed that bridge this gap by teaching parents positive communication skills that are paramount to parent-child bonding and reduce recidivism (Gonzalez et al.). All facilitators in this study spoke of the need for counselling interventions that specifically offered teaching moments in the process of addressing incarcerated mothers' emotional needs. In this regard, Mrs. Ramjattan pointed to the significance of her empowerment classes as a source of grieving, venting, and purging for women who are already burdened by the estrangement from their children and the social scrutiny that accompanies it. She explains:

> *I offer them a pre-release program ... I let them know that the journey better prepares them by boosting their self-esteem so that they know they can make it, that they learn from their mistakes and that they are ready to go out. I teach them about issues of forgiveness, forgiving themselves, helping people, trying to talk about how they hurt people, how people hurt them.*

Similarly, Hope's counsellor Mary spoke of the multiple approaches to addressing incarcerated mothers' emotional needs. She noted:

> *We teach them how to talk about family relationships. We also make them feel like they are part of the larger society. To do that, we bring national celebrations to*

*them.... We also encourage them to have some strength
of mind—to think differently, to reflect on the possibility of a new beginning. While most of them cry even
before we leave the session for the day, we always feel at
these moments that there is a need for us to do more for
them. We have other psychologists who could work with
them to do sessions on anger management, promoting a
positive self-esteem, strengthening communication with
their children, parenting strategies. These help to better
equip them to bond with their children while doing it in
a humanizing way.*

Mary also noted that "sometimes we just engage in active listening
and allow the mothers to purge their emotions in the process. We
use these opportunities to help them find suitable ways to cope."
Facilitators insisted that these coping sessions engender a sense of
social belonging and positive thinking, as well as promote critical
parenting skills as useful coping and rebuilding strategies. Arditti
and Few support the need for parenting programs that connect to
the emotional issues that women face if they are to reinvest in their
children and their role as mothers. In such cases, Snowden and
Kotze propose that therapists be more open to the experiences and
meanings that these mothers associate with their roles, rather than
rely on their own understanding of the mothers' circumstances.
This approach allows for new ideas to emerge around behavioural
control and purposeful action.

Given the intensity of the social burden and often silenced pain
associated with the mothers' incarceration, Mrs. Ramjattan also
spoke of the need for non-traditional programs (including drama,
poetry, monologue, and dance) as alternative healing strategies for
incarcerated mothers. Specifically, she stated:

*Although the sessions deal with the issues that they face,
we saw that movies also encourage them to deal with these
issues of forgiveness and understanding. What I personally
have done is to use the basic teaching of science, mathe-
matics and grammar not just for certification but also as
a means of expressing themselves in a creative way.*

According to Mrs. Ramjattan, these offer non-traditional methods of enhancing the mothers' attempt to rehabilitate during incarceration and ultimately reintegrate themselves into the general society post release. Judith, a musician by profession, also supported this strategy and the specific use of music as a way of promoting "emotional freedom and purging." In *Agency through Collective Creation and Performance: Empowering Incarcerated Women On and Off Stage*, Janet Wilson presents a refreshing interpretation of acting and performance as ways of giving voice to the personal stories of incarcerated women, in addition to making visible more authentic representations that can diminish the weight of the shame and blame produced by maternal incarceration.

However, facilitators also call attention to the social, technical, and administrative constraints of intervention that serve as major setbacks to the effectiveness of such counselling sessions. Mary noted that "most weekends, our visits are reduced to two or three hours and with rigid supervision. In some cases, we do not get the cooperation of some officers. If there are multiple groups on the same day, they would just turn us away." Judith also voiced that "when we go in there on Saturdays, I get the sense that we are disturbing their rhythm. We feel as if we are not always welcomed there." Mrs. Ramjattan similarly noted that she "was not allowed to have a one on one session with incarcerated mothers" and that "at times during group sessions I am interrupted and asked to finish off because of some unrelated interruption in the prison system." In such cases, the group's approach to facilitation constrains their abilities to foster interaction and personalization with incarcerated mothers. Thus, while Mrs. Ramjattan "would like to consistently address their needs and get the project done, the situation and conditions of their incarceration does not allow this and I always feel that this program occupies a back seat." It is in such cases where facilitators feel unwelcomed, and where social relations and movable terms of engagement have a tremendous impact on the frequency and intensity of intervention sessions, that the contexts of such phenomena require further investigation. It also points to the need for a more structured organization of these interventions, greater sensitization and holistic training in restorative rather than punitive justice, and programs that include participation from prison officials, mothers, and perhaps the mothers' families.

MATERNAL VISITS

Since many incarcerated mothers receive few visits from their children (Glaze and Maruschak), the visits become a critical experience that shapes the subjectivities embedded in their maternal identities (Ferraro and Moe). It is against this background, and the overwhelming negativities of these limited visits for both parents and children, that all facilitators promoted the need to strengthen the interaction and attachment between incarcerated mothers and their children. This is the crux of Hope's prison project; Jennifer disclosed that the program allows children to "visit their parents within the prison walls twice a year—at Christmas and Mother's day. On those days, children get to spend time with their mothers, to be cuddled, to interact and start a reconnection process with their mothers."

However, all facilitators noted an inherent paradox: while the visits ushered in moments of joy, they also left many mothers and their children with noticeable grief afterward. For instance, Emmy shared how "mothers are just happy to see their children ... they touch their faces, hug them, it is all very touching." However, Mary also reported that the visits left an overwhelming feeling of sadness and inadequacy among the mothers. She communicated:

> *Although mothers get excited sometimes with the news of [their children's] coming, they are often left hurt and embarrassed when the child does not react in any way to them or does not even want to remain near the mother. The problem here is that being incarcerated didn't help the relationship in the first place.*

Facilitators also reported how the lack of social support for the children of incarcerated mothers complicates the effectiveness of this initiative, in addition to the lagging feeling of sorrow post-visit. Mrs. Ramjattan thus expressed:

Mothers look forward to [visits with their children] but wish they had more visits. They can't wait. They want to see [their children], to cuddle them, and just hear what is going on in their lives. However, when they are leaving they cry and some of them just withdraw. The children cry too and that makes the mothers feel even worse. What we need is more support for their families in their absence, to see them more often, to cuddle them for longer periods. I wish that visits would be more often; even during classes they talk about how they are very depressed.... They feel that they are angry with themselves and I encourage them to see this as an empowering process to be strong enough to prevent temptation or some return back to the life of crime post release.

The underlying complexity of the situation facing incarcerated women is evident within this narrative. It suggests that there are conflicting emotions surrounding mothers' visits with their children. However, further probing from facilitators highlights how such emotions do not stem from the mindset of the mothers or their attitudes towards their children, but from the multiple social constraints and stigmas that affect the visiting experience for both mother and child. For example, Judith elaborated that "these visits are short and governed by strict supervision." Mr. Stayer also pointed to the "closed nature of the environment and the mindset of officials." In his analysis, dealing with these social and physical constraints requires greater "sensitization of the public, broader programs that treat the person's perception of mother-child relationships, and some re-training of prison officials before these interventions can begin to bear fruits." Mrs. Ramjattan also called for more research, monitoring, and evaluation of existing prison programs, sensitization programs, and holistic development of intervention programs that allow children to grieve with their mothers during incarceration. She stated that "we need a class for children to come to the prison so that they can adjust to what they are going through ... to make room for their children and to be in a workshop where they can talk about what they are going through, to play, to laugh together."

This suggestion squares with the need to work with communities to establish programs and services that support children, particularly those who are at risk of criminal activity (Gilham). This kind of intervention presents a win-win situation where communities and public officials can support the rebuilding of maternal skills for incarcerated women while addressing the complex social factors that place their children at risk of developing emotional and behavioural problems. However, Gilham notes how this approach requires that prison workers and intervention facilitators push for "legislation that supports families when parents are incarcerated, which focuses on liberal and non-traditional visitation privileges" (100).

This presents a unique challenge for Caribbean countries. For instance, Saavedra et al. highlight how there is "no country in the region [that] even systematically documents or registers the number of children of prisoners" (7). This lack of data has considerable implications for the implementation of holistic programs that support families during the incarceration of a parent. The lack of coordination of intervention programs also complicates such involvement. Thus, facilitators in this study observed that, while social welfare departments, family services, NGOs, and the police service provide information on the placement and general welfare of children of incarcerated parents, there were no agencies responsible for developing or sustaining the holistic wellbeing of these children during their parents' incarceration.

On the whole, while parental outreach programs exist, they remain highly unsystematic with little coordination between institutions, agencies, and individuals. Saavedra et al. thus call for much needed harmonization of such initiatives, particularly for Caribbean societies where the "judicial and penal system remain adult-centric" (23). Citing the United Nations Declaration of the Guiding Principles of Drug Demand Reduction (1998), Singh also emphasizes the need for building resource capacity through stakeholder partnerships with government organizations, community groups, and NGOs. This need to systematically coordinate and integrate intervention strategies for incarcerated mothers and their children remains a critical challenge for prison and judicial reform in the region.

CONCLUSIONS

Parenting interventions that support incarcerated mothers have received little empirical attention in the Caribbean. However, with an increasingly vulnerable and growing population, there is an "urgent need ... for the development, implementation and evaluation of programs designed to ease the deleterious effects of parental incarceration on the family unit" (Wilson et al. 115). This chapter sought to examine the processes and dynamics that underlie the outcomes of prison parenting programs for incarcerated mothers in Trinidad and Tobago. Findings indicate that incarcerated mothers remain largely powerless in their desires to maintain a maternal bond with their children, to determine arrangements for childcare during incarceration, or remove the stigmatization of their incarceration and the potential effects it may have on their children.

Thus, while parenting programs offer creative counselling and educational interventions that promote positive communication, mind-sets, and interaction as critical aspects of building confidence in their maternal selves, facilitators noted that the administrative dynamics of the prison, as well as the weight of the blame assigned to incarcerated mothers, served as major barriers to parenting programs' effectiveness.

Where international "research on the impacts and benefits of parenting programs in prison strongly supports the implementation of parenting curricula" (Purvis 16), these findings point to the need for greater examination of the conditions, perceptions, and relations that underlie prison parenting programs. Such empirical research must be perceived as a fundamental stage in the design and implementation of parenting interventions for incarcerated mothers and their families.

Resultant reform must also address the inherent diversities in and stratified nature of the circumstances, backgrounds, and needs of all involved. If taken seriously, these reforms hold the potential for making visible not only the intricacies and social injustices surrounding the experiences of incarcerated women and their families, but also of lessening the social burdens of their incarceration.

WORKS CITED

Abidin, R. Richard and John F. Brunner. "Development of a Parenting Alliance Inventory." *Journal of Clinical Child Psychology* 24.1 (1995): 31-40. Print.

Allen, Suzanne, Chris Flaherty and Gretchen Ely. "Throwaway Moms: Maternal Incarceration and the Criminalization of Female Poverty." *Journal of Women and Social Work* 25.2 (2010): 160-72. Print.

Arditti, Joyce and April Few. "Maternal Distress and Women's Re-entry into Family and Community Life." *Family Process* 47.3 (2008): 303-321. Print.

Bloom, Barbara and David Steinhart. *Why Punish the Children: A Reappraisal of the Children of Incarcerated Mother in America.* San Francisco: National Council on Crime and Delinquency, 1993. Print.

Clark, Judith. "The Impact of the Prison Environment on Mothers." *The Prison Journal* 75.3 (1995): 306-329. Print.

Creswell, John. *Qualitative Inquiry and Research Design: Choosing Among Five Traditions.* Thousand Oaks, CA: Sage, 2013. Print.

Enos, Sandra. *Mothering from the Inside: Parenting in a Women's Prison.* Albany, NY: State University of New York Press, 2001. Print.

Esnard, Talia and Kimberly Okpala. "Mothering at the Margins: The Case of Incarcerated Women in Trinidad and Tobago." *Criminalized Mothers, Criminalizing Mothering.* Ed. Joanne Minaker and Bryan Hogeveen. Toronto: Demeter Press, 2015. 292-322. Print.

Ferraro, Kathleen and Angela Moe. "Mothering, Crime, and Incarceration." *Journal of Contemporary Ethnography* 32.1 (2003): 9-40. Print.

Gabel, Katherine. "Behavioural Problems in Sons of Incarcerated or Otherwise Absent Fathers: The Issue of Separation." *Family Processes* 31.3 (1992): 303-314. Print.

Gabel, Katherine and Denise Johnston, eds. *Children of Incarcerated Parents.* New York: Lexington Books, 1995. Print.

Gilham, Jo Jerry. "A Qualitative Study of Incarcerated Mothers' Perceptions of the Impact of Separation on their Children." *Social*

Work in Public Health 27.1-2 (2012): 89-103. Print.

Glaze, E. Lauren and Laura M. Maruschak. *Parents in Prison and Their Minor Children*. Washington, DC: U.S. Department of Justice Bureau of Justice Statistics, 2008. Print.

Gonzalez, Patricia, Tony Romero and Christine Cerbana. "Parenting Education for Incarcerated Mothers in Colorado." *Journal of Correctional Education* 58.4 (2007): 357-373. Print.

Government of Trinidad and Tobago (GOTT). *The Cabinet Appointed Task Force for Prison Reform and Transformation*. 2002. Web. 04 Aug. 2015.

Government of Trinidad and Tobago (GOTT). *Data on Women Arrested/Charged for Serious Crimes for the Years 2007-2012*. Maximum Security Prison, Arouca: GOTT, 2012. Print.

Government of Trinidad and Tobago (GOTT). National Drug Council in collaboration with the Prison Service of Trinidad and Tobago. "Women in Prison in Trinidad and Tobago: Relationship between Drug and Criminal Offending." *Drug Abuse Monitoring Project Among Inmates*, 2004. Web. 30 Mar. 2013.

Hagen, Kristine and Barbara Myers. "The Effect of Secrecy and Social Support on Behavioural Problems in Children of Incarcerated Women." *Journal of Child and Family Studies* 12.2 (2003): 229-242. Print.

Hairston, Creasie. "Mothers in Jail: Parent-Child Separation and Jail Visitation." *Affilia* 6.2 (1991): 9-27. Print.

Hancock, Dawson and Bob Algozzine. *Doing Case Study Research: A Practical Guide for Beginning Researchers*. New York: Columbia University Press, 2006. Print.

Harriott, Anthony, Heraldo Munoz, Freddy Justiniano, Niky Fabiancic, and Leida Merado. *Caribbean Human Development Report 2012: Human Development and the Shift to Better Human Security*. New York: United Nations Development Program (UNDP), 2012. Print.

Inter-American Commission of Women (CIM). *Women and Drugs in the Caribbean: A Policy Working Paper*. Washington, DC: Inter-American Commission of Women, 2014. Web. 4 Aug. 2015.

Jackson, Arrick, Ashley Blackburn, Peggy Tobolowsky and Dana Baer. "An Examination of Guilt, Shame, Empathy and Blaming among a Sample of Incarcerated Male and Female Offenders."

Southwestern Journal of Criminal Justice 8.1 (2011): 4-29. Print.

Johnston, Denise. "Parent-Child Visits in Jails." *Children's Environments Quarterly* 12.1 (1995): 25-38. Print.

Johnston, Denise and Katherine Gabel. "Incarcerated Parents." *Children of Incarcerated Parents*. Ed. Katherine Gabel and Denise Johnston. New York: Lexington Books. 1995. 3-20. Print.

Kennon, Suzanne, Virginia H. Mackintosh and Barbara Myers. "Parenting Education for Incarcerated Mothers." *Journal of Correctional Education* 6.2 (2009): 10-30. Print.

King, Anthony. "The Impact of Incarceration on African American Families: Implications for Practice." *Families in Society: The Journal of Contemporary Human Services* 74.3 (1993): 145-53. Web. 10 Nov. 2012.

Klein, Axel, Marcus Day and Anthony Harriott. *Caribbean Drugs: From Criminalization to Harm Reduction*. London: Zed Books, 2004. Print.

Loper, Booker Ann and Elena Hontoria Tuerk. "Improving the Emotional Adjustment and Communication Patterns of Incarcerated Mothers: Effectiveness of a Prison Intervention Program." *Journal of Child and Family Studies* 20.1 (2011): 89-101. Print.

Makariev, W. Drika and Phillip R. Shaver. "Attachment, Parental Incarceration and Possibilities for Intervention: An Overview." *Attachment and Human Development* 12.4 (2010): 311-331. Print.

McKim, Allison. "Getting Gut-Level: Punishment, Gender, and Therapeutic Governance." *Gender and Society* 22.3 (2008): 303-23. Print.

Miller, M. Keva. "The Impact of Parental Incarceration on Children: An Emerging Need for Effective Interventions." *Child and Adolescent Social Work Journal* 23.4 (2006): 472-486. Print.

Mohammed, Patricia and Anthea Perkins. *Caribbean Women at the Crossroads: The Paradox of Motherhood among Women of Barbados, St. Lucia and Dominica*. Kingston, Jamaica: Canoe Press, 1999. Print.

Mumola, Christopher. *Bureau of Justice Statistics Bulletin: Incarcerated Parents and Their Children*. Washington, DC: U.S. Department of Justice, 2000. Print.

Myers, J. Barbara, Tina M. Smarsh, Kristine Amlund-Hagen and

Suzanne Kennon. "Children of Incarcerated Mothers." *Journal of Child and Family Studies* 8.1 (1999): 11-25. Print.

Newman, Claire, Catherine Fowler and Andrew Cashin. "The Development of a Parenting Program for Incarcerated Mothers in Australia: A Review of Prison-Based Parenting Programs." *Contemporary Nurse* 39.1 (2011): 2-11. Print.

Pemberton, Rita. "Petticoats, Pathogens, Pollutants: Women, Law and Sanitation in Late Nineteenth-Century Trinidad." *Engendering Caribbean History: Cross-Cultural Perspectives.* Ed. Verene Shepherd. Kingston: Ian Randle Publishers, 1995. 491-498. Print.

Purvis, Mayumi. "Paternal Incarceration and Parenting Programs in Prison: A Review Paper." *Psychology and Law* 20.1 (2013): 9-28. Print.

Reissman, Catherine. *Narrative Analysis.* Newsbury Park, CA: Sage, 1993. Print.

Saavedra, Enrique, Paula Lappado, Matilde Bango and Federico Mello. *Invisible No More: Children of Incarcerated Parents. Cases from Latin America and the Caribbean.* Argentina: Church World Service, Latin America and the Caribbean, 2013. Print.

Sandifer, Jacqueline. "Evaluating the Efficacy of a Parenting Program for Incarcerated Mothers." *The Prison Journal* 88.3 (2008): 423-45. Print.

Schram, Pamela. "An Exploratory Study of Stereotypes about Mothers in Prison." *Journal of Criminal Justice* 27.5 (1999): 411-26. Print.

Scobie, Olivia and Amber Gazso. "It Was Easier to Say I Didn't Have Kids: Mothering, Incarceration and Relationships with Social and Criminal Justice Policies." *Incarcerated Mothers: Oppression and Resistance.* Ed. Gordana Eljdupovic and Rebecca Jaremko Bromwich. Toronto: Demeter Press, 2013. 148-159. Print.

Seymour, Cynthia. "Children with Parents in Prison: Child Welfare Policy, Program, and Practice Issues." *Child Welfare* 77.5 (1998): 469-93. Web. 26 Sep. 2012.

Singh, Wendy. "Drugs and the Prison System: Impact of Legislative Changes on the Prison Crises in the Commonwealth Caribbean Region." *Caribbean Drugs: From Criminalization to Harm Reduction.* Ed. Axel Klein, Marcus Day and Anthony Harriott.

London: Zed Books, 2004. 101-119. Print.

Snowden, Jenny and Elmarie Kotze. "I'm Not a Bad Mother: Stories of Mothering-on-the-Edge." *The Australian and New Zealand Journal of Family Therapy* 33.2 (2012): 142-156. Print.

Thompson, Patricia and Nancy Harm. "Parenting from Prison: Helping Children and Mothers." *Issues in Comprehensive Pediatric Nursing* 23.2 (2000): 61-81. Print.

Wilson, Janet. "Agency through Collective Creation and Performance: Empowering Incarcerated Women On and Off Stage." *Making Connections: Interdisciplinary Approaches to Cultural Diversity* 14.1 (2013): 1-15. Print.

Wilson, Kristina, Patricia Gonzalez, Tony Romero, Kimberly Henry and Christine Cerbana. "The Effectiveness of Parent Education for Incarcerated Parents: An Evaluation of Parenting from Prison." *Journal of Correctional Education* 61.2 (2010): 114-132. Print.

III.
Mother-Blame in Popular Culture

9.
Blaming the Mother

The Politics of Gender in Cindy Sheehan's Protest of the Iraq War

LINDA PERSHING

IN THIS ESSAY, I offer a critical analysis of the representations of motherhood that accompanied Cindy Sheehan's peace activism from 2003 to 2007. My analysis is based on field research and participant observation in peace actions and events that were organized by Sheehan from 2005 through 2007, including Camp Casey in Crawford, Texas; the cross-country Journey for Humanity in summer of 2007; and vigils and protests that were held in Washington, DC, New York City, San Diego, and San Francisco. I investigate the ways in which Sheehan's identity as a mother became a focal point for extensive and often derogatory cultural commentary about her. Sexist characterizations coupled with stereotypes about mothering—particularly in times of war and military conflict—provided detractors with an easy way to dismiss her critique of the U.S. military's invasion and occupation of Iraq. From the perspective of a feminist scholar of folklore and popular culture, I examine negative reactions to Sheehan as a mother, therein deciphering and interpreting significant aspects of sexism that shaped folk expression and public discourse about her. In the following exploration I focus on two interrelated stereotypes that were pervasive in characterizations of Sheehan: the "loud-mouthed bitch" and the "bad mother."[1]

CINDY SHEEHAN'S AWAKENING AS A PEACE ACTIVIST

Before the U.S. military invasion of Iraq in 2003, Cindy Sheehan spent much of her adult life living in middle class neighbourhoods in Southern and Northern California while raising her four children. In addition to her labour as a mother, she worked at various times as a loan adjustor and Catholic youth minister, and spent a few months at the Department of Health and Human Services. Her 24-year-old son Casey enlisted in the army and served as a mechanic and army specialist with the First Cavalry Division. His battalion was deployed to Iraq in March 2004. On April 4, Casey was killed in an ambush in Sadr City. He was shot in the head with such force that the round slammed through his Kevlar helmet and ricocheted several times through his skull (Raddatz; Sanchez; also see Figure 1).

Figure 1. Banner of Casey Sheehan, killed in the Iraq War on April 4, 2004. The banner was displayed at the peace encampment Sheehan founded near George W. Bush's ranch in Crawford, Texas. Photo: Linda Pershing.

Sheehan was devastated by the death of her eldest child. As was the custom, her family met with President George W. Bush for a ten-minute consolation session. As Sheehan recounts in *Peace Mom*, Bush had not bothered to learn their names before talking with them on June 18, 2004, and he referred to Casey generically as "the loved one." She recalled: "His entire tone was one of being at a tea party, and the first thing he uttered was, 'So, who are we honorin' here?' We all looked at one another in disbelief" (82).

She noted that Bush had no interest in looking at photos of Casey or hearing about his life. Instead, as Sheehan recalls:

> He took my right hand in both of his and said, 'Mom'—he called me Mom—'I can't imagine losin' a loved one. Whether it is an aunt, uncle, niece, nephew, brother, sister.' I stopped him and said, 'Mr. President ... Casey was my son. I think you can imagine it—you have two daughters—try to imagine one of them being killed.' I saw a brief flicker of humanity in his eyes, then it was gone. I said, 'Trust me, Mr. President, you don't want to go there.' And he said, 'You're right. I don't.'...I was stunned at his coldhearted statement and all I could mutter was, 'Well thanks for putting me there.' (83, emphasis added)

In the months following Casey's death, Sheehan began to question the Bush Administration's rationale for going to war with Iraq. She learned as much as she could about the war, read critiques that appeared on progressive and peace movement websites, and soon came to the conclusion that the "war" was actually an illegal invasion and occupation. She soon concluded that Bush's claims about "weapons of mass destruction" and his arguments about the connections between the World Trade Center attacks and Iraq were fabrications. In the summer of 2004, she joined an organization called Military Families Speak Out, where she met with others who advocated for withdrawing U.S. troops from Iraq. As she processed her grief and became more knowledgeable about the occupation, Sheehan began writing about the war and speaking at peace events.

By October 2004, Sheehan commented to a reporter that she did not understand the reasons for the U.S. invasion of Iraq, and that she did not believe Iraq posed an imminent threat to the U.S. ("Cindy Sheehan Is Working"). During the November 2004 presidential race, staff members of the Internet political action committee RealVoices.org asked Sheehan to share her story in a commercial they were making to oppose the war ("A Mother's Tears"). She recounts in *Peace Mom* how the national advocacy organization MoveOn.org bought the commercial and aired it in swing states, hoping that growing concern about the war would help unseat Bush in the upcoming election (93-94).

In less than a year, Sheehan's life changed completely. She dedicated her time to peace activism, collaborating with others whose family members had been killed in Iraq. In January 2005, they tried to arrange a meeting with Secretary of Defense Donald Rumsfeld. When he refused, they organized one of their first political actions: a protest of the war, staged at the Pentagon. As a result of the media attention created by this small event, television journalist Diane Sawyer invited Sheehan to do an interview on *Good Morning America*, scheduled for the day of Bush's second inauguration (Sheehan, *Peace Mom* 108-9). Soon Sheehan was giving speeches across the U.S. She grounded her commentary in her experience as a mother whose son was killed in an increasingly unpopular war (Pershing, "Cindy Sheehan"). In March 2005, she appeared on the cover of *The Nation* magazine, featured in an article titled "The New Face of Protest?" about the growing movement by soldiers and their families who opposed the U.S. military action in Iraq (Houppert "The New Face").

Figure 2. Sheehan (on right of the banner) and supporters leading a march down the country road to Bush's Prairie Chapel Ranch. After August 2006, Sheehan returned to Crawford repeatedly, when George W. Bush was at the ranch. This photo was taken during Sheehan's March 2006 vigil in Crawford. Photo: Linda Pershing.

In August 2005, Sheehan was invited to serve as a keynote speaker at the annual Veterans for Peace convention in Dallas, while George W. Bush was enjoying a five-week vacation at his Prairie Chapel Ranch in nearby Crawford, Texas. On August 3, she was watching the news and learned that fourteen Marines had been killed in one attack. Six marines from the same Ohio unit died just a few days earlier. Commenting on the rising death toll, George Bush explained at a press conference, "The families of the fallen can rest assured that their loved ones died for a noble cause" (Nichols). Sheehan recalled her reaction: "I was heartbroken for the families and for the lives cut so cruelly short by Bush's lies. I was heartbroken for myself sitting in the living room surrounded by Casey's things and medals and awards and pictures and immersed in all of the lost dreams and lost opportunities and the future" (Sheehan, *Peace Mom* 135). In response, she typed the following email message and sent it out to her contact list of about three hundred people:

> I am going to Dallas this weekend to speak at the Veterans for Peace convention. After I am finished, I am going down to Crawford, and I am going to drive up as far as I can go and I am going to demand to meet with the m.f.'er and I am going to ask him for what noble cause did he kill Casey and to demand that he stop using Casey's sacrifice to justify more killing. (136)

The next time she checked her email, she found six hundred responses from people across the country. The word spread quickly about Sheehan's plans to request a meeting with the president. On August 6, she and twelve members of Veterans for Peace, along with members of the feminist peace organization CodePink and a few others, travelled to Crawford in a caravan of a bus and approximately twenty cars. As they approached the ranch, county sheriffs blocked their path (see Figure 2). Sheehan sat in a ditch on the side of the road and declared that she was not leaving until the president came out to meet with her (see Figures 3, 4, 5). As luck would have it, she was in the right place at the right time. Approximately 75 reporters were already in Crawford to

Figure 3. Supporters at the Crawford vigils stand with Sheehan near the roadside entrance to Bush's ranch. They hold a banner created by members of the feminist peace group CodePink, who joined Sheehan in Crawford. Photo: Linda Pershing.

Figure 4. Sheehan staging a vigil at the roadside entrance to Bush's ranch. The intense heat of central Texas made actions of this kind especially grueling. Photo: Linda Pershing.

cover Bush's activities, and they descended upon this grieving mother who had the audacity to mourn so publicly on the president's doorstep. Within twenty-four hours, her face flashed across television and computer screens, into homes across the U.S. and around the world. This middle-aged mother who called the president into question emerged as the new symbol of the contemporary peace movement, drawing crowds of supporters, as well as counter-protesters and a slew of journalists (see Figure 6). Suddenly, this obscure

168

Figure 5. After police banned them from setting up an encampment on the side of the road near Bush's ranch in Crawford, Sheehan and supporters were arrested for camping in roadside ditches. Here Sheehan is at the nearby Waco, Texas, courthouse protesting the arrest and attempt to curtail her civil rights. Photo: Linda Pershing.

suburban homemaker was being featured on every national news source (Aszklar). Soon nicknamed the *"Peace Mom,"* Sheehan was credited with galvanizing a nation and injecting life into a sluggish peace movement at a time when approval ratings for Bush's war policy dropped to forty percent ("Approval Ratings").

ANALYSIS OF FOLK AND POPULAR RESPONSES TO CINDY SHEEHAN

Public response to Cindy Sheehan was instantaneous and emotional, with comments ranging from "Cindy Sheehan is the modern day Joan of Arc and she is confronting an ominous and soulless [sic] military machine" to "Cindy Sheehan is a traitor to her own son's voluntary service and ultimate sacrifice" ("Cindy Sheehan Is"; also see Figure 7). By the end of August 2005, over fifteen thousand people from across the U.S. and several other countries had travelled to this remote Texas location to support Sheehan's cause and join her makeshift peace encampment, which soon stretched for miles along the sides of the country road in Crawford, Texas. Celebrities and activists such as Eve Ensler, Jesse Jackson, Al Sharpton, and Martin Sheen joined the encampment and the resulting media circus to support her. The Bush Administration tried to ignore her, while critics lambasted Sheehan as emotional, misguided, a lunatic, a traitor, a "media whore," and even as satanic (see Horowitz; Rich; Rothschild; and The People's Cube). An Internet tracking source reported

From left to right. Figure 6. Sheehan was besieged by dozens of reporters who were eager to cover the story of a mourning mother who wanted to meet with the President. Here she wears a T-shirt quoting one of Bush's famous misstatements when talking about U.S. military "strategery," rather than "strategy." Figure 7. Supporters and peace activists from across the country joined Sheehan at the encampment and at peace vigils to express their solidarity. Photos: Linda Pershing.

that on August 18, 2005—roughly the mid-point of Sheehan's month-long vigil outside Bush's ranch—a full fifty percent of all online blogs included discussions about Cindy Sheehan (Blog Pulse). By June 28, 2007, a Google search for the key words Cindy Sheehan resulted in approximately 1,580,000 web entries.

The mass media coverage of Sheehan was extensive, and thousands of other expressive forms—such as jokes and cartoons, websites, online blogs, and urban legends—sprang up to characterize her as a "loud-mouthed bitch" and, consequently, as an unequivocally "bad mother." Such discourses provide rich terrain for feminist analysis and reflection. Sheehan's fundamental question to President Bush—for what "noble cause" did my son die?—made her a focus for both admiration and scorn. Thinking back about the reactions to her efforts in Crawford, Sheehan later reflected:

August '05 was the happiest, yet the 2nd most stressful time of my life. The people who saw my sunburned face, wild hair and chapped lips every time they turned on their TV never saw me tossing and turning in my tent or trailer on a nightly basis, totally stressed out about the [Karl] Rovian smear campaign and worrying about what lies were going to be told about me, or what attack was coming next. ("Turn, Turn, Turn.")

Sexist stereotypes about women and mothers came to the fore immediately when her Crawford vigil hit the news. Gender commentary about Sheehan demonstrates what still occurs in the U.S. when women move beyond traditional roles as caregivers and mothers to critique government policies during times of war. Similar examples include the public outcry that followed criticisms of Bush's policies delivered by Natalie Maines, a member of the popular Dixie Chicks country musical group, and by television talk show host Rosie O'Donnell ("Rosie O'Donnell Attacks Bush").[2] Disparagement of these women who spoke against the U.S. invasion of Iraq often centered on gender constructs, and community activist Victoria Mares-Hershey accordingly commented that "politicians, journalists and political analysts have vilified Sheehan as everything close to a mad housewife, hysterical feminist, naïve peacenik and political opportunist, disgracing her country and the memory of her son." She countered these characterizations with her own assessment:

Cindy Sheehan looks like democracy. Brash, starkly direct, given to emotional outbursts, rabble-rousing and doing it in the street, she disturbs the people's comfort zone and rationalizations, keeping democracy alive. Brutally honest, irritatingly persistent, "sugary icing on a cake of steel." ...She camps at the commander in chief's front door and asks him to be accountable.

SHEEHAN THE "LOUD-MOUTHED BITCH"

The first theme that quickly emerged during Sheehan's August 2005 Crawford vigil reflects an attempt to denigrate and discount her because she adopted a confrontational style that many people consider unbecoming to, and inappropriate for, mothers of soldiers during times of war. In stereotyping her as a "loud-mouthed bitch" through jokes, blogs, and cartoons, pundits argued that Sheehan, because her son was in the U.S. military, had no business speaking against the war. Some complained that as a military mother, she "didn't know her place," that she needed to "get over" the death of her son and learn to grieve privately and silently, like a dutiful and patriotic military mother. Commentary of this type was especially vicious, signalling the misogyny that emerges when a woman whose primary identity has been as a mother and wife refocuses her energy on political activism. Incessant use of the term "bitch" to describe Sheehan illustrates how she had transgressed socially acceptable roles for mothers. An online commentator using the name DANCALL objected:

I thought it was understandable for this woman to implode, especially after her son, a true American Hero, was violently killed in a war. But this bitch has stepped over the line. All kindness and understanding are now gone. Ms. Sheehan, you are one stupid bitch. You have not only dishonored your son, your family and your country, you have shown yourself for the stupid bitch you are. (DANCALL)

The number of nasty invectives that detractors used to denounce Sheehan was remarkable, and they exacted a considerable toll on her. In addition to labelling her a "bitch," critics described her as an "ignorant cow," "whore," "slut," "dyke," "cunt," and countless other derogatory terms, many of which specifically reference women's sexuality (see, for example, Hendrie).[3]

"Momma Moonbat" was another term frequently used on websites and blogs to describe Sheehan. "Moonbat" has become an all-purpose insult used in libertarian and conservative online discourse to describe liberals, peace protestors, and other ideological opponents. In April 2006, a blogger identifying himself as Max Power ranted:

In my opinion Cindy Sheehan i[s] a hate filled whore who

couldn't keep her son's umbilical on and so, is running his name through the mud and bitching as loud as she can to try to make the world feel sorry for her... It is also of my opinion that she has some far leftist speechwriters who are trying their best to get her elected to Congress so she can bitch at us some more and infest the world with her feminist, shortsighted, snaggle toothed, diatribes.... Finally, it is my opinion that she fucks goats. (Power)

Denunciations such as this one often included sexual slurs. Mother-based insults about Sheehan were rampant on the Internet, where public discourse and debate often occur without personal accountability or consequences. Similarly, ageist and violently sexist accusations about opportunism, insanity, immorality, and symbolic necrophilia characterized many online commentaries about Sheehan (Rothschild; also see Engelhardt; Huffington; Manjoo). The virulent sexism that is embedded in these epithets is remarkable. In response to the common use of such expletives, commentator Janet Contursi observed:

What is interesting about those horrible comments about Cindy Sheehan is the sexual/gender language used to condemn her. This says more about the speakers and our society than it does about the issue. I wonder if the outrage would be so strong if the dead soldier's father, rather than his mother, was out there protesting. And, by the way, where the hell is he??? (August 15, 2005, response to Rothschild)

Furthermore, I found no equivalent sexist discourses about fathers who became outspoken critics of the war after their sons or daughters were killed in Iraq (such men include Andrew Bacevich, Carlos Arredondo, Bill Mitchell, and Fernando Suarez del Solar).[4] In a similar vein, threats of violence were common if Sheehan refused to silence her message. One unnamed critic announced, "Cindy is a communist whore and should therefore shut the hell up.... In short, I think she is a shameless bitch who needs to either a) shut up or b) be shot" (response to Rothschild). However, the suggestions of violence against Sheehan had very real implications.

Figure 8. After the August 2005 encampment in Crawford, Sheehan was invited to lead peace marches and actions across the country. Here she speaks at a January 2006 peace rally orga- nized by students at University of California San Diego. Photo: Linda Pershing.

Figure 9. One of Sheehan's strategies was to make the numbers of U.S. military personnel killed and wounded in the Iraq War visible to the public. This sign was displayed and updated on a daily basis at the Camp Casey, the peace encampment in Crawford, Texas. Photo: Linda Pershing.

In the summer of 2005, Sheehan had a body guard accompany her during a national protest tour. An Iraq War veteran who objected to Sheehan's message told one of his professors at a community college in Ventura, California, that he should bring a "Molotov Cocktail" to her upcoming speaking event on campus "so that he could take care of the problem himself." The day before Sheehan's presentation, he was arrested for accidentally exploding a bomb at his house. Police found an AK-47 assault rifle and several pipe bombs during the arrest.[5]

While some bloggers described Sheehan as a "bitch," numerous journalists and writers also characterized her as a loose cannon. Sheehan's public speaking style is disarming—she is direct, out-spoken, and candid, rather than choosing her words carefully for the sake of diplomacy or social conformity. This approach drew many people to rally around her, but it also has potentially deadly implications for women in public life. In August 2005, while staging her first vigil at Crawford, she responded to criticism about her speaking style: "I have been known for some time as a person who speaks the truth and speaks it strongly. I have always called a liar a liar and a hypocrite. Now I am urged to use softer language to appeal to a wider audience" (Sheehan, "Hypocrites and Liars"). She frequently used pejorative terms like "neo-con," "BushCo," the "Bush cabal," and the "Bush regime" to refer to the president and his administration. Reflecting on Sheehan's direct style, Victoria Mares-Hershey commented that "Cindy is a woman holding up a mirror to America and saying, as difficult as it may be, it's time to 'tell the truth.'"

Critics often complained that Sheehan's expletives and profanity were inappropriate for the mother of a soldier who died in the war, and that she could have communicated her message in less offensive, more "feminine" ways. In contrast, supporters noted that her use of language was refreshing and honest:

> They would attempt to tame her by shearing away her language, not just the profanity for which she was known, but the very fierceness of her words. She had no hesitation about calling the President "an evil maniac," "a lying bastard," or the administration "those lying bastards," "chickenhawks," "warmongers," "shameful cowards," and "war criminals." She called for the President's "im-

peachment," for the jailing of the whole top layer of the administration (no pardons). She called for American troops to be pulled out of Iraq now. And most of this largely disappeared from a much-softened media portrait of a grieving antiwar mother.... She is as blunt and impolite in her mission as the media is circumspect and polite in its job, as most of the opposition to George Bush is in its "opposition." And it was her very bluntness, her ability to shock by calling things by their actual names, by acting as she saw fit, that let her break through and that may help turn a set of unhappy public opinion polls into a full-scale antiwar movement. (Englehardt)

Furthermore, after years of being in the limelight, Sheehan has become impressively articulate about public policy issues and assessments of U.S. political leaders. Artist Linda Eddy captured in her political cartoon what many of Sheehan's critics have expressed: a desire to silence her. Eddy drew a caricature of Sheehan with a large bandage—decorated like a U.S. flag—affixed across her mouth, along with the slogan, "Cindy Sheehan doesn't speak for me." It was marketed on an array of consumer products from coffee mugs to baby bibs to T-shirts (Eddy). A female David to Bush's Goliath, Sheehan was cast in the role of the classic "bitch": an angry—and consequently bad—mother who would not shut up and would not go away.

SHEEHAN THE "BAD MOM"

From the moment Sheehan entered the public spotlight, commentators denigrated her for challenging patriarchal notions of "good" motherhood—particularly ideals of the "patriotic mother" who honours her son's sacrifice when he is killed in a war. Challenging the euphemisms that render the carnage of war invisible, Sheehan often comments that Casey was not "lost" or "fallen" but rather was murdered by a shot to the head (see Ferner). Her actions contrasted sharply to those of Grace Darling Seibold, who founded the American Gold Star Mothers during World War I. When George Seibold was killed in action in 1918, his mother

Figure 10. Sheehan (second from the right holding the banner) organized and led peace actions focusing on the experiences of mothers whose children had been killed in the Iraq War. Sheehan named this event "Mother of A March," scheduled on Mother's Day 2007 in Washington, DC. Photo: Linda Pershing.

created an organization for grieving mothers who suffered with pride for the "supreme sacrifice" their soldier sons made dying for their country. The nationalistic and xenophobic organization got its name from the gold star medal that families received and often proudly displayed in the front windows of their homes when their loved ones died in the war.[6] In 2007, the charter of the American Gold Star Mothers proclaimed that the organization is designed to "maintain true allegiance to the United States of America ... [and to] inculcate lessons of patriotism and love of country in the communities in which we live" ("Gold Star Moms").

Rather than continue this tradition, Sheehan challenged the presumption that mourning mothers should support the war in which their children were killed. In the months after Casey died, Sheehan moved through various stages: experiencing intense grief, expressing anger, raising difficult questions, calling for accountability from public officials, asking others to join her in this effort, and developing a more complex political analysis of the Iraq War. Rather than mourn her son's death in private, Sheehan made her grief public, therein verbalizing her pain and subsequently using her experience to formulate criticism of U.S. foreign policy, nationalism, corporate greed, militarism, and a host of other political issues. In an essay she wrote in August 2005, Sheehan commented about the Bush Administration: "I think they seriously 'misunderestimated' [making fun of a term George W. Bush used] all mothers. I wonder if any of them had authentic mother-child relationships and if they are surprised that there are so many mothers in this country who are bear-like when it comes to wanting the truth....?" (Sheehan, "Hypocrites and Liars").[7] In response, opponents attacked her moral character, family loyalty, and her legitimacy as a mother. Patriotic mothers are expected to hold true the cherished memory of their children by making the ultimate sacrifice—that of their children's lives—for a nationalistic cause. Critics lambasted Sheehan when she refused to play the role accordingly.

Cynthia Enloe, a leading scholar in the study of the historical and political relationships between women and militarization, comments on the complex dynamics which constrain mothers' responses to nationalism and patriotism. Reflecting on mothers' civic engagement, she astutely identifies the pressure for women to conform to the ideal of the patriotic mother who stoically grieves after her son (rarely is the death of a daughter-soldier mentioned) dies in war while continuing to support the government that sent him to fight. This ideal conflicts with the unpopular notion of a mother as a patriotic citizen, whose active concern for her country also entails, and even necessitates, critique of government practices and wartime policies. Enloe reflects:

> Many women have a very ambivalent relationship to patriotism precisely because the conventional prescriptions for being recognized as woman-and-patriot are grounded in notions of feminine "respectability." In exposing this ambivalence and its causes, feminists have made the very model of the patriot less tenable. Most militarizing states need women to seek to be patriots, yet need them to do so without stepping over the bounds of "proper" femininity, since that would then dispirit a lot of men, who would feel that their own masculine turf was being challenged. In a patriarchal state a woman can aspire to be a "patriotic mother" but not a "patriotic citizen." On the other

hand, we now have increasing historical documentation of women who have challenged this orthodox, gendered idea of patriotism. (Enloe 171-72)

Detractors criticized Sheehan because she spoke out, not only about her grief as a "Gold Star Mother" but also about larger political and social dimensions of the war. As Enloe observes, speaking from the vantage point of motherhood is a double-edged sword because crossing the line between grief and political commentary often puts mother-activists at risk for public criticism. When Sheehan became a top news story, commentary about her "abandonment" of her children and husband surfaced almost immediately, despite the fact that most of Sheehan's adult life had been devoted to caring for her family. Discourses that constructed her as a "bad" wife and mother ignited in August 2005 when she led the vigil outside Bush's Crawford ranch. At the same time, Patrick Sheehan, her spouse of 28 years, filed for divorce. According to Cindy, their estrangement was fuelled by the stress of Casey's death and her decision to take up full-time activism against the war (Sheehan, *Peace Mom* 123-32). People who had no personal knowledge of Sheehan's life circulated rumors and lies in an attempt to discredit her.[8]

One particular narrative that gained momentum over the Internet claimed that Cindy filed for divorce many years before the war and left her son to be raised by her former husband when she became a political activist for the Democratic Party. According to this fictional account, Patrick Sheehan remarried, and he and his second wife raised Casey as a young child because Cindy was no longer interested in caring for him ("The 'Real' Cindy Sheehan"). Soon after Sheehan started her Crawford protest, pundits reported that she had always been a neglectful and selfish mother. Narratives of this type were complete fabrications, casting Sheehan as an unfit mother who valued her political ambitions over the care of loved ones. Stories about Sheehan abandoning her family reflect and perpetuate the sexual double standard about parental responsibility that remains pervasive in U.S. discourse, since fathers who are activists and social critics are rarely scrutinized for spending time away from home or "abandoning" their families. These stories were ultimately fabricated with the knowledge that, no matter what a woman accomplishes in her life, claiming that she is a "bad mother" is a very effective way to discredit her.

Based on these allegations, some commentators argued that Sheehan's "failure" as a mother relegated her to subhuman status. A blogger by the name of ransr made the following accusation:

> We can agree that motherhood is good and that the loss of a child is awful. Something that is not meant to be. HOWEVER, this woman is not [a] mother. She abandoned her son as a child. She did nothing for him except to use his death as an opportunity for her 15 minutes of fame. I can think of nothing good to say of a woman who abandons her young. Even animals don't do that. (Comcast Community Forums)

Many conceptualized her "ineptitude" as a mother and wife as Sheehan's defining characteristic. An Internet commentator named Bindarra complained, "The real futility of Cindy Sheehan was this: as she grieved the loss of her son, she abandoned her husband and other children, who needed her more than ever" (Pareene). In this sense, Sheehan's most egregious crime was daring to leave the domestic realm and move into civic space to become a public figure. A blog entry titled "Cindy needs to go home" epitomizes this sentiment, as a writer using the name gsyvrud calls for Sheehan to return to an imagined, private home life in which women are rendered invisible:

> I think of other parents who lost children in wars such as Iraq, Vietnam, Korea, or WW2 ... who accepted their loss and grief and went on to remain solid citizens of the USA without having to blame and bad-mouth a President or others—public or military officials ... for their children's deaths. At Memorial Day ceremonies all across our nation yesterday, those parents ... visited the graves of their loved ones and honored them along with their communities in which they live. Their quiet devotion to their childrens'

memories and their support of our nation—no matter who is the President ... is a far greater and a far better testimony than Cindy Sheehan could ever hope to make with her foul-mouthed protests and constant publicity seeking. *She needs to go home, and hopefully, disappear from the public arena for the remainder of her life.* (Syvrud, emphasis added)

On the whole, the notion that a woman's value, first and foremost, is defined by her caretaking role as a wife and mother was deeply ingrained in popular commentary, which constructed Sheehan as a "bad mom." In times of war, mothers are expected to support American militarism and grieve the deaths of their soldier sons with piety and patriotic fervour. Sheehan's refusal to do so allowed critics to dismiss her as a neglectful, selfish, and disingenuous wife and mother.

Figure 11: Cindy Sheehan often wore T-shirts and buttons calling for the impeachment of President George W. Bush and Vice President Dick Cheney. Among friends and peace activists, she celebrates her fiftieth birthday on July 10, 2007, at Camp Casey in Crawford, Texas. Photo: Linda Pershing.

CONCLUSION

Cindy Sheehan became a lightning rod for heated debates about U.S. foreign and public policies, war and peace, civic rights, free speech, and a host of other important issues. Contentious disputes about mothering were central to the public's reception of this activist who, in many ways, challenged patriarchal notions of "good" motherhood and womanhood more generally. However, in spite of the vitriolic backlash that her presence inspired, her efforts also garnered considerable support. For instance, journalist Stephanie Salter offered an insightful analysis of the many attempts to discredit Sheehan through claims that she was "exploiting" her son's death in the Iraq War to further her own agenda:

> As for exploiting her son's death, what does that look like? If Casey Sheehan had not been killed in a war in Iraq, his mother likely would not be out stumping against that war. To acknowledge that fact is no more exploitive than when parents whose children have been kidnapped or molested react by lobbying for tougher laws and longer sentences. (Salter)

Some supporters saw Sheehan as a significant prophetic voice that unexpectedly arose from the life of a white, Catholic, middle-class mother to become an outspoken political critic. While opponents tried to dismiss her by dredging up sexist stereotypes, portrait artist Robert Shetterly developed a very different perception:

> Cindy Sheehan has painted a very accurate portrait of herself, her anger, her frustration, her determination to give meaning to Casey's death, her implicit belief that if the American people know the truth, they will do the right thing. Many people would now edit and censor her words, pull her teeth, make of her a grief-struck pawn of the left. The degree to which they attack her is the degree to which the power of her truth terrifies them. (Shetterly)

Another journalist similarly noted that the "trouble" with Cindy Sheehan—the real basis of the complaints and efforts to discredit her—was that she was a mother of a dead soldier who spoke out and took action to protest the war, refusing to conform to the stereotype of the patriotic, silently suffering, war-supporting mother:

> The problem with Cindy Sheehan was that she wouldn't let herself be put in a box. She wouldn't sit on a porch and

grieve the way mothers are supposed to, with a wisp of a star in the window, just behind the curtains, letting the world know, if it cared, that she'd lost a son.... She wouldn't be quiet and she wouldn't stay home and she wouldn't quit shouting out that the war in Iraq that took her son's life was and remains an atrocious mistake. (van Doorn)

Because Sheehan refused to be silenced, she became a target for many of the types of character assassination that commonly befall mothers in public life. Through political cartoons and jokes, bloggers' rants and urban legends, critics branded her as a loud-mouthed bitch and a bad mother in an attempt to discredit her critique of the war. Critics often interpreted Cindy Sheehan's actions and public presence using discourses of mother-blame. Her resistance signified a defiance of conventional, patriarchal norms by claiming space in public life and countering cultural assumptions about military mothers' support for the wars in which their children fought and died.

ENDNOTES

[1]Special thanks to Kathie Alvizo, Nishelle Bellinger, Lindsay Riedel, and Lori Walkington, who assisted with the research and interview transcription.

[2]Maines spoke out briefly against President Bush during a concert in London, England. The Dixie Chicks experienced an enormous backlash, and much of the criticism was extremely sexist. In reaction to Maines' comment, many Southern and country music radio stations banned Dixie Chicks songs and called for people to gather and burn their CDs ("Dixie Chicks Pulled"; Dixie Chicks: Shut Up).

[3]At the time, the misogynist connotations of the term "mother fucker" did not seem to concern Sheehan. Her understanding of sexism in language and culture developed noticeably as she became a public speaker and leader. For example, she began using inclusive language to refer to deity (Sheehan, *Peace Mom*, 129) and articulated her support for "matriotism" as an alternative to

patriotism (see Sheehan "Matriotism").

[4]See Goodman; Houppert (2005, 2006); Pershing "Do Not Go Gentle" and "From Sorrow to Activism"; Rockwell.

[5]Email message from Cindy Sheehan to the author (June 23, 2007).

[6]For many years, only mothers who were born in U.S. were admitted to the American Gold Star Mothers, even if they had legally immigrated to the U.S. and their children had died in service to the U.S. military ("'Gold Star' Moms to Admit Non Citizens"). See Shields concerning Ligaya Lagman, a Filipina who has been a legal resident and taxpayer of the U.S. since 1982. Her son, Army Staff Sergeant Anthony Lagman, died fighting in Afghanistan, but she was barred from entrance to the American Gold Star Mothers because she was not a U.S. citizen. With pressure, the American Gold Star Mothers changed their policies and admitted her in 2005.

[7]Here Sheehan ridiculed Bush's propensity for butchering the English language. His use of the term "misunderestimate" is one of many such vocabulary errors documented in "Don't Misunderestimate Bushisms."

[8]For example, see this Internet commentary assailing Sheehan, entitled "Bad Mom." An author named Marie wrote: "I really don't like her and I think her issues run really deep and have to do with the way she treated her son and maybe that is why she is so rabid and willing to ignore his death and go on, and on, and on, and on, and on, and on … 'bout the war. I do agree with Al, she needs counseling. But, not 'cause her son died. I think, maybe, perhaps, could be, that she was a REAL bad mom. And MAYBE she is trying to justify her being a bad mom by doing the things she is doing.… Here is what I think about Cindy Sheehan: She is a HORRID mother and I have ZERO respect for her. I also think she is a TERRIBLE WOMAN. I think she is a BAD person with questionable motives" ("The 'Real' Cindy Sheehan").

WORKS CITED

"Approval Ratings for President and Congressional Leaders Continue to Drop, According to Latest Harris Poll." *PRNewswire* 24 Aug. 2005. Web. 11 Dec. 2007.

Aszklar, Lisa. "Media Bias: A Content Analysis of the Cindy Sheehan Antiwar Protest of Aug. 2005." MA thesis. George Mason University, 2006. Print.

Blog Pulse. 13 Dec. 2007. Web. 19 Dec. 2007.

"Cindy Sheehan." *Uncyclopedia*. n.d. Web. 6 June 2014.

"Cindy Sheehan Is." *United for Peace of Pierce County*. 18 Aug. 2005. Web. 19 June 2007.

"Cindy Sheehan Is Working To Bring Our Troops Home: 'Mr. President. You Have Daughters. How Would You Feel If One of Them Was Killed?'" *Buzzflash*. 7 Oct. 2004. Web. 10 June 2007.

Comcast Community Forums. "Cindy Sheehan." 29 May 2007. Web. 17 June 2007.

DANCALL. Comment in response to "Cindy Sheehan's Farewell." *The Nation,* 31 May 2007. Web. 20 June 2007.

"Dixie Chicks Pulled from Air after Bashing Bush." *Showbiz*. 14 Mar. 2003. Web. 10 Dec. 2007.

Dixie Chicks: Shut Up and Sing. Dir. Barbara Kopple and Cecilia Peck. Woolly Puddin' Films, 2006. DVD.

"Don't Misunderestimate Bushisms." *CNN*. 15 Jan. 2003. Web. 28 June 2007.

Eddy, Linda. "Cindy Sheehan Doesn't Speak for Me." *Rightwing-stuff*. n.d. Web. 5 June 2014.

Englehardt, Tom. "Cindy, Don, and George: On Being in a Ditch at the Side of the Road." *Sign of the Times*. 2005. Web. 17 June 2007.

Enloe, Cynthia. *The Curious Feminist: Searching for Women in a New Age of Empire*. Berkeley: University of California Press, 2004. Print.

Ferner, Mike. "What One Mom Has to Say to George Bush." *Mike Ferner Blog*. 12 Aug. 2005. Web. 13 Dec. 2007.

"Gold Star Moms/Who We Are/History." *Gold Star Moms*. 2007. Web. 20 June 2001.

"'Gold Star' Moms to Admit Non Citizens: Group Came under Fire for Barring Filipina Mother of Slain GI." *U.S. Times*. 28 June 2005. Web. 25 June 2007.

Goodman, Amy. "The Endless War Memorial: Father of Slain Soldier Joins Times Square Protest to Read Names of Iraq War Dead." *Democracy Now*. 13 Mar. 2007. Web. 26 Dec. 2007.

Hendrie, Phil. "Anti-war Mom: Another Ignorant Cow." *Free*

Republic. 11 Aug. 2005. Web. 5 June 2014.

Horowitz, David. "Cindy Sheehan 'Doesn't Respect Her Own Son's Life.'" *Media Matters.* 17 Aug. 2005. Web. 19 June 2007.

Houppert, Karen. "Cindy Sheehan: Mother of a Movement?" *The Nation.* 25 May 2006. Web. 29 June 2007.

Houppert, Karen. "The New Face of Protest?" *The Nation.* 28 Mar. 2005. Web. 29 June 2007.

Huffington, Arianna. "It Takes a Village to Smear Cindy Sheehan." *Huffington Post.* 12 Aug. 2005. Web. 14 Dec. 2007.

Manjoo, Farhad. "Smearing Cindy Sheehan." *Salon.* 13 Aug. 2005. Web. 4 June 2014.

Mares-Hershey, Victoria. "Portrait of Cindy Sheehan also a Picture of Democracy." Reprinted from *Portland Press Herald.* 30 Aug. 2005. Web. 21 June 2007.

"A Mother's Tears." YouTube. Prod. by RealVoices.org, 2004. Web. 13 Dec. 2007.

Nichols, John. "The President's Vacation from Reality." *The Nation.* 15 Aug. 2005. Web. 27 June 2007.

Pareene, Alex. "The Surge Worked: Cindy Sheehan Gives Up and Goes Back to Russia." *Wonkette.* 3 June 2007. Web. 5 June 2014.

The People's Cube. Cindy Sheehan as Satan (graphic). n.d. 2 June 2014.

Pershing, Linda. "Do Not Go Gentle into That Good Night: The Tragic Death of Brian Arredondo." *Journal of American Folklore* 127.503 (2014): 82-90. Print.

Pershing, Linda. "Cindy Sheehan: A Call to Maternal Thinking in the Contemporary Peace Movement." Ed. Andrea O'Reilly. *The Legacy of Sara Ruddick's Maternal Thinking.* Toronto: Demeter Press, 2009. 144-172. Print.

Pershing, Linda, with Nishelle Y. Bellinger. "From Sorrow to Activism: A Father's Memorial to His Son Alexander Arredondo, Killed in the U.S. Occupation of Iraq." *Journal of American Folklore* 123.488 (2010): 179-217. Print.

Power, Max. "Cindy Sheehan the Movie: Cindy and the Dragon." Blue Damage. 20 Apr. 2006. Web. 5 June 2014.

Raddatz, Martha. *The Long Road Home: A Story of War and Family.* New York: Penguin, 2007. Print.

"The 'Real' Cindy Sheehan." *Urban Legends. About.com.* 6 Sept.

2005. Web. 4 June 2014. Renew America Forum. 17 Mar. 2006. Web. 28 Mar. 2006.

Rich, Frank. "The Swift Boating of Cindy Sheehan." *New York Times*. 21 Aug. 2005. Web. 26 June 2007.

Rockwell, Paul. "From Grief To Protest: How Peace Loving Fathers Honour Their Fallen Sons." *In Motion Magazine*. 11 June 2004. Web. June 29, 2007.

"Rosie O'Donnell Attacks Bush and Screams for His Impeachment." YouTube. 2007. Web. 13 Dec. 2007.

Rothschild, Matthew. "The Savaging of Cindy Sheehan." *The Progressive*. 11 Aug. 2005. Web. 29 June 2007.

Salter, Stephanie. "Cindy Sheehan an Ordinary Woman on a Path That's Extraordinary." *The Tribune-Star*. 14 Apr. 2007. Web. 22 June 2007.

Sanchez, Maria. "Sheehan's Father Finds Meaning Amid Grief." *Sydney Herald*. 28 June 2007. Web. 7 July 2007.

Sheehan, Cindy. "Hypocrites and Liars." *Common Dreams*. 20 Aug. 2005. Web. 22 June 2007.

Sheehan, Cindy. "Matriotism." *Common Dreams*. 26 Jan. 2006. Web. 9 June 2007.

Sheehan, Cindy. *Peace Mom: A Mother's Journey through Heartache to Activism*. New York: Atria Books, 2006.

"Turn, Turn, Turn." *Common Dreams*. 19 June 2007. Web. 22 June 2007.

Shetterly, Robert. "Painting Cindy." *Lew Rockwell*. 20 Aug. 2005. Web. 22 June 2007.

Shields, Mark. "Grief of a Gold Star Mother." *CNN*. 18 June 2005. Web. 12 June 2007.

Syvrud, Kay. "Give Me Strength! Nancy Pelosi and Cindy Sheehan." Buffalo Gal. 29 May 2007. Web. 3 June 2014.

van Doorn, John. "Cindy Sheehan Steps Away." *North County Times*. 2 June 2007. Web. 1 July 2007.

10.
Tiger Mothers and the Birth of a New Maternal Epithet

A Feminist Critical Discourse Analysis of Popular Responses to Amy Chua's *Battle Hymn of the Tiger Mother*

SARAH SAHAGIAN

WHY DO SO MANY people revile Amy Chua with the passion of a thousand and one suns? Because I assure you, many people do. To prove this hatred exists in the world, I googled "Amy Chua is a Monster" on this day, March 30, 2014. I received 195,000 hits. Clearly, there are an inordinate number of people who believe Chua to be, for lack of a better word, monstrous. But *why*? Chua is a Yale Law professor who studies the intersection of racial politics and free markets in her academic life. Overall, she is a conventionally successful career woman with two degrees from Harvard, a husband by the name of Jed Rubenfeld, who is a fellow Yale Law professor, and two daughters.

Do people hate Chua because she seems to have achieved the feat of "having it all," whatever that means? Do people hate her because her books on economic structure and ethnicity, such as her 2014 work *The Triple Package,* often veer into deeply troubling racial essentialism?

Interestingly, much of the vitriol levelled at Chua actually comes from people's distaste for the way she parents her daughters, Lulu and Sophia. In 2011, Chua published a *New York Times* best-selling memoir, *Battle Hymn of the Tiger Mother.* It is a memoir that was translated into numerous languages and started a global media controversy. Of course, not everyone in the world read the book, but for a while it seemed like even those who hadn't so much as flipped through a copy had opinions about it.

When considering the case of Chua, I am reminded of the re-nowned scholars of motherhood Molly Ladd-Taylor and Lauri

Umansky. They argue, "'Bad' mothers have moved noticeably toward center stage in American culture" (2). They also contend the "bad" mother concept is quite elastic, which means mothers are blamed "for everything, pure and simple" (2). Ladd-Taylor and Umansky cite such examples as "the welfare mother, the teen mother, the career woman who has no time for her kids, the drug addict who poisons her fetus, the pushy stage mother," and "the overprotective Jewish mother" (2). Building on this work, I would argue that a recent addition to this pantheon of bad mothers is none other than the tiger mother.

In this chapter, I discuss Chua's own reflections on what she calls "Chinese parenting." Then, I analyze the backlash her work has received in both popular American media and American academia. I then move into a summation about the significance of the "tiger mother" as racial stereotype. Of course, because this is one short chapter, I am only able to provide a few examples of the sort of criticism levelled at Chua. In light of this, I have selected both popular media and academic responses I find particularly reflective of the criticism Chua's mothering memoir has received.

Ultimately, this chapter takes the form of a feminist critical discourse analysis, whereby I hope to demonstrate how much of the criticism against Chua has racialized and deeply mother-blaming roots. I argue the sort of mother-blame directed at Chua perpetuates the Western ideal of the sacrificial patriarchal mother who is called upon to do the work of childrearing without complaint and with no real authority with which to make parenting choices. The furor over *Battle Hymn* is the product of an intersectionally racist and sexist panic, a panic by members of an American public threatened by Chua's confident, self-identified "Chinese mothering" style. Ultimately, I illustrate how the troubling discourse surrounding Chua's mothering has reached such heights that it has resulted in the addition of the *tiger mother* epithet to the list of stock bad-mother archetypes.

THE ORIGINAL "TIGER MOTHER" IN HER OWN WORDS

While the term *tiger mother* did not exist in the popular lexicon prior to Chua writing her memoir, there are now academic studies claiming to prove the inferiority of so-called tiger mothers. There are also countless opinion pieces devoted to taking them down. Who are these so-called tiger mothers and what do they stand for? The answer varies greatly depending on whom you ask. For her part, however, Chua does not use *tiger mothering* in her memoir as a term to describe her disciplined, work-intensive approach to parenting. In actuality, it is a reference to the fact that Chua was born in the "year of the tiger" according to the Chinese zodiac. In her memoir, Chua instead uses the term "Chinese parenting" to refer to her childrearing philosophy.

In *Battle Hymn*, Chua explains some core tenets regarding what she perceives as "Chinese parenting" norms. She writes, "What Chinese parents understand is that nothing is fun until you're good at it. To get good at anything, you have to work, and children on their own never want to work, which is why it is crucial to override their preferences" (31). Chua goes on to argue that this intensive parenting is worth it in the end:

> ...if done properly, the Chinese strategy produces a virtuous circle. Tenacious practice, practice, practice is crucial for excellence; rote repetition is underrated in America. Once a child starts to excel at something—whether it's math, piano, pitching, or ballet, he or she gets praise, admiration and satisfaction. This in turn makes it easier for the parent to get the child to work even more. (32)

Chua's use of the term "Chinese parenting" of course results in a gross ethnocultural generalization—a generalization, one must note, for which she provides little proof in her memoir. The sum total of her evidence takes the form of her anecdotal experience and a vague footnote about studies Chua claims support her ideas, though she provides no meaningful discussion of their methods or conclusions. Also telling is that despite her frequent reference to "Chinese parenting" as if it were a monolithic category of childrearing, Chua's memoir acknowledges that *not all* Chinese parents raise their children in a similar manner. She also acknowledges that many non-Chinese parents of different ethnicities practice an approach to childrearing similar to hers (4). While not everyone interprets Chinese culture in the same way, and while indeed it is offensive to pretend Chinese parenting is a monolith, it is important to remember that *Battle Hymn* is a work of life writing. It is not a parenting manual or a longitudinal research study. *Battle Hymn* is a memoir about how its author, Amy Chua, mothers and perceives mothering. It documents the biased associations with Chinese culture she attaches to her personal approach to parenthood.

As her memoir proceeds, Chua candidly showcases both her parenting triumphs, as well as moments of conflict and even crisis. In terms of what she perceives as her parenting successes, Chua recalls:

> But probably most important, we stuck with the Chinese model because the early results were hard to quarrel with. Other parents were constantly asking what our secret was. Sophia and Lulu were model children. In public, they were polite, interesting, helpful, and well spoken. They were A students, and Sophia was two years ahead of her classmates in math. They were fluent in Mandarin. And everyone marveled at their classical music playing. (62)

During a family vacation to Russia, Chua argues bitterly with her younger daughter Lulu. After many arguments over issues, such as Lulu's anger at her mother for insisting Lulu perform the violin at her Bat Mitzvah, the conflict reaches crisis level. The crisis occurs when Lulu refuses to try caviar at a restaurant in Red Square. In response, Chua says to her daughter:

> Do you know how sad and ashamed my parents would be if they saw this, Lulu—you publicly disobeying me? With that look on your face? You're only hurting yourself. We're in Russia, and you refuse to try caviar! You're like a barbarian! And in case you think you're a big rebel, you are *completely ordinary.* There is nothing more typical, more predictable, more common and low, than an American teenager who won't try things. (226)

Lulu, however, does not take her mother's criticism lying down. Lulu retorts by telling Chua, "Shut up" and soon thereafter declares, "I *hate* you! I HATE YOU" (226). The fight escalates from there, with Chua telling Lulu, "You are a terrible daughter" (226). Lulu's response is equally biting: "I know—I'm not what you want—I'm not Chinese! I don't want to be Chinese. Why can't you get that through your head? I *hate* the violin. I HATE my life" (227).

While Chua readily admits her approach to parenting does not make her immune to mother-daughter conflicts, her memoir suggests her mothering style produces positive results overall. After their blowout in Russia, Chua writes, "I couldn't lose Lulu. Nothing was more important. So I did the most Western thing imaginable: I gave her the choice. I told her that she could quit the violin if she wanted and do what she liked instead, which at the time was to play tennis" (233).

However, what happens after Lulu is permitted to quit the violin is also interesting. Despite her decision to pursue tennis instead, Lulu continues to employ the strong work ethic her mother teaches her when she is studying classical music. Chua recalls one afternoon when she picked her daughter up from a tennis tournament only to hear the words, "Guess what, Mommy—I won!" (240).

Chua is impressed with Lulu's commitment to tennis. After watching her daughter in a particularly long training session, Chua compliments her on how much her backhand has improved; however, Lulu insists, "No, it's not right yet.... Can we get a court tomorrow?" (431). Of her own volition, Lulu soon becomes as intense about practicing the sport she chose for herself as Chua was about Lulu practicing the instrument Chua chose for her at the memoir's start.

However, simply because Chua now allows her daughter to decide on her own activities does not mean that she abandons her approach of attempting to guide Lulu toward successful results. Chua ends her memoir with this passage:

> I've resorted to espionage and guerilla warfare. I secretly plant ideas in her tennis coach's head, texting her with questions and practice strategies, then deleting the text messages so Lulu won't see them. Sometimes, when Lulu's least expecting it at breakfast or when I'm saying good

night—I'll suddenly yell out, "More rotation on the swing volley!" or "Don't move your right foot on your kick serve." And Lulu will plug her ears, and we'll fight, but I'll have gotten my message out, and I know she knows I'm right. (244)

Chua admits to having conflicts with her daughters. She admits to allowing Lulu to choose tennis over the violin in order to improve their relationship. However, Chua ends her maternal narrative at a moment of success: not only is Lulu excelling at her passion, Chua's maternal authority is not effaced. When Chua tells us, "I know she knows I'm right," the text suggests Lulu is able to become her own person with her own interests without her mother being rendered irrelevant. This memoir is not the story of maternal marginalization. Instead, it can be read as a narrative about a mother's resiliency, as Chua admits her fallibility without becoming overcome by guilt or insecurity.

Of course, there are some who read this book and interpret Chua's parenting style as overly strict and far too labour-intensive. I would argue that it is, however, important to remember Chua's intense approach to motherhood is fairly *de rigueur*. After all, what does it mean to be an "intense mom" in the era of intensive motherhood? Is that not how we are all encouraged to parent? In her work, Sharon Hays explains that the discourse of intensive mothering has become the dominant childrearing paradigm. Under this discourse of intensive mothering, she writes, "there is an underlying assumption that the child absolutely requires consistent nurture by a single primary caretaker and that the mother is the best person for the job" (414). Other features of intensive mothering, according to Hays, are that it is "expert-guided, emotionally absorbing, labour-intensive, and financially expensive" (414). This description closely reflects Chua's approach to motherhood, which involves her spending inordinate amounts of money on her daughter's extra-curricular lessons and overseeing often hours-long musical practice sessions.

It would appear that many facets of Chua's mothering reflect cultural norms for those class-privileged enough to practice intensive mothering. Chua does differ, however, when it comes to the patriarchal expectation that not only should mothers do the bulk of childrearing but they should do so in an uncomplaining and self-effacing manner. According to Andrea O'Reilly, "'Good' mothers in patriarchal motherhood ... are defined as white, middle-class, married, stay-at-home moms" (69 "Outlaw(ing) Motherhood"). Chua deviates from this norm by the fact of her Chinese ethnicity, which she embraces and celebrates in her memoir. She also deviates in one other important way—she may be a remarkably intensive mother but she is not a sacrificial mother. O'Reilly explains sacrificial mothering as the following:

> The patriarchal ideology of motherhood makes motherhood deeply oppressive to women because sacrificial motherhood ...requires the repression or denial of the mother's own selfhood; as well as it assigns her all of the responsibility for mothering but gives no real power from which to mother. (*Rocking the Cradle* 44)

Chua departs markedly from this definition of sacrificial motherhood because she does not deny herself. The very act of writing a memoir, where she explains her thoughts and opinions on motherhood, acknowledges this selfhood. Nor does Chua relinquish her "power"; she may allow her growing daughters more freedom of choice by the memoir's end but she still makes her feelings known concerning Lulu's tennis practices.

While I do not mean for this paper to be an endorsement of Chua's memoir or all of her parenting decisions, I would argue many of the criticisms commonly levelled at Chua are problematic. I will now analyze some salient examples of the backlash to *Battle Hymn of the Tiger Mother.* I will do so in order to illustrate the aggressive nature of the mother-blame aimed at Chua in the popular media's reception of her memoir.

THE POPULAR MEDIA'S TAKE ON CHUA'S MEMOIR

While Chua herself does not use the words *tiger mother* as a generalizable term in her memoir, shortly after the book's publication, the rest of the world began to do so. Chua's specific nickname for herself was suddenly transformed into a new archetype of bad mother as everyone rushed to decry her in print.

In one particularly scathing piece in the New York-based newspaper *The Observer*, Lee Siegel takes Chua to task. He writes:

> Though she is now a "writer," Ms. Chua is blind and deaf to the most transparent psychological event. When Sophia, her oldest daughter, jumps out of their car "to grab a tennis racket" as Ms. Chua is backing out of the driveway, Ms. Chua runs over the girl's leg and breaks her ankle. Rather than attributing her daughter's recklessness to the hysterical anxiety her mother's pressure is inducing in her, Ms. Chua strides ahead. Being laid up "at least gave her a lot of time to practice the piano," she shrugs.

Siegel takes an event described in Chua's memoir as an accident, her running over Sophia's foot when the girl unexpectedly leaps out of a moving vehicle, and morphs it into evidence of Chua's failure as a mother. Rather than chalking Sophia's accident up as a foolish but human mistake made by a teenager, Siegel interprets the event in such a way as to render Chua entirely at fault. The fact that Chua eschews the logic of sacrificial motherhood and has no guilt surrounding the event renders her "blind" and "deaf" in Siegel's eyes. In other words, Siegel critiques Chua for not finding ways to assume events over which she has no control are somehow all her fault. She is "blind" and "deaf" to the social expectations that a mother blame herself.

Siegel's keenness to interpret Sophia's fluke accident as proof of Chua's inadequacy illustrates how, in the mother-blame game, it would seem as if the mother herself can never get ahead. In the words of Paula Caplan, reflecting on her experience studying mother-blame, "It seemed there was nothing that a mother could do that was right...." (592).

Lee Siegel is not the only high-profile newspaper columnist who publicly decries Chua as a lacking mother. In January of 2011, David Brooks wrote an article for *The New York Times* titled "Amy Chu Is a Wimp." In it, he details his objections to Chua's parenting style:

I just wish she wasn't so soft and indulgent. I wish she rec-ognized that in some important ways the school cafeteria is more intellectually demanding than the library. And I hope her daughters grow up to write their own books, and maybe learn the skills to better anticipate how theirs will be received.

Brooks' overall tone is condescending, suggesting Chua, who has raised two daughters, has no understanding of children's development. By nonsensical contrast, Brooks feels confident enough in his own comprehension of parenting to lecture a mother of children he does not know. Brooks' snide comment about his "hope" that Chua's daughters will grow up to write their own books also implies Lulu and Sophia must have salacious stories about their upbringing to share. It suggests that the relatively happy ending to Chua's book is a false one, that by being a demanding and confident mother, she could not possibly be a successful one who is appreciated by her daughters. Not only this, but Brooks progresses from mother-blame to victim-blaming by suggesting Chua is the one who bears the responsibility for the vitriolic backlash she has received from people like himself. Brooks is the columnist who resorts to puerile name-calling by referring to Chua as a "wimp" in an international newspaper and yet according to him, we should believe Ms. Chua brought his bullying on herself.

In the *Huffington Post*, psychologist Dr. Jim Taylor also uses his mass media platform to skewer Chua in an op-ed. His tone is particularly scathing, illustrated by a description of what he imagines it would feel like to be mothered by Chua: "Living with that ticking time bomb of a mother would feel as safe and secure as living in Baghdad." Taylor's hyperbolic tone is telling. We see how freely he feels entitled to condemn Chua as a mother.

So what exactly about Chua's mothering style does Dr. Taylor find as terrifying as living in a war-ravaged city mired in poverty? Taylor writes: "Chua's concern for her daughters' self-esteem omits two other contributors to healthy and resilient self-esteem. First, children need to feel loved by their parents. Though I'm sure Chua loves her daughters as much as the next parent, it appears that she doesn't express that love in healthy ways." Ultimately, Taylor, who has never been mothered by Chua, feels confident diagnosing her love for her daughters as unhealthy. He feels confident reading against Chua's happy ending of family harmony and the preservation of maternal authority, contending her daughters will be traumatized by living with her. Here, Chua, who dares to share a story with a relatively successful ending, comes up against the patriarchal assumption that she should instead sacrifice herself on the altar of blame. There is no room for tales of a resilient and confident Chinese-American mother under Dr. Taylor's presumptuous, mother-blaming gaze. Like Siegel and Brooks, Taylor's op-ed represents *Battle Hymn* as a tale of maternal monstrosity. Ultimately, it is problematic how these three men, who have neither been parented by Chua nor co-parented with her, feel confident using such harsh language to criticize her mothering.

THE ACADEMY TAKES ON TIGER MOTHERING

It is important to remember, however, that Chua has not simply inspired negative reactions in the popular media. Her memoir also became a catalyst for academic research produced by American universities critiquing the effectiveness of so-called tiger mothers. These studies research—and ultimately judge—Chinese-American parents who are perceived as strict and authoritarian. For example, in a study conducted by Su Yeong Kim et al. and published in the *Asian American Journal of Psychology*, the authors use their research findings to come down en masse against what they term "tiger parenting." They write, "The current study suggests that, contrary to the common perception, tiger parenting is not the most typical parenting profile in Chinese families, nor does it lead to optimal adjustment among Chinese American adolescents" (Kim et al. 7). The authors base these findings on a study involving a "three-wave longitudinal design spanning eight years, from early adolescence to emerging adulthood" (7). The study reports on six parenting dimensions such as "warmth and shaming," as well as "six developmental outcomes," including "GPA and academic pressure" (7). Ultimately, Chua's memoir has sparked the creation of academic research that aims to take down all sorts of disparate

Chinese-American parents for what is perceived as their flawed, non-Western approach to parenting.

From their research, Kim and her colleagues conclude that tiger mothering has negative effects on children. According to their study's results, "a tiger parenting profile is associated with lower GPA and educational attainment, as well as less of a sense of family obligation; it is also associated with more academic pressure, more depressive symptoms, and a greater sense of alienation" (7). We see from such research that Amy Chua is no longer the only tiger mother whose parenting is judged by society. Significantly, however, Chua herself has become a symbol for everything academics use ethnically essentialist studies to declare is "wrong" with Chinese mothering, blaming this racially stereo-typical notion of strict parenting for a host of ills experienced by children and teens with Chinese ancestry. Ironically, one of these problems cited by Kim and her fellow researchers includes lower GPAs—a problem from which, Chua makes clear, her A-student daughters do not suffer. This contradiction, however, does not stop researchers from associating Chua's nickname and approach to parenting with any obstacles a Chinese-American high school student may encounter.

Psychology Professor Cixin Wang of UC Riverside also uses academic research to take down so-called tiger mothers. When discussing her research on Chinese adolescents in a 2014 interview for UCR Today, Wang readily employs the term tiger mother. Wang states, "Our research shows that Tiger Mother type of parenting, specifically controlling, punitive, and less supportive type of parenting is really not working in the sample of Chinese adolescents" (qtd in Nealon). Wang later adds, "It also shows that it is important for Chinese parents, who tend to be less emotionally expressive and use less praise in parenting, to show their approval, love and support for their children" (qtd in Nealon). Here, Wang not only stereotypes Chinese parents as "less emotionally expressive" but by virtue of using Chua's nickname, Wang anoints Chua as the poster child for this proposed maternal failing. The woman who proudly boasts in print about how polite and academic her girls are is thus paradoxically chastised for bestowing insufficient "praise" as a parent.

The debunking of so-called tiger mothering by professional researchers affiliated with universities is worrisome. A term Chua never uses in the original text of her memoir to refer to anyone but herself has been appropriated. Now, the term refers to any number of racially stereotypical faults researchers may associate with Chinese parents. The term *tiger parenting* has been co-opted by these academics as a byword for what they perceive as excessively intensive, overly strict parenting in Chinese-American diasporic groups, illustrating the extent to which Chua herself has been vilified. It also illustrates the power and omnipresence of this new bad-mother archetype.

THE TIGER MOTHER STEREOTYPE AS A SYMBOL OF RACIAL AND CULTURAL PANIC

It is obvious from analyzing the writing and research of Chua's critics in academe and the popular media that the tiger mother trope circulates as a racist maternal stereotype. That stereotype is one of the Asian-American mother who drives her children to succeed at all costs, and with little attention paid to the well-being of said children. Why is this new racialized bad-mother stereotype so very problematic? To explain why, let us remember Rey Chow's writing on ethnic stereotypes. Chow reminds us that such stereotypes can function as "political weapons capable of generating belief, commitment and action" (53). In other words, racialized, prejudice stereotypes can and do result in real world discrimination.

It is clear that the tiger mother trope has already formed a racist and harmful bad-mother archetype; however, we must also ask ourselves why people are so threatened by so-called tiger mothers. Why is there a panic in the media and academia over whether Chinese mothers are good parents? To answer this, I refer to an observation made by sociologist Hilary Levey Friedman. She writes:

A few weeks before the Chua controversy, educators had been stunned by the superlative test scores coming out of Shanghai on the Program for International Student Assessment (PISA). Some commentators thought *Battle Hymn*

could be America's new "Sputnik moment"—except that
Amy Chua was born in the United States.... (70)

In her work, Rey Chow discusses how the "figures of the Jew, the
Jap, and the wetback have all produced substantive political consequences, from deportation to incarceration to genocide or ethnic
cleansing" (53). In the case of Amy Chua, intense mother-blame
is another such consequence of ethnic stereotypes.

Ultimately, we see from the criticism Amy Chua has encountered, and how the term *tiger mother* has even been appropriated
by those who oppose Ms. Chua and her views on parenting,
that it is clear Chua's memoir has been used as the blueprint to
describe a certain kind of bad mother. This new bad-mother stereotype is the racially charged and sexist image of a pushy Asian
woman read by her opponents as an insufficiently loving tyrant.
She is a woman whose confident tale of maternal authority and
overall success is aggressively opposed by newspaper critics and
researchers alike.

Indeed, that panic in the U.S. media regarding Chinese culture,
and by extension China as a nation, is an important theme in the
Chua controversy, for while she is an American citizen, she proudly
identifies her mothering style with her own personal perception
of Chinese values. The panicked desire to assert American superiority is decidedly pointed in the words of Melinda Liu. Writing
for *Newsweek*, she contends:

> What the "Chinese mom" debate swirling around Amy
> Chua's book fails to adequately consider is the fact that
> American classrooms—and society in general—are more
> conducive to individual expression and innovation. The rote
> learning that she stresses might work when her daughters,
> outside the home, are encouraged to think independently.
> But in China, where authoritarian parenting is coupled with
> an ossified higher education system, creativity is stifled.

Liu makes generalizations about the practices of parents in
China, a nation of more than a billion individuals, and contends
that this strict and "authoritarian" approach to parenting impedes

independent thinking. Thus, despite international test scores, Liu nonetheless finds a way to declare American culture comparatively superior.

Of course, all of these distinctions between Chinese parenting and a more Western, "American" approach, are separated by flimsy walls. Friedman reminds us that American parents who are not of Chinese heritage can also be strict and authoritarian. She points out the racist double standard regarding the widespread criticism of Chua in the American Media, writing, "...let's not kid ourselves into thinking that that 'Chinese' Tiger Moms like Amy Chua own the title of pushiest parents in the world. Various American parents compete for that title as well..." (71). American outrage over the supposed evils of Chinese parenting is thus, in the end, both alarmist and hypocritical.

CONCLUSION

Ultimately, while Ladd-Taylor and Umansky point out that society decries drug-addicted mothers and other women portrayed as absent and neglectful on one side of the bad-mother spectrum, Chua is on the other side of that spectrum. She is found lacking precisely because of her maternal intensity. In the age of intensive mother-hood, however, the fact that one of the most hated mothers spends inordinate amounts of time and money preparing her children for the world proves how adaptable a phenomenon mother-blame is. In the end, it is a phenomenon capable of finding fault in every mother who has ever existed—or will ever exist.

Whether you agree with her approach to parenting or not, I would argue the rage and mother-blame directed at Chua in both the media and academic spheres is particularly problematic. The vilification of Chua as an unloving and poor mother illustrates how dangerous an activity mothering really is. The appropriation of the term "tiger mothering" as a new gendered ethnic stereotype associated with Asian women demonstrates how perilous it is to discuss one's approach to motherhood in a public forum like a memoir. It is perhaps even more dangerous to portray oneself as an overall effective and successful mother who refuses to become a sacrificial character because in Chua's case, her opponents have simply used this display of maternal confidence to prove she is all the more insensitive.

In the end, Chua was punished for her candor by becoming one of the least popular mothers on the Internet. In an era where intensive mothering is the norm, the media and academic discourse surrounding tiger mothers functions as a cautionary tale. It illustrates how easy it is for even a highly privileged, married, heterosexual mother of two to be transformed into a maternal monster. It also illustrates how readily America will blame mothers, especially mothers who are perceived as un-American.

When it comes to the mother-blame game, any mother can be considered a loser. The meteoric rise of *tiger mother* as byword for *bad mom* is proof the game is rigged.

WORKS CITED

Brooks, David. "Amy Chua Is a Wimp." *The New York Times.* 17 Jan. 2011. Web. 10 Nov. 2014.

Caplan, Paula J. "Don't Blame Mother: Then and Now." *Maternal Theory: Essential Readings.* Ed. Andrea O'Reilly. Toronto: Demeter Press, 2007. 592- 600. Print.

Chow, Rey. "Brushes with the Other-as-Face: Stereotyping and Cross-Ethnic Representation." *The Rey Chow Reader.* Ed. Paul Bowman. New York: Columbia University Press. 2010. 48-55. Print.

Chua, Amy. *Battle Hymn of the Tiger Mother.* New York: Penguin Books. 2011. Print. Friedman, Hilary Levey. "Lions, Tigers, and Bear Moms—Oh My!" *Contexts* 10.3 (2011): 70-71. Print.

Hays, Sharon. "Why Can't a Mother Be More Like a Businessman? *Maternal Theory: Essential Readings.* Ed. Andrea O'Reilly. Toronto: Demeter Press, 2007. 408-430. Print.

Kim, Su Yeong et al. "Does 'Tiger Parenting' Exist? Parenting Profiles of Chinese Americans and Adolescent Developmental Outcomes." *Asian American Journal of Psychology* 4.1 (2013): 7-18. Print.

Ladd-Taylor, Molly and Lauri Umansky. Introduction. *'Bad' Mothers: The Politics of Blame in Twentieth Century America.* New

York: New York University Press, 1998. 1-28. Print.

Liu, Melinda. "Amy Chua's Chinese Mom Controversy: The Response in China." *Newsweek*. 19 Jan. 2011. Web. 10 Nov. 2014.

Nealon, Sam. "Hold On, Tiger Mom." *UCR Today*. 22 Sept. Web. 22 Nov. 2014.

O'Reilly, Andrea. *Rocking the Cradle*. Toronto: Demeter Press, 2007 Print.

O'Reilly, Andrea. "Outlaw(ing) Motherhood." *What Do Mothers Need?* Toronto: Demeter Press, 2013. 63-80. Print.

Siegel, Lee. "Declawing the Tiger: A Spanking for Amy Chua." *The Observer*. 19 Jan. 2011. Web. 16 Nov. 2014.

Taylor, Jim. "What Tiger Mothers Do Wrong (And Right)." *The Huffington Post*. 21 Jan. 2011. Web. Nov. 8 2014.

11.

"Because My Mother Was a Liar and a Whore"

Adulterous Mothers and Paternity Uncertainty in Jo Nesbø's *The Snowman*

BERIT ÅSTRÖM

T HE DEVIOUS WOMAN deceiving her husband into raising another man's child as his own is a recurring stereotype in patriarchal society. The idea that unsuspecting men are "the hapless victims of lying women," as one fathers' rights activist claims, seems deeply entrenched in public discourse (Cannold 251), and the claim that up to thirty percent of children in the West are attributed to the wrong father is often repeated by the media (Gilding 1).[1] Because paternity uncertainty is presumed to be so widespread in Western society, it becomes a useful plot device in crime fiction; it often provides a motive for murder, or a red herring. In *Malice in the Cotswolds* (2013), for example, author Rebecca Tope constructs a scenario where a barren wife discovers that her husband is the father of their neighbour's child, which prompts her to kill both father and son. Similarly, Fay Sampson uses unknown paternity to discuss societal attitudes towards teenage pregnancy in *Father Unknown* (2012). Åsa Larsson employs the well-established theme of the unknown, illegitimate heir killing off legitimate heirs in *The Second Deadly Sin* (2014). Likewise, in Alison Bruce's *Cambridge Blue* (2010), misattributed paternity becomes a reason for blackmail, which in turn prompts murder, whereas Camilla Läckberg interrogates notions of identity through the theme of misattributed paternity in *The Ice Princess* (2011). In Jo Nesbø's *The Snowman* (2010), the novel investigated in this chapter, the murderer kills in order to punish women who deceive their husbands into raising their lovers' children.

In crime fiction, murder is a threat to society that must be neutralized and disposed of (Plain 3). In the case of serial killers, this is
usually accomplished by depicting the killer as a unique aberration
that can be neatly contained and removed (Freccero 48; Simpson 2).
In *The Snowman*, however, the positions of murderer and victims
as threats to society are reversed. Drawing on sociological research
on cultural attitudes toward misattributed paternity, this chapter
analyzes how Norwegian author Jo Nesbø uses the readers' cultural preparedness to believe in the perfidy of mothers to normalize
and recuperate the murderer. This preparedness is reflected in the
way reviewers in Britain and North America have commended the
novel for both plotting and characterization but have neglected to
interrogate the characterization of the victims. The novel presents
its adulterous mothers as oversexed, untrustworthy, and disloyal,
whereas the murderer is shown to be a suffering victim of one
such mother. By lying about the paternity of their children, the
mothers have invited their own destruction. In this way, Nesbø's
novel represents adulterous mothers as a greater threat to society
than a man who cuts women to pieces. This chapter will thus begin
by contextualizing the societal notion of the adulterous mother in
relation to scientific research, discussing in particular how concepts
from the field of evolutionary psychology are reiterated in the novel,
which thereby lends plausibility to the plot, before moving on to
an analysis of how the novel presents the victims as blameworthy.

ADAPTING AN URBAN MYTH

Although no medical research supports a claim for rates of
misattributed paternity higher than three percent in any Western nation (Gilding 4), the idea that there are vast numbers of
children attributed to the wrong father has a strong hold on the
cultural imagination in North America, Europe, and Australia, as
is evidenced by its repeated use in, for example, novels, film, and
television. Sociologist Michael Gilding, whose research includes
studies of paternity testing, terms the idea of widespread paternity
uncertainty an "urban myth," which he argues is sustained by
three groups: fathers' rights activists, DNA-testing laboratories,
and evolutionary psychologists (7-8). For example, fathers' rights

activists in the U.S. and Australia use the myth to support their demand for changed legislation (Cannold 2008), which would ensure that biological fathers have access to their own children, as well as to protect non-biological fathers from having to pay child support (Henry 52). The DNA-testing laboratories naturally have a vested interest in acquiring customers and accordingly have little reason to question the accuracy of the inflated figures.[2] The evolutionary psychologists, finally, use the supposed high rates of misattributed paternity to support their claims that women have sex outside established relationships as part of an evolutionary strategy to make sure that "men of high genetic quality" father their children (Schmitt 280). In short, if women cannot marry a partner with desirable genes, they can marry a less suitable partner and then conceive by the more attractive partner. As Leslie Cannold has noted, although misattributed paternity can take a number of different forms, the one most often addressed by fathers' rights activists and legal reformers is what she terms "'cuckold' paternity fraud." The reason for this focus, she argues, is that it is a crime that women perpetrate against men, and so it triggers patriarchal paranoia about women's perfidy (250, 254). Unscrupulous women are said to exploit the "emotional vulnerability" of "innocent" men (Henry 52, 59). The resilience of this urban myth, despite the lack of scientific support, suggests that it taps into a cultural suspicion of women, drawing on an assumption that all women are inclined to be promiscuous and purposefully trick their partners into supporting other men's offspring.

The Snowman, in which a number of women are killed for committing cuckold paternity fraud, draws on the urban myth of mothers' duplicity. The murderer, Mathias Lund-Helgesen, discovers as a teenager not only that his mother has a lover but that this lover is his biological father from whom he has inherited a disfiguring, slowly crippling, and ultimately fatal disease. He promptly murders his mother. Through his work with DNA testing, Lund-Helgesen later discovers a number of other mothers who have similarly deceived their husbands. He decides to punish them, and during the course of the novel he murders nine women and attempts to kill a tenth, the former girlfriend of the investigating police officer, Harry Hole.

Early in the novel, Hole listens to a radio broadcast about seal behaviour in which one speaker refers anecdotally to a supposed Swedish study showing that fifteen to twenty percent of children have a different father than the one they think (Nesbø 12). This statistic is repeated as a fact by Hole and Lund-Helgesen on several occasions throughout the novel, and it is never contested by them or any other character (308, 488, 535). Rather, they accept the claim as scientific fact, likely because it fits with the cultural beliefs that all women are potential liars and all men are thereby potential victims. This notion is succinctly expressed by one fathers' rights organization that contends, "Any man can be deceived into believing they are [a child's] father" (Cannold 250), and as the murderer points out to Hole, there is a 20 percent chance that he himself is an illegitimate son (Nesbø 535). No woman can be trusted, not even Hole's own mother. Within the novel, there are no "good" mothers. As Andrea O'Reilly notes, "good" mothers are culturally constructed as "altruistic, patient, loving, selfless, devoted, nurturing," and "not sexual" (4). All the mothers in *The Snowman* fail in some of these respects, but mostly in that they are all sexual beings who enjoy extramarital sex. This marks them as bad mothers—not only in the eyes of the murderer but also in the society constructed in the novel. Nesbø thus draws on the urban myth of the adulterous mother when creating the mother characters and also uses concepts from the field of evolutionary psychology to create a framework of plausibility for the interpretation of their actions.

EVOLUTIONARY PSYCHOLOGY AND
MISATTRIBUTED PATERNITY

Attempting to discern the causes of human behaviour, evolutionary psychology sometimes relies on cross-species comparisons, focusing on "nonhuman analogs" and disregarding factors such as "morality, the arts, language, culture" (Tooby and Cosmides 12). Humans and human behaviour are analyzed in the same terms as those applied to sea horses, tamarinds, and marmosets, for example (Schmitt 263). Thus, people are conceptualized as biological males and females, and their sexual activities are understood as mating rituals. Similarly, non-human animal mating is referenced in terms more suited to human societies: a male animal may be "cuckolded," a situation that is "inflicted" on it "by a female's sexual infidelity" (Shackelford et al. 374).[3] Animal behaviour is discussed as if it were the result of reflective thinking, whereas human behaviour is reduced to unreflective instinct.

This blurring of categories also occurs in *The Snowman*. For example, there are repeated references to the alleged behaviour of a particular type of seal. During the radio broadcast that Hole listens to at the beginning of the novel, it is said that in order to ensure the best genetic inheritance for their pups, female seals never mate twice with the same male (Nesbø 12).[4] The males counteract this evolutionary strategy by trying to kill the females as soon as the pups can fend for themselves. If they can kill the female before it mates with a new male, they can minimize competition for their own progeny. Here the seals' behaviour is anthropomorphized: the females are referred to as "promiscuous" and their mating behaviours are compared to playing the "stock market" (12). The males, as Hole remarks, are "cold and rational" and, aware of the females' strategies and plans, they carry out their own evolutionary strategies (354).

Like some evolutionary psychologists, the speakers in the radio program transpose the behaviour of the seals onto humans, claiming that human females who cheat on their husbands think like the female seals. They ultimately disregard the facts that these animals are not in monogamous relationships, that they do not attempt to mate with more than one partner during any given breeding season, and that they do not attempt to make one male rear the offspring of another. In this regard, any human female who stays with one male whilst conceiving by another would not follow the same evolutionary strategy. Yet, in the context of the narrative, both seal and human females are presented as promiscuous, callous, and scheming. In this discussion of anthropomorphization, moving back and forth between species, no difference is drawn between female seals and women. There is an unspoken implication that if it is sound evolutionary strategy for seals and women to attempt to acquire the best genes for their offspring, and for male seals to kill the females in order to give their own offspring an advantage, it is also sound evolutionary strategy for human males to kill adulterous wives.

The explanation for adultery in humans promoted by evolutionary psychologists suggests that a woman who is unable to secure the man she wants will settle for a less desirable husband, who will provide for her and her offspring. She will then make sure that she conceives by a man with superior genes (Schmitt 264). The same evolutionary mechanisms are presented as motivating the reasoning and actions of the victims and their partners in *The Snowman*. For instance, two of the victims' husbands, Filip Becker and Rolf Ottersen, are described in particular detail as boring but stable. Becker is a professor of physics; he is cold, strict, and very conservative (Nesbø 43). Ottersen, an engineer by training, runs a shop together with his wife where they sell arts and crafts from various African countries. Ottersen is presented as laughable; he is referred to as "a bag of bones" and "a wading bird," (104) as well as "a stork" and "a scarecrow" (399). It is suggested that no woman could love these men; they can provide financial stability but are socially insignificant. As such, their wives exploit them for economic benefits but then pursue more exciting lovers to father their children.

The man that Birte Becker and Sylvia Ottersen allow to father their children is Arve Støp, the owner of a successful magazine and "one of the most knowledgeable, arrogant and entertaining opinion-formers in the country" (12). In comparison with their husbands, he is much more desirable, but he is not interested in monogamous relationships. He prefers short affairs with married women who are less likely to want to settle down with him (364). When Støp finds out that he has fathered children, he thinks to himself that "he should feel deeply depressed" since he is the carrier of a very serious disease, but he feels "excited" and "almost happy" (402). Støp does not play any part in the children's upbringing, nor does he contribute financially, apart from paying for yearly medical check-ups. Thus, like Birte Becker and Sylvia Ottersen, he is acting exactly in the way postulated by evolutionary psychologists, securing his own genetic survival with minimum effort. In this way, the novel draws on concepts from the field of evolutionary psychology to make the characters' actions plausible. It further taps into the mother-blaming discourse of Western society when suggesting that the victims are responsible for their own deaths.

BLAMING THE MOTHERS

In crime fiction, people are murdered for any number of different reasons: to prevent them from changing a will, to stop blackmail, to make sure that business deals go through, to ensure that revenge is achieved, or to make sure that a secret is not revealed.[5] It is not unusual for victims to be constructed as responsible for their own deaths in some way, for example by abusing or threatening to expose the wrongdoings of the would-be murderer. According to Mathias Lund-Helgesen, the murderer in *The Snowman*, the women he kills are also responsible for their own deaths, primarily by deceiving their husbands about their children's paternity. The narrative also bears him out, thus confirming that these women were bad mothers and wives who deserved to die.

Sociologist Lyn Turney has noted how women who commit paternity fraud are socially constructed as "predatory" and "deceptive," thus exemplifying "female sexuality out of control" ("Paternity Secrets" 229). As previously noted, the cultural perception of a good mother is that she is not overtly sexy or sexual. Birte Becker, the first victim brought to Hole's attention in the novel when she is reported missing, fails in this regard. When Hole goes through her clothes and effects, his observations suggest that her jewelry, dresses, and underwear are either childishly sparkly or inappropriately sexy: "Everything here was a bit Vegas" (Nesbø 48). The impression of inappropriate sexiness is strengthened by repeated observations of her physical attractiveness, such as her son noticing how men look at her when they are out together (27). Later on there are comments about her *"Penthouse* body" (304) and specifically about her "Pamela Anderson-attractive" breasts that appear to have been surgically enhanced (363, 393). In sum, her attractiveness is framed in terms of vulgarity and pornography. This impression is confirmed when it is made clear that she has cheated on her husband with a large number of men throughout her marriage (306). Not only was she habitually promiscuous but there is no indication that she felt any kind of guilt for her actions.

When she becomes pregnant and her lover refuses to marry her, "she did what she had to do. She found her child a father and a secure home" (400). At no point does she stop to think about any moral or legal implications—she simply does what she has to do.

When her husband is first introduced in the narrative, the impression is that he is a cold and cruel person, bullying both his wife and son. He also despises his wife, who is presented as naive bordering on simple-minded, as well as of a lower socioeconomic status. When he wishes to explain to their son why a certain grammatical construction that she uses is incorrect, he states, "Mummy doesn't speak properly. Do you understand? Mummy comes from a place and family where they're not bothered about language" (26).

Yet, as the story unfolds, the narrative appears to transfer sympathy from her to him. At the same time, as more and more damaging facts are disclosed about her personality and actions, revealing her as immoral and promiscuous, he makes an emotional journey from rejecting the child, claiming to have no son (336), to embracing him wholeheartedly: "I love you so much.…You're my boy. Do you hear? My boy" (542).

The murderer's first victim is his own mother, Sara Kvinesland. Nothing is said of her appearance but her personality is revealed as an example of "female sexuality out of control." She is obsessed with her lover—to the extent that she leaves her teenage son waiting in the car for forty minutes on a cold day so that she can have sex with him. She is also cold and indifferent toward her husband, and when he pleads with her not to leave him, she responds with a "bitter laugh" (5, 471). She is thus not "selfless," "patient," nor "devoted," but intent on pursuing her own pleasure at the expense of her son and husband. When the boy realizes that she has betrayed his father and lied to both of them, he kills her by hitting her four times over the head with a jack until her skull caves in, causing her to drive into the river. He then leaves her to drown in the car (Nesbø 472-473).

The woman who is most censored by the narrative is Sylvia Ottersen. Sylvia is described by her twin sister as "stubborn, hot-headed, spoilt," and manipulative (149). She has also left her husband and their twin daughters on two occasions for other men, although she returned each time after being abandoned by her lovers (149). She initiates an affair with Arve Støp in her and her husband's shop moments after they meet, and the language used not only indicates that she is unconcerned with concealing her sexual activities but also suggests a certain coarseness about the whole arrangement: "She let him fuck her in the back room and didn't even bother to lock the shop door" (397). Indeed, at their final sexual encounter, Støp realizes that she has arranged it so that her husband should walk in on them and she is angry with Rolf when he is late. She then uses the resulting pregnancy to extort money from Støp in order to keep the failing shop going.

On the whole, the victims of the murderer are presented as bad mothers and wives, oversexed and deceitful. They perpetuate the cultural belief that women are inclined to commit paternity fraud by marrying for financial security while having extramarital sex with more desirable men. Having established the victims as over-sexed, callous, and grasping, the novel further suggests that their actions and choices are physically damaging.

MOTHERS AS VECTORS FOR DISEASE

The evolutionary strategy used by the adulterous mothers in the novel ultimately proves unsuccessful. Sara Kvinesland, for exam-ple, conceives by a man who has scleroderma, a painful disease that thickens the skin. This will restrict movement until "you're suffocated by your own skin" (477). Likewise, in having children by Arve Støp, Birte Becker and Sylvia Ottersen have exposed their children to Fahr's syndrome, which is "a bit like Alzheimer's" (187). Thus the adulterous women are not only deceiving their husbands, they are also endangering their future offspring by having sex with men who carry tainted genes. "What secret flaws did he have," Lund-Helgesen wonders to himself about the woman's lover when he encounters the first case of misattributed paternity, thus suggesting that all lovers may be tainted (479). Yet, even though the men are the actual carriers of disease, they are not regarded as a threat; rather, it is the women who choose inappropriate partners who are pathologized as spreaders of disease. So even though Lund-Helgesen thinks of Arve Støp as a "lecher," (493) his revenge is directed only toward the women: he kills his mother but does not approach her lover. The women are the danger; they are the ones that have to be stopped. Lund-Helgesen refers to them as "disease," and it is his job to cleanse society of them (536). In this he sees himself and Harry Hole as colleagues fighting an up-hill struggle together: "The disease you and I are fighting can't be eradicated," he tells Hole during their final conversation, after he has been caught (536). The adulterous women become not only a problem for the individual men they lie to, but to the whole of society, and rather than preventing men with hereditary diseases from procreating, the women must be "eradicated."

SYMPATHY FOR THE KILLER

Just as the novel goes to some length to portray the victims as culpable and deserving of their deaths, the narrative presents the murderer as pitiable and absolves him of responsibility for his actions. In this, it adopts some of the strategies sociologist Karen Morgan has noted in her analysis of how UK newspapers attempt to deal with the supposedly abnormal situation of husbands killing their wives.[6] Although most violent deaths experienced by women in the UK are the result of violence from a current or previous male partner, relative, or friend, the public expectation is that women are killed by strangers (Morgan 491). Thus, the fact that someone within the community, a "normal" husband, may commit murder must be explained away and neutralized. Newspapers employ various strategies to achieve this, such as focusing on the husband's pain and suffering or placing at least some of the blame on the victim. This is often done by stating that the woman's actions, such as infidelity, drove him to murder or triggered his rage. In effect, the women must "take the blame for the violence" and reconcile "what is seen as the anomaly of a violent husband with the ideology that violence comes from dangerous strangers" (493).

In *The Snowman*, Mathias Lund-Helgesen, although a stranger to his victims, is at the same time representative of the men and children who are hurt and damaged by deceitful women. He is part of a community of victims. Utilizing some of the same strategies as those analyzed by Morgan, the novel creates a more nuanced image of Lund-Helgesen. Like the men Morgan mentions who have killed their adulterous wives, Lund-Helgesen is driven to murdering his mother, as he makes clear when Hole asks him why he killed her: "Because my mother was a liar and a whore" (Nesbø 535). Whilst waiting for her, the teenage Lund-Helgesen becomes bored, leaves the car to make a snowman, and accidentally sees her having sex with her lover (471). As he watches them, everything falls into place and he not only realizes that the man, who exhibits the same rare genetic anomaly as he does, is his father but that this affair is the reason his mother treats her husband so harshly. He further realizes the extent of other lies she has told him about his identity. At a stroke, he has lost everything. The boy decides that his father must never know about this and that he must protect him (472). In order to accomplish this, he must kill his mother. Through the focus on the boy's intense feelings of betrayal and rejection, it is suggested that his actions are not only caused by her actions but they are a natural and understandable reaction. She has driven him to murder.

Morgan similarly notes how "reduced competence" is used as an explanation for male spousal violence. Expressions such as "animal frenzy," "frenzied attack," and "crazed animal" are used to suggest that the husband was temporarily unable to control his actions (Morgan 494). This kind of rage also characterizes Lund-Helgesen's first murder as an adult, when he loses control in "a frenzy of fury and panic" (Nesbø 484). With subsequent murders, he learns to stay in control, but the notion of reduced competence remains. He realizes that these murders are attempts to reconstruct the initial murder of his mother, and he diagnoses himself as suffering from "a serious personality disorder" (485). This realization does not cause him to stop the murders, however. He is a methodical albeit ferocious serial killer, and he is not really responsible for his own actions.

Another way in which newspaper discourse naturalizes the husband as killer is by focusing on his feelings of pain and grief so that "he is represented as (at least) equally deserving of sympathy as his victim" (Morgan 493). As noted, the narrative describes how the sight of his mother and her lover causes the destruction of Lund-Helgesen's whole world. When he later discovers by chance that the putative father of a girl suffering from a hereditary rheumatic illness is not her biological father, he is overwhelmed with sympathy for the husband and the child, and he cries all night (Nesbø 479). Thus he is not constructed simply as a cold and manipulative serial killer; rather, he is a multidimensional and complex character that suffers from what unscrupulous women do to their families.

The debilitating illness that Lund-Helgesen has inherited from his biological father will kill him slowly and painfully. Therefore, he has planned to kill himself after the last planned murder, that of Hole's former girlfriend. However, Hole manages to stop him from committing suicide and is very eager that Lund-Helgesen should live (540). It is clear from their final conversation that Hole wants Lund-Helgesen to die an agonizing death from his congenital disease rather than "choose another death" (536). However, when the police psychologist jokingly asks if "taking the life of a person who wants to live" is worse than "taking death from a person who wants to die," Hole has a noticeably visceral reaction that suggests a sense of guilt (547). He has prevented Lund-Helgesen from killing himself, thus condemning him to a drawn-out, torturous death, which he now seems to regret. Thus, the reader is again invited to sympathize with the murderer.

Regarding narrative sympathy, there is a substantial difference in how the murderer and his victims are represented. The narrative often uses free indirect speech rather than dialogue to reveal characters' feelings and thoughts, but Lund-Helgesen is given much more space to do this than the women he kills. Birte Becker, for example, is only narrated through her lover, Arve Støp, who conceptualizes her as a "simple but quick-witted" woman who is all too eager to foist Støp's child onto an unsuspecting man (400). Her own feelings and motivations are not described. Similarly, readers only encounter Sylvia Ottersen through her sister's hostile description and Støp's narration of their relationship. She comes across as a predatory and grasping woman who despises her husband and sets out to humiliate him. Her own feelings are only described in a few sentences just before she is about to die. Sara Kvinesland is given slightly more narrative space, which primarily describes how her search for sexual gratification always comes at the expense of her child's welfare and how much her husband annoys her. She is constructed as a selfish and unpleasant person who merits no sympathy. On the whole, the narrative constructs these mothers as unilaterally morally defective and culpable, whereas Lund-Helgesen is revealed to be a multidimensional character deserving of sympathy. In short, although Lund-Helgesen's crimes consist of murdering nine women and almost succeeding in killing a tenth, whereas his victims are only guilty of allowing their husbands to falsely believe they are biological fathers to the children they raise, the reader is invited to empathize with the murderer, if not condone his actions.

CONCLUSION

By drawing on cultural notions of women as greedy, selfish, and manipulative liars who exploit innocent men for their own benefit, *The Snowman* constructs its victims as blame-worthy and at least partially responsible for their own deaths. Simultaneously, by presenting a more nuanced image of the murderer than of the women, the reader is invited to sympathize with him. Thus the threat to society is not the serial killer but the women who drive him to commit murders in an effort to eradicate the moral and physical disease they spread.

The novel thus makes use of societal notions already in play in order to create a believable plot, but in doing so, it also perpetuates the idea that no wife is above suspicion and that every husband is a prospective victim of paternity fraud. Since such ideas inform the rhetoric of fathers' rights organizations in the U.S., Britain, and Australia, in addition to calls for changes in U.S. legislation, it is important to both contextualize and problematize these representations of mother-blame in crime fiction.

ENDNOTES

[1] The thirty-percent figure comes from an unpublished study carried out in Britain in 1973, a study that has since been severely criticised for lack of scientific rigour (Gilding 2-3). Yet the figure is still quoted as an established fact (Schmitt 266).

[2]Since the middle of the 1990s, DNA-testing laboratories have marketed their services directly to potential customers (Turney, "Paternity Testing" 74). One company, Paternity Direct, also offers "infidelity testing," encouraging clients to send in, for example, toothbrushes, chewing gum, and facial tissues for testing to establish potential infidelity.

[3]Some texts are strikingly emotive, for example depicting human reproduction on a genetic level as warfare—"a mother-father battle" (Campbell 632)—or suggesting a notion of blame. Arguing that jealousy is an evolutionary response, Shackelford et al. state that "male sexual jealousy could only evolve if female sexual infidelity was a recurrent feature of human evolutionary history" (375). It is thus women's fault that men are jealous.

[4]Whether the Berhaus seal actually exists and behaves in the way described is uncertain but also not relevant to this discussion.

[5]For example, in Ruth Rendell's *A Judgement in Stone*, the protagonist, who works as a housekeeper, kills her employers in order to keep her illiteracy a secret.

[6]Although Morgan's study is restricted to the UK, I would argue that the underlying societal impulse to exonerate men in cases of domestic violence is common to most Western countries.

WORKS CITED

Bruce, Alison. *Cambridge Blue*. London: Robinson Publishing, 2010. Print.

Campbell, Anne. "Aggression." *The Handbook of Evolutionary Psychology*. Ed. David M. Buss. New Jersey: John Wiley & Sons, 2005. 628-655. Print.

Cannold, Leslie. "Who's the Father? Rethinking the Moral 'Crime' of 'Paternity Fraud.'" *Women's Studies International Forum* 31 (2008): 249-256. Print.

Freccero, Carla. "Historical Violence: Censorship and the Serial Killer: The Case of *American Psycho*." *Diacritics* 27.2 (1997): 44-58. Print.

Gilding, Michael. "Rampant Misattributed Paternity: The Creation of an Urban Myth." *People and Place* 13.2 (2005): 1-11. Print.

Henry, Ronald K. "The Innocent Third Party: Victims of Paternity

Fraud." *Family Law Quarterly*. 40.1 (2006): 51-79. Print.

Läckberg, Camilla. *The Ice Princess*. London: Harper, 2011. Print.

Larsson, Åsa. *The Second Deadly Sin*. London: MacLehose Press, 2014. Print.

Morgan, Karen. "Cheating Wives and Vice Girls: The Construction of a Culture of Resignation." *Women's Studies International Forum* 29 (2006): 489-498. Print.

Nesbø, Jo. *The Snowman*. Trans. Don Bartlett. London: Vintage, 2010. Print.

O'Reilly, Andrea. Introduction. *Mother Outlaws: Theories and Practices of Empowered Mothering*. Toronto: Women's Press, 2004. 1-28. Print.

Plain, Gill. *Twentieth-Century Crime Fiction: Gender, Sexuality and the Body*. Edinburgh: Edinburgh University Press, 2001. Print.

Rendell, Ruth. *A Judgement in Stone*. London: Arrow Books, 1978. Print.

Sampson, Fay. *Father Unknown*. Sutton: Severn House, 2012. Print.

Shackelford, Todd K., Nicholas Pound, Aaron T. Goetz, and Craig W. Lamunyon. "Female Infidelity and Sperm Competition." *The Handbook of Evolutionary Psychology*. Ed. David M. Buss. New Jersey: John Wiley & Sons, 2005. 372-93. Print.

Schmitt, David P. "Fundamentals of Human Mating Strategies." *The Handbook of Evolutionary Psychology*. Ed. David M. Buss. New Jersey: John Wiley & Sons, 2005. 258-291. Print.

Simpson, Philip L. *Psycho Paths: Tracking the Serial Killer through Contemporary American Film and Fiction*. Carbondale: Southern Illinois University Press, 2000. Print.

Tooby, John and Leda Cosmides. "Conceptual Foundations of Evolutionary Pscyhology." *The Handbook of Evolutionary Psychology*. Ed. David M. Buss. New Jersey: John Wiley & Sons, 2005. 5-67. Print.

Tope, Rebecca. *Malice in the Cotswolds*. London: Allison & Busby, 2013. Print.

Turney, Lyn. "Paternity Secrets: Why Women Don't Tell." *Journal of Family Studies*. 11.2 (2005): 227-248. Print.

Turney, Lyn. "Paternity Testing and the Biological Determination of Fatherhood." *Journal of Family Studies* 12.1 (2006): 73-93. Print.

12.
Lean In or Leave Before You Leave?

False Dichotomies of Choice and Blame in Public Debates about Working Motherhood

JENNIFER L. BORDA

S HERYL SANDBERG HAS SPENT the last five years managing the business operations of the corporate behemoth Facebook, after successful stints as a top-level executive at Google and as Chief of Staff to the U.S. Treasury Secretary. Yet Sandberg did not become a household name as a result of C-level positions at two of the most famous and profitable technology companies in the country, nor as one of very few women included in the *Forbes* 500 list. Rather, Sandberg has earned "celebrity status" in the last two years because of her viral videos and best-selling non-fiction book, *Lean In* (2013).

The primary aim of this chapter is to better understand the construction of Sandberg's popular discourse regarding working women and motherhood, as well as the public dialogue sparked by *Lean In*. Here I analyze the academic and public discussions that have emerged in the press as a response to Sandberg's initiatives and demonstrate how they critique her "brand" of neoliberal postfeminism, which essentially blames mothers for their failure to succeed in the workplace. By pointing out the limitations of Sandberg's proposed solutions for female empowerment in the professional realm, her critics have effectively shifted the focus from working mothers' "choices" to the very real constraints that working women face. I argue that the public debates and dialogue fuelled by Sandberg's book open up possibilities for re-imagining ways of talking about the patriarchal bias in workplace culture that keeps women, and especially mothers who work outside the home, from achieving professional success. I conclude that this public discourse reveals the potential for diverse voices to envision a more inclusive and just notion of gender equality—both at home and in the workplace—that moves beyond mother-blame and provides opportunities to increase social capital for working mothers.

SANDBERG'S ASCENSION

Having ascended to the highest levels of her profession in both the corporate and public sectors, Sandberg is well positioned to reflect on her achievements, as well as the many hurdles she has encountered, as a female business leader in the overtly male-dominated workplaces of Washington, DC, and Silicon Valley. For the past few years, Sandberg has interpreted her own experiences within this cultural framework, and she has produced a series of guidelines to help other women manage both their careers and their "gendered" identities in their workplaces and personal lives. Her December 2010 TED Talk, "Why We Have Too Few Women Leaders," which has been viewed more than 4.5 million times, advises women who work in the corporate realm to "sit at the table," "keep their foot on the pedal," and to not "leave before you leave." This video was re-purposed into a 2011 Barnard College Commencement Address in which Sandberg urged the newly minted female grads to "lean way into their careers" because they hold "the promise for a more equal world."

Both videos went viral, and Sandberg seemingly recognized an emerging demand: a growing demographic of women workers seeking guidance, strategies, and motivation for productively navigating the conflicting demands of professional careers and personal desires. The last two generations of women living in what has been characterized as a "postfeminist" age have earned advanced degrees in record numbers and many have prioritized the pursuit of a promising career and bright financial future in their twenties. Yet one challenge has complicated their career trajectory: how to keep their professional careers on the fast track without compromising their personal ambitions, including having children. Sandberg's ability to seize on this cultural moment by parlaying her mini-lectures into a business memoir/self-help/motivational strategy guide is a testament to her own business acumen. *Lean*

In rocketed to the top of both the *New York Times* and Amazon. com bestseller lists, and it remained in various top 10 lists for more than a year.

THE *LEAN IN* REVOLUTION

Lean In is based on the premise that women are bound to stereotypes that have pervaded gender relations throughout the last century, the vestiges of which remain despite the gains of liberal feminism in the 1970s and 1980s. Sandberg argues that women have let these stereotypes fuel doubts, cultivate perceived deficiencies, and reinforce the constraints of expected "feminine" behaviours, which in turn have come to define women's identities, choices, and career paths. The book is bolstered by numerous empirical studies, as well as a slew of anecdotal evidence based on Sandberg's own experiences and those of similarly successful people in business and economics. For example, Sandberg cites the 2011 McKinsey report that notes "men are promoted based on potential, while women are promoted based on past accomplishments" (*Lean In* 8).

Sandberg also recounts the Heidi/Howard case study at Harvard University in which students were given two identical application packages, yet half of the candidates were identified as "Heidi" and the other half as "Howard." Students viewed the candidates as equally competent but asserted that Heidi was not "the type of person you would have to hire or work for." According to Sandberg, this clearly demonstrates how "success and likeability are positively correlated for men and negatively correlated for women" (40). As an examination of how women's status in contemporary U.S. workplace culture differs from men, the book has been instrumental in bringing some of the complexities and contradictions experienced by working women—and specifically working mothers—to the forefront of public discourse.

However, while the book has been internationally well received, many outspoken critics believe that Sandberg wrongly blames working women—and especially working mothers—for making poor professional and personal choices based on these stereotypes. These choices, according to Sandberg, land women in "mommy-tracked" positions during their thirties and consequently result in a lack of opportunity for advancement during the more critical period of women's mid-stage careers. Framed within the postfeminist rhetoric of "choice," Sandberg's advice simultaneously emboldened and enraged readers and, upon its release, became fodder for hundreds of editorials, blog discussions, and online reader comments. More than a year later, the deliberation about working women and mothers, workplace culture, and whether anyone can actually achieve work-life balance has continued to rage on in public discourse.

LEAN IN'S "CHOICE FEMINISM"

According to Sandberg, women are guilty of conforming to the expectations of their sex, and the ambition gap between men and women is the reason why there are so few women leaders in business (*Lean In* 15-26). Sandberg's advice to women is framed by a social constructionist approach to gender: by citing various psychological studies, she asserts that women are not "naturally" different from men, but girls have been socialized in ways that prevent them from embracing their own ambition and cultivating successful careers (21-24). Sandberg writes, "We internalize the negative messages we get throughout our lives—the messages that say it's wrong to be outspoken, aggressive, more powerful than men. We lower our expectations of what we can achieve" (8). The problem, Sandberg explains, is not so much that gender bias exists in the workplace culture but that so many women have let these external forces dictate their individual choices both personally and professionally. The decisions women most often make for themselves regarding issues like career progression, household management, and domestic partnership arrangements are really to blame for keeping women from climbing the corporate rungs. Specifically, Sandberg argues that these "internal barriers" are just as important as the "institutional barriers" that others have argued keep women from achieving professional success (8-9). Yet Sandberg advocates that women should focus on addressing internal obstacles *rather than* institutional changes—such as family-friendly workplace policies—"because they are under our own control" (9).

Furthermore, in order for women to "internalize the revolution," Sandberg insists that they relinquish their fears of not being liked, making wrong choices, being judged, being a bad mother/wife/daughter and that they stop internalizing failure by eschewing self-doubt. She urges women to recognize their own "impostor syndrome" and transform their insecurities into a "fake it until you make it" form of confidence by seizing opportunities and taking risks (28-30). For women to really succeed in business, Sandberg declares, they need to approach career progression as men always have, such as putting themselves forward for a promotion even if they meet only sixty percent of the requirements, making themselves seen and heard, and learning to withstand criticism (58-63). Sandberg also advises that all workers, and corporations as a whole, would benefit by everyone bringing their "whole" selves to their jobs by being honest, talking about personal lives/situations, and reflecting on decisions that are driven by emotion (88-91).

In the second half of the book, Sandberg begins to rely less on statistical information and research as she weaves in more anecdotal stories and personal revelations. It is here that she also begins to advise working women on blurring "the line between personal and professional" (90) in their integration of career and family. Yet her advice may be read in direct contradiction with a more balanced life in which one's personal roles and identities are prioritized as much as one's roles and identities as a worker. Sandberg's guidelines here include do not plan too far in advance (especially for motherhood), and do not look for an exit or put on the brakes but continue to accelerate by keeping a foot on the gas pedal until a decision must be made (93-103).

Throughout the book, Sandberg cautions women about putting family before career, which is sound advice for women who do not yet have children or a spouse. Of course, Sandberg admits that once children enter the picture, women can only continue to lean in if they can "make their partner a real partner" and reject the notion that mothers must bear the primary responsibility of childcare (108-115). Sandberg does briefly acknowledge how difficult it is for women to achieve true equality in the home, which has been far more challenging than doing so in the workplace. For example, she attests to the ease of replicating the gendered patterns from our childhood households but at the same time urges women to reverse such learned behaviours (116-120). She makes it clear to her readers that an equal partnership at home is crucial if women hope to "integrate" their families with their professional success. Yet it is also clear that such integration does not occur without cost, and the sacrifices of having a family should be managed so that women's paths to executive-level success are not compromised.

CHOICE RHETORIC AND MOTHER-BLAMING DISCOURSES

In Chapter 9, Sandberg exposes the myths of "having it all" and "doing it all," writing, "Mothers don't want to be perceived as less dedicated to their jobs than men or women without family responsibilities. We overwork to overcompensate" (129). Yet she also acknowledges that most women take the same mentality to their work as mothers, and many women currently embrace the standards of "intensive mothering." Sandberg explains intensive mothering as a sociological term for the cultural elevation of the importance of women spending large amounts of time with their children—even more than stay-at-home mothers of previous generations (135). However, Sandberg does not offer a solution that guides women to strike a balance between these opposing forces. Rather, she advises that working mothers should take advantage of technology to work at home longer into the night and earlier in the morning while their kids are asleep; to become highly productive outside of work hours by sneaking in work where they can, such as in the soccer field restroom; to identify real priorities at home and at work; and to understand success as "making the best choices we can ... and accepting them" (139).

As such, in Sandberg's vision, the underlying problem does not lie with institutional structures and sexist double standards that constrain women as mothers and as workers; rather, women are held back by the "choices" they make as they attempt to negotiate these roles. Over the past decade, a number of scholars have begun to explore how "choice" rhetoric is mediated through trending news stories, popular culture, and the evolution of liberal feminism at the end of the twentieth century. Many of these scholars agree that such discourses represent the influence of postfeminism in mainstream Western culture (Dow; Vavrus; McCarver). In her book *Prime-Time Feminism*, Bonnie Dow argues that by the late twentieth century, representations of feminism "as a set of political ideas and practices [was] transformed into a set of attitudes and personal lifestyle choices" (209). Because of this, feminism is interpreted and represented in the mass media as "a lifestyle, an attitude, an identity," rather than as an ideology or political praxis (209). Linda Hirshman coined the term "choice feminism" in 2005, arguing that this discourse originated with second wave liberal feminists who wished to shift from judgmental rhetoric concerning abortion to a more supportive one. The consequence is that anything a woman does—including having children, working outside the home, and staying at home—is "counted as feminist as long as she *chose* it" (Hirshman).

In her study of online discussions about Sarah Palin after her U.S. Vice Presidential nomination, Virginia McCarver examines "the root of choice rhetoric's power and ubiquity in dominant cultural narratives and the publicly celebrated veins of the women's movement" (21). She contends that, within postfeminist discourse, "feminism and choice are closely identified, to such an extent that being a feminist means exercising one's choices and supporting another woman's choices, no matter what they may be" (34). Yet McCarver reveals that embedded within choice rhetoric are neoliberal cultural narratives of freedom, autonomy, and personal agency, since "a woman's choices are private, individual, and to be respected" (23). Women are thus theoretically free to make their own decisions with fortitude, while shouldering the responsibility of any consequences. McCarver cautions that the focus on themes such as independence and individual responsibility distracts from the limited options, poor alternatives, and double binds that often constrain women's choices. She analyzes the "You Can't Have It All" script found in online commentary, which was used to criticize Palin's choice to mother her five children, including a special needs newborn, while running for the second highest political office in the nation. McCarver demonstrates how this discourse "ascribes failure or difficulty in navigating the challenges of work and family to women rather than to the social reality of limited resources or inadequate alternatives" (31).

Similarly, Dana Schowalter elaborates on trending news stories in the media that favour working mothers who "can solve their problems without government-solutions" (229). She explains that "the ideal postfeminist citizen is one who adopts individualized solutions to the problems she experiences as she attempts to balance her work in the home with work outside the home. When she fails to 'have it all,' this woman is encouraged to blame only herself" (229). Such rhetoric of choice and blame, particularly those surrounding women, work, and motherhood/family, are deleterious to women because they often "mask a series of narrow scripts, each delineating a limiting and unfavourable 'choice' dangerous to women, feminist, and gender relations in its obfuscation of oppression and patriarchy" (21).

Sheryl Sandberg's approach to improving women's status in the workplace is an extension of the choice rhetoric explored by McCarver and Showalter, therein blaming women as individually responsible when they do not achieve workplace success. While Sandberg claims a feminist agenda, her advice to women is very individualized and devoid of context. As Catherine Rottenberg notes, "This turn inward helps to produce an individuated feminist agent who, alone, is accountable for garnering her own 'revolutionary' energy" (9). Sandberg contends that if we "internalize" the revolution, the shift to equality will happen one person at a time. Her theory represents a kind of "trickle down" feminism or the notion that if enough women make it to the top playing by the rules, more women in leadership will lead to better changes for all women. This ideology informs policies which, at the bottom line, are most beneficial to procuring the strengths and ambition of individual female executives in training. Rottenberg notes that what *Lean In* reinforces is "precisely the entrepreneurial subject who is encouraged to take her own personal initiative in order to improve her career prospects, particularly in the corporate world" (10).

It is no wonder that Sandberg became a media darling after her book's release. As bell hooks notes in the blog *The Feminist Wire*, Sandberg's "faux feminism" is basically a neoliberal or corporate feminism, and "Sandberg's definition of feminism begins and ends with the notion that it's all about gender equality within the existing system." That is, rather than challenging the system that has kept men in power, Sandberg's work replicates the masculine model of white male privilege by encouraging individual responsibility and enterprising thinking—such as spotting opportunities, taking risks, and networking effectively—to promote more women to the upper echelons of the business world. Susan Faludi similarly writes that "Sandberg's admirers would say that *Lean In* is using free-market beliefs to advance the cause of women's equality. Her detractors would say (and have) that her organization is using the desire for women's equality to advance the cause of the free market. And they would both be right" (5). Faludi deems Sandberg's message a "corporate brand of feminism" that cajoles women to work harder, to keep their focus, and achieve individual empowerment rather than embracing a collective solution to workplace inequality that would bolster all women. Rottenberg further argues that this neoliberal feminism uses key liberal ideas, such as equality, opportunity, and free choice, to produce a particular kind of feminist subject "who is not only individualized but entrepreneurial in the sense that she is oriented towards optimizing her resources through incessant calculation, personal initiative and innovation" (4-5).

For working mothers, Sandberg's key to success is managing the precarious balance between home/family and professional demands by employing the economic model of efficiency, innovation, and cost-benefit analysis to individual circumstances (Rottenberg 12). Any failure to achieve such balance is an indication that the woman has made an improper calculation or misallocation of resources and is therefore to blame for her poor choices. Also, much of Sandberg's advice involves tips for negotiating a workplace culture based on a model of the masculine worker, presumably with a wife at home managing the housework and kids, and fails to recognize that all workers have private as well as professional lives. Consequently, these "choices" made by Sandberg's enterprising women workers/ working mothers serve to underscore corporate goals, values, and balance sheets without adversely impacting the patriarchal corporate culture.

WOMEN RESPOND TO *LEAN IN*

The immediate response to Sandberg's treatise was full of righteous sentiment weeks before *Lean In* had been officially released. Many reviews and editorials surfaced in the traditional press, as well as in independent and online sources. Some referred to the onslaught as a "backlash" in which women were aiming to discipline the "uppity" Sandberg. Yet, when read in the aggregate, many of these critiques cohere around three main themes, all of which reflect the limitations of the "choice" rhetoric which frames Sandberg's book: 1) not all working mothers have a choice, 2) working mothers' choices are often constrained by gendered expectations of women's competing roles as workers and mothers, and 3) rather than require individual solutions that strengthen business imperatives, real change will come only when workplace culture and policies are revised to benefit all workers and families.

Months after the book's release, a number of women came to Sandberg's defense, including a host of editorials posted on the *Forbes* website touting the value of Sandberg's advice for female executives. Still, critiques of Sandberg have continued to accumulate. What has emerged from this online debate is a more robust understanding of working mothers' experiences, the complexities of their diverse situations, and the need not only for self-awareness of individual limitations but for collective effort that would elevate all working women through structural and political change. Jodi Kantor writes in *The New York Times* that a theme which had already emerged in criticisms of *Lean In* was that Sandberg "places too much of the onus on women who are already struggling to fill impossible demands, and too little on government and employers to provide better childcare, more flexible jobs and other concrete gains." In another *New York Times* article, Anne Ladky, executive director of an advocacy group for low-income women in Chicago, explains, "The reality is that a lot of women don't have any bargaining power" (quoted in Rampell). That is, for many women, the choice is not as clear as leaning in or leaving before you leave; rather, many women must work to maintain a job at all costs because they have families to support.

While Jill Filipovic's online editorial for *The Guardian* was mostly appreciative of Sandberg's efforts, she also notes that women remain poorly compensated and disproportionately steered toward "pink collar" jobs that often involve care work. She further observes that most US jobs do not offer paid sick days, vacation days, or maternity leave and that "federally-funded childcare seems like a pipe dream; livable wages, comprehensive benefits and collective bargaining agreements for all workers feel similarly far off." Filipovic concludes that "these are collective social problems.... This isn't all in our heads, and it can't be fixed with an individual attitude adjustment." Similarly, Stephen Marche notes in an essay for *The Atlantic* that the load for most people—all workers, but especially working parents—is already unbearable, but even more so for those facing class inequities. The solution, he argues, "is establishing social supports that allow families to function."

Other commentators suggested that the tenor of Sandberg's advice, such as talking about mentors, glass ceilings, and work-life balance, privileges a neoliberal approach to change at the expense of systemic transformations that would truly equalize opportunity for all workers, including working parents. Anand Giridharadas looks into the future to examine what more women at the table might mean and identifies an issue overlooked by Sandberg: "that men have built a world of work that is fundamentally unbalanced, excessively focused on money and power, and dismissive of the body's need for renewal." In an online editorial for *The Washington Post*, columnist Rosa Brooks agrees that ubiquity has come to define the quality of one's work. She writes, "If you're not at your desk every night until nine, your commitment to the job is questioned. If you're not checking e-mail 24/7, you're not a reliable colleague. But in a world in which leaning in at work has come to mean doing more work, more often, for longer hours, women will disproportionately drop out or be eased out." She further explains that "if we truly want gender equality, we need to challenge the assumption that more is always better ... and we need to challenge those assumptions wherever we find them, both in the workplace and in the family."

While Sandberg explains the "trap" of the "having it all" myth in terms of limited resources, increased demands, choices, and trade-offs by noting that "being a parent means making adjustments, compromises, and sacrifices every day" (*Lean In* 122), many of the responses to her book suggest that her economic metaphor fails to interrogate the inhumane work expectations and personal sacrifices that comprise the capitalist corporate regime. Applebaum notes in her review of *Lean In* that Sandberg's personal anecdotes "show her working harder, longer hours than anyone else and accepting bigger, tougher challenges. Generally, she advocates adjusting one's life to the punishing routine of corporate success rather than vice versa." Similarly, in an online op-ed for *The Atlantic*, Chimene Keitner observes, "If 'ambition' means seeking success along a single dimension, at the expense of other goals and values, it's no wonder that some members of today's educated elite (who have some degree of choice in the matter) seem to be disavowing the concept. Instead of abandoning ambition, we should seek to redefine it."

As these writers clearly indicate, the very notion of "leaning in" or closing the ambition gap between men and women means upholding the patriarchal and corporate-defined mandate of work above all else. Several commentators signalled that Sandberg's focus on gender stereotypes about women's leadership qualities overshadows the gendered nature of women's lives as both workers and mothers. Melissa Gira Grant asserts, "Sandberg's understanding of leadership so perfectly internalizes the power structure of institutions created and dominated by men that it cannot conceive of women's leadership outside of those narrow spaces." Within this framework, the biggest threat to women finding "the will to lead" is their desire to have a child. Kate Losse, a former Facebook employee, writes in an online article for *Dissent* titled "Feminism's Tipping Point: Who Wins from Leaning In?" that "for Sandberg, pregnancy must be converted into a corporate opportunity: a moment to convince a woman to commit further to her job." Regarding Sandberg's contention that working mothers must lean in and remain in the workplace at all costs, Losse writes, "Sandberg encourages women to maintain a commitment to the workplace without encouraging the workplace to maintain a commitment to them."

BEYOND MOTHER-BLAME:
ENVISIONING EMPOWERING ALTERNATIVES

Rather than perpetuate the tyranny of the modern workplace by blaming individual women for failing to succeed therein, many of *Lean In*'s critics reveal how an unrelenting focus on work negatively impacts women as a whole and specifically limits the choices available to working mothers. *Forbes* "Women in Tech" online contributor Kate Brodock suggests that Sandberg's advice to women that they step up, work harder, not check out early, and lean forward is "still wrought with the tension between being successful and having a healthy work-life balance" and that "women have been put under a different set of expectations in terms of having a job and having a family" because their biological roles as mothers have tied them to traditional family roles. Similarly, Bryce Covert comments in a blog for *The Nation* that this issue really affects all parents, but men traditionally have addressed the competing demands of home and work *at the expense of* women's careers and ambitions. He concludes that "the problem is that too many women already lean out—and that far too few men do the same. We need to start by asking men to recalibrate if we're going to revolutionize the workplace." Brodock similarly concludes that "the idea of becoming successful only if you spend all of your waking hours working is not only wrong, but irresponsible and very misguided. *We need to change this for everyone.*"

Along these lines, some of the most thoughtful responses to *Lean In* suggest embracing a more inclusive feminism than Sandberg's business manifesto, one with a broader definition of success that bridges women's diverse identities and circumstances. For example, bell hooks asks her readers to "dig deep" and go "beyond lean in" in an effort to "remember that visionary feminist goal which is not a woman running the world as is, but of women doing our part to change the world so that freedom and justice, the opportunity to have optimal well-being, can be equally shared by everyone—male and female." Lisa Belkin also advises that "one does not opt-out OR in, lean in OR back, work OR not, choose family OR career" but rather we improvise according to our changing circumstances and evolving lives. Giridharadas similarly describes a high-powered meeting in Manhattan meant to discuss what a new wave of the women's movement may achieve in the workplace and notes that everyone conceded that the key "was to frame the new ways of working as performance enhancements," including flexible arrangements for workers and other means of enhancing worker renewal. Along this trajectory, Cali Yost argues that companies can improve their bottom line by implementing a new model that "moves beyond the outdated limits of 'balance' and 'having it all'" by realizing that "work+life fit" is an issue for parents and non-parents alike and by offering "greater flexibility and creativity to manage our responsibilities on and off the job."

CONCLUSION

Ultimately, the binary existence imagined in Sheryl Sandberg's book between those who lean in and those who lean out, or between those who strive to create a "balanced" life and those who do not, perpetuates blame when women fail to achieve the highest levels of professional success in their childbearing and childrearing years. While *Lean In* speaks to the gendered stereotypes that have kept women from shattering the highest of glass ceilings, her argument that women should amend their behaviour to accommodate established models of masculine success in the corporate world only perpetuates the neoliberal capitalist culture that elevates work above all else. Further, Sandberg's unwillingness to critique institutionalized workplace culture and standards functions to reify the differing social expectations and double standards that unfairly penalize women workers, and working mothers even more so, because the responsibilities for figuring out how to "have it all" is left to individual women rather than corporate leaders. Rather than reframe the debate to reveal how gendered expectations create double binds that lead to women's limited choices along the corporate career path, Sandberg's treatise urges women to embrace the masculine model of corporate success and find a way to conform their personal lives to their professional ambitions. In contrast, the responses to Sandberg as they have evolved in the traditional press, online platforms, and independent media coalesce to interrogate or, in Joan William's terms, "unbend" gendered systems that structure market work and family work by re-conceptualizing notions of work around our collective social values (4-8). By re-imagining the workplace in this way, we can also re-imagine women's and mothers' relationships to work, to their families, and to each other without requiring them to make impossible choices or to suffer the consequent burdens and blame.

WORKS CITED

Applebaum, Anne. "How to Succeed in Business." *The New York Review of Books.* 6 June 2013. Web. 22 July 2013.

Belkin, Lisa. "The Rest Of The Work/Life Conversation That The New York Times Article Started." *Huffington Post* blog. 9 July 2013. Web. 10 July 2013.

Brodock, Kate. "Women Can't Have It All, But Maybe No One Can." *Forbes Online.* 25 June 2012. Web. 5 Mar. 2013.

Brooks, Rosa. "Recline, Don't 'Lean In' (Why I Hate Sheryl Sandberg)." *The Washington Post* blog. 25 Feb. 2014. Web. 3 Mar. 2014.

Covert, Bryce. "Men of the World, Lean Out!" *The Nation* blog. 26 Feb. 2014. Web. 3 Mar. 2014.

Dow, Bonnie J. *Prime-Time Feminism: Television, Media Culture, and the Women's Movement Since 1970.* Philadelphia: University of Pennsylvania, 1996. Print.

Faludi, Susan. "Facebook Feminism, Like It or Not." *The Baffler* 23 (2013): n.pag. Web. 3 Mar. 2014.

Filipovic, Jill. "Sheryl Sandberg is More of a Feminist Crusader than People Give Her Credit For." *The Guardian.* 1 Mar. 2013. Web. 5 Mar. 2013.

Giridharadas, Anand. "Women Are at the Table, So Now What?" *The New York Times.* 14 June 2013. Web. 3 Mar. 2014.

Grant, Melissa Gira. "Sheryl Sandberg's 'Lean In' Campaign Holds Little for Most Women." *The Washington Post.* 25 Feb. 2013. Web. 3 Mar. 2014.

Hirshman, Linda. "Homeward Bound." *The American Prospect.* 21 Nov. 2005. Web. 3 Mar. 2014.

hooks, bell. "Dig Deep: Beyond Lean In." *The Feminist Wire.* 28 Oct. 2013. Web. 29 Oct. 2013.

Kantor, Jodi. "A Titan's How-To on Breaking the Glass Ceiling." *The New York Times.* 21 Feb. 2013. Web. 5 Mar. 2013.

Keitner, Chimene. "Why Nobody Can Win the Having-It-All Race." *The Atlantic.* 17 July 2012. Web. 5 Mar. 2013.

Losse, Kate. "Feminism's Tipping Point: Who Wins from Leaning In?" *Dissent: A Quarterly of Politics and Culture.* 26 Mar. 2013. Web. 3 Mar. 2014.

Marche, Stephen. "Home Economics: The Link between Work-Life Balance and Income Equality." *The Atlantic*. 19 June 2013. Web. 10 July 2013.

McCarver, Virginia. "The Rhetoric of Choice and 21st-Century Feminism: Online Conversations about Work, Family, and Sarah Palin." *Women's Studies in Communication* 34 (2011): 20-41. Print.

Rampell, Catherine. "Coveting Not a Corner Office, but Time at Home." *The New York Times*. 7 July 2013. Web. 10 July 2013.

Rottenberg, Catherine. "The Rise of Neoliberal Feminism." *Cultural Studies* (2013): 1-20. Web. 6 June 2014.

Sandberg, Sheryl. Barnard College commencement speech. *Barnard College*. 17 May 2011. Web. 5 March 2013.

Sandberg, Sheryl. "Why We Have Too Few Women Leaders." *TED.com*. Dec. 2010. Web. 5 March 2013.

Sandberg, Sheryl with Nell Scovell. *Lean In: Women, Work, and the Will to Lead*. New York: Knopf, 2013. Print.

Schowalter, Dana. "Silencing the *Shriver Report*: Postfeminist Citizenship and News Discourse." *The Communication Review* 15 (2012): 218-231. Print.

Vavrus, Mary Douglas. "Postfeminist Redux?" *The Review of Communication* 12.3 (2012): 224-236. Print.

Williams, Joan. *Unbending Gender: Why Family and Work Conflict and What To Do About It*. Oxford: Oxford University, 2000. Print.

Yost, Cali. "The 10 Keys to Building the Flexible Workplace of the Future." *The Atlantic*. 17 July 2012. Web. 5 Mar. 2013.

IV.
Sharing Mother-Blame Stories:
Strategies for Resistance

13.
Twice Shamed and Twice Blamed

Assumptions, Myths and Stereotypes about "Giving Up a Child" and "Taking In a Child"

LEE MURRAY AND KERRI KEARNEY

*I*T'S A BOY! *The baby is fine despite his fast delivery. He is dark, cute, funny-looking, red, yelling, and I want to hold him. The doctor is gentle but firm as he explains that if I hold my baby, I won't be able to give him away. I promise to give him away. I hold my baby boy and I fall in love. He is gorgeous. I keep my son in my room for the next five days. They keep taking him back. I sneak into the nursery during the day and I take him out. I go back at night and hold him and rock him and talk to him and sing to him. I tell my baby everything I think he needs to know. I read to my baby. I sing some more and kiss and hug him constantly.*

All they *care about is if I will be able to give my son away. I assure them daily that I will. I know I can; I think it is the best decision, at this time, for my baby and probably for me. They continue to take my baby back to the nursery, and I continue to take him back to my room. I am mad at the nurses, at the doctor, and at myself. I am a young teen mom and an "illegitimate mom," but I know what I want; I want to spend time with my baby. Finally I have had enough and I emphatically say, "If I give my baby away I will have only these five days to give him all the love I can, and it needs to last him for a while so leave me alone,* PLEASE!*" And they do.*

And I give my baby away (Murray "Secrets").

A couple of decades later, in another country, a very different scene unfolds for another young woman:

I walk alone down the quiet, wide hospital corridor—awash in a cauldron of boiling emotions as my instincts jangle out a message of impending danger. From some distant emotional space in which I am protectively huddled, I feel my hand pushing the hospital bassinet that houses a newborn baby girl. I hear the "swoosh" of wheels turning ... swoosh, step, swoosh, step. The sound seems to echo loudly on a hospital floor that has otherwise fallen absolutely silent.

We turn the last corner between us and the room of my child's birthmother.

Even as my intellect tells me this meeting is vital for my child, and my heart tells me it is vital for her birthmother, a voice inside my head says that once she sees the baby, she will not be able to let her go. Once she sees me in the flesh, she will consider me inept or incapable; she will see through my pretenses that I am a good mother despite my "asking" other women to birth my children. The dread hangs heavy in the pit of my stomach, and it contrasts sharply with the confident face I am determined to project to the audience of nurses trying hard, and failing, not to stare. "Judge not what you do not understand," I think defensively as I move by. "All is well with me" (Kearney and Bailey).

SHARING "OTHER MOTHERING" STORIES

Some mothering experiences are deliberately and carefully buried. And often they are deeply buried. Then a sudden or unexpected connection with another person triggers a thought or a feeling that brings forth a conversation from that secret space, resulting in the sharing of our stories. In 2010, we, the co-authors of this chapter, published back-to-back articles (Kearney and Bailey; Murray "Secrets"). Publicly sharing our experiences solidified our mutual fascination with the peculiar juxtaposition of our socially assigned "other mother" roles (mothering that is situated outside the nuclear, two-parent, heterosexual family with biological children from the present union—preferably marriage) and popular interpretation of our mothering experiences. We discovered that we share not only mutual mothering struggles and joys but also similar shame and blame reactions to our other mothering stories. Interwoven with other voices from the adoption literature, we discuss here our stories from the perspectives of "giving away a child" and "taking in a child" with a goal of questioning the assumptions, myths, and stereotypes about mothering in the adoption triangle.

THE LITERATURE AND A CONSIDERATION OF SOCIAL UNDERSTANDING

Our stories are written in the context of a North American society during contemporary times; therefore, the majority of the literature reviewed here is also written in the context of a North American society. More specifically, one of our mothering stories is situated in the United States and the other in Canada. Our stories are meant to represent only our personal experiences, which serve to challenge normative motherhood discourses in North American society. Popular writings, dominant perceptions, and contemporary adoption literature often associate enduring pain with mothering roles in the adoption triangle. They predict anguish for mothers who have "given their babies away" and resultant regret that lasts a lifetime (see Bloch Jones; Cushman, Kalmuss, and Namerow; DeSimone; Fessler; Ge et al.; Janus; Lauderdale; Miller and Coyl; Rosenberg and Groze; Solinger). They similarly presume that mothers who adopt their children experience shame and pain (see Johnston; Lane; Scully; Tsigdinos; Waits). To be sure, these roles are not free from pain, but perhaps this pain is partially derived from social expectations that mothers *should* experience shame and blame. To be a mother in the adoption triangle is perceived as a bad thing; thus the unwed pregnant teen is a bad girl, and the woman who adopts—either because she cannot get pregnant or does not desire to be pregnant—fails to realize an integral component of being female.

While perspectives concerning the diversity of mothering roles have changed over time, we propose that even contemporary Western "conventional" knowledge about adoption (both research-based literature and social understandings) perpetuates experiences of pain, shame, and blame that may have little relevance to many mothers' lived experiences. We do not seek to revise the maternal narratives of women whose experiences *do* support these commonly held beliefs. For example, both Fessler and Schaefer describe how birthmothers who "give up" their children experience life-long grief after being pressured, often by family, to do so. The 2013 U.S. film *Philomena*, which is based upon Martin Sixsmith's investigative book, similarly shows a young mother whose baby was essentially stolen from her and who, 50 years later, anxiously searches for a son she has grieved for every day. In her 2000 book, Bloch Jones gives the apparently inevitable shame, guilt, and extreme grief of birthmothers its own name: "Birthmother Syndrome." Each of these sources reassures us that shame, blame, pain, and even coercion characterize the experiences of birthmothers. And for many birthmothers, this may be the case.

In contrast, for the mother who adopts, infertility is often understood to be intertwined with her personal choices. The issue of infertility is riddled with shame and blame, although some authors of popular press books (see Lane; Scully; Waits), perhaps as a defense mechanism, take a humorous approach to the loss. Sokol takes a different approach; he first shares the painful experience of his wife's infertility and then their decision to adopt. This story exemplifies the common social understanding that the choice to adopt comes after failed (first choice) attempts to get pregnant. This understanding, present in all of the above texts, strongly suggests that adoption begins from a point of pain, shame, and perhaps blame.[1]

A second and similarly common theme about mothers who adopt is also present in Sokol's book: "It comes down to how much love you have inside and to know if you are capable of giving true parental love, sacrifice and dedication to a child that is not your own" (10). His is not an unusual statement about the social perception that children who are adopted are somehow not their parents' "own" children. Logic dictates, then, that mothers of children who were adopted are also somehow not their "own"; they are not "real" or "natural" mothers to their children. It seems redundant but still important to point out that being considered a less-than-real mother might bring about a certain amount of pain, and perhaps even shame, for women in this role.

In contrast to the aforementioned research and societal understandings of these issues, we suggest that mothers' experiences in the adoption triangle are much more complex and that a *lack of expected pain* may be an unspoken part of their stories. This chapter accordingly highlights how we experienced shame and blame for not doing it "right" the first time and additional shame and blame for not feeling the appropriate guilt, anguish, and grief as a result of our mothering decisions. We acknowledge the particularity of our experiences, as well as the fact that there are men involved in our journeys who need to voice their own experiences. In sharing our personal experiences of "other mothering," this chapter presents a counter-narrative to accepted beliefs about mothering roles and mothering wisdom.

THE ILLEGITIMATE MOM: LEE'S STORY

Even today, hearing adoption referred to as "taking in an unwanted or abandoned child" shakes me up. Dave, my now forty-four-year-old biological son, was not unwanted, nor was he abandoned. But as his birthmother, society grants me no redemption. I consistently experience the imposition of the "bad mother" label. First I placed my child for adoption and then I proceeded forward with a life that eventually included raising other children and gaining an advanced degree. But perhaps most important is that I did all of this with a sense that the decision I made turned out okay, both for my child and for me.

Although, as a teen, I was "bad" for getting pregnant and "bad" for giving my baby away, I was not that different from my peers. Several of my high school friends were pregnant before they were married. However, they did the "right" thing by marrying their children's fathers, and I did not *want* to get married. This made me particularly bad. The wisdom of the time also supported placing the child for a secret adoption. The illegitimate mother could revoke her sin, restore a semblance of normalcy, delete the illegitimate child from existence, and expunge her sexual past. But I never saw Dave as a mistake. I was naïve and made a mistake in judgment, but I neither wanted to delete nor deny Dave's existence—nor did I want to have my bad behaviour expunged.

When Dave was born, we spent an amazingly happy and sad week together. And then I did not meet him again until he was married and raising two children. I am sure both Dave and I consider from time to time what our lives would have been like if I had made a different decision, but that will always remain a wonderment. Would we go back and change things if we could? I do not think I would. And although Dave may wonder how his life may have been different, he has expressed many times how much he enjoys life as it is.

I kept my inner turmoil about being a birthmother—my feelings, questions, and experiences—a secret for many, many years. My awkwardness and reluctance to tell came, and still comes, from a place deep inside me where explanation is difficult to find. I have a level of peace with the past, and yet the normative discourse says I should still suffer and feel bad about my behaviours, decisions, and feelings related to Dave's birth. If I were "normal" I would feel more remorse or resentment; perhaps my story is a bit different because my parents were so supportive of my decisions, which was rare at that time. I do feel a degree of shame about getting pregnant and choosing adoption for my baby, but I feel doubly shamed by society because my life is not permeated by never-ending regret, disappointment, and turmoil—all the things that I am *supposed* to feel.

I see Dave and his family on an irregular basis because of physical distance but also because we are both busy with our lives. I understand and truly accept that his love for me as a mother figure is subject to limitations. I do love him as my son, but part of my decision to allow others to parent him meant being realistic about the outcome. I am not suggesting I was mature enough at the time of his birth to recognize this, but it was a realization that came over time. Part of the outcome of my decision meant that I would always be closer to the three children I raised, and to my resultant grandchildren, than I am to Dave and his family. And he is, as expected, closer to the family who raised him.

I always assumed that Dave was happy and that he made his adoptive parents very happy. Perhaps it was the naïveté of my assumptions that carried me through without a lot of battle scars. Perhaps the alternative would have caused unbearable grief and loss. I do not know. I also assumed that Dave's parents would be a couple who could not have children and, even as an adult, I never recognized that as an assumption until Kerri and I began to share our stories.

BYPASSING "NORMAL" MOM: KERRI'S STORY

I never felt the internal drive to be pregnant that my friends expressed, but I learned to act as if I did. Yes, I very much wanted to be a mother and pregnancy provided the obvious path to achieve this. I was raised with the idea that I would find "Mr. Wonderful," marry, and have biological babies (in that order), all gracefully accomplished on the way to happily ever after.

I married while completing graduate school, and a few years later I was surprised when I did not get pregnant. I became disconcerted as time passed, but I do not remember feeling panicked or devastated. I did not admit this, however; in response to others' enquiries and comments, I tried to say the right things and demonstrate the appropriate level of grief. I really was starting to wonder what in the world was *wrong* with me—mentally and emotionally, not physically. The message was clear to me that if I was not getting pregnant, I should be immobilized by deep grief. I was initially resistant to this message but society was quietly teaching me to feel shame for my circumstances.

After twelve months of purposeful attempts had not produced a pregnancy, my "condition" got its own official name—infertility. My husband made his thoughts clear about six months later:

> *"I'm not pregnant." I shared the disappointing news and waited for a hug and just a bit of encouragement. My husband just stood there, still and silent, his expression unreadable. Never breaking eye contact, he took one deliberate step back, and then he began an overt, slow, silent, and methodical scan of my body all the way to my toes, and back up again. I stood absolutely still, frozen in shock at the cold appraisal. Once again looking me straight in the eyes, he said without apparent emotion, "Well …you're not a man. And it appears you are not a woman. So I guess the real question is what are you?"*
>
> *Later that day, moving robotically, I took my clothes, my beloved dog, and my rebellious female parts, and I drove away in my car. I left everything else behind. Permanently.*

To this day the memory of that particular conversation is razor sharp and vividly coloured in my memory banks. By then, I had learned my role and I did, indeed, feel fully frozen with shame—twice shamed—first because I could not get pregnant as a *real* woman would and second because I did not feel deep grief about my lack of pregnancy. I did feel frustration, as well as a sense of failure. I also felt sad that I was not yet a mother. But I did not feel grief. Not only did I fail at pregnancy but I could not even muster the correct reaction to my womanly failure. This incident was the closing bell on a troubled marriage, a decision for which I shouldered full blame. I soon began divorce proceedings with a sense of personal failure, shame, and deep anger.

As a newly single person living in a time where technology provided multiple options for pursuing pregnancy, the decision to adopt felt more right for me than pregnancy ever had. Before I remarried five years later, my husband-to-be agreed to adopt at least one child. But, as he was raised in a traditional home similar to mine, I believed he needed time and space to consider his own feelings about biological children against my "strange" position that biology was an artificially imposed requirement for families. Three years into our marriage, I reluctantly entered infertility treatment against a ticking biological clock and, even today, I cannot separate what part of that decision was for my husband and what part was meant to address the shame I felt from not getting pregnant in my twenties. Would getting pregnant now absolve me of some of my sins? After it was confirmed that a medical reason for my infertility could not be identified, I soon bargained my way out of treatments and began the adoption process. But the decisions I made solidified others' notions that I deeply grieved my infertile state and that adoption was my second choice. Indeed, this was the only socially acceptable understanding of my journey.

DISCUSSION

Illegitimate pregnancy, unwed mothers, infertility, adoption—all have been hush-hush topics at some point in history and, in varying degrees and contexts, still are. All depart from the normative discourse, the preferred ideal, of motherhood and families. But as women who share these experiences begin to address them more openly, it is possible that they will shoulder additional shame and blame. Their voices are often silenced a second time—they are twice shamed—if they do not demonstrate the "appropriate" sentiments in light of their womanly failures. This chapter seeks to lessen the twice-shamed effect of being different. Both of our experiences carry with them some level of pain, grief, and sorrow; however, the eternal glove of despair and regret does not fit as snuggly as society believes it should.

BIRTHMOTHERS

Terms such as relinquishment, surrender, self-sacrifice, anger, anguish, longing, regret, survival, loss, powerlessness, low self-esteem, guilt, grief, shame, and blame permeate the birthmother literature. My (Lee's) experience, at least in part, is a counter-narrative to the presumptions that birthmothers are pressured to place their babies for adoption, they lack family support, and their lives are forever shadowed by deep regret and sorrow.

While contemporary writings speak strongly of pain and regret, the majority (see Bloch Jones; Cushman et al.; DeSimone; Fessler; Sixsmith) consist of *someone else* telling birthmothers' stories. Very few feature a birthmother telling her story from a first person and firsthand experience (Murray "Secrets"; "Epilogue"). Perhaps this speaks to the constrained voices and experiences of birthmothers; it also suggests that we have not heard the whole story.

Fessler does include firsthand accounts of birthmothers, but in authoring her text she also selected which stories to include and exclude. To her credit, she does indicate that she is not representing *all* birthmothers in her book. Similarly, Bloch Jones states that her book "is certainly not about *all* birthmothers" (xv). Notably, birthmothers who are absent include those who are chronically ill, addicted, emotionally unwell, and collectively "whose lives were so habitually dismal that relinquishment easily blended with other problems and passed almost unnoticed" (Bloch Jones xv). It is suggested in Bloch Jones' statements that birthmothers with "dismal" lives willingly, and without regret, placed their babies for adoption. In my opinion, this is a major assumption about their experiences. While there was pain and sorrow related to my experience as a teen birthmother, I did not feel enduring pain or regret. None of the stories of birthmothers from Bloch Jones' book fit my life experience then or now.

Both the literature and popular writings describe parents and authorities encouraging, convincing, and forcing birthmothers to give up their babies for adoption. The birthmothers are described as being powerless, hopeless, and helpless. They also describe themselves as not being mature enough, strong enough, or forceful enough to resist adoption plans. For many this was the origin of their grief, despair, and anger. My decision to place my baby for adoption changed many times during my pregnancy but, ultimately, I had family support to make my own decision. Without family support I may not have had the resolve to follow through with what I thought was the "best" decision at the time. I have not felt the resentment, anger, anguish, or prolonged grief that is considered typical for birthmothers; perhaps this is because I was not forced to "relinquish" or "surrender" my child.

I believe there were and are other birthmothers who benefit from family support. I believe there are others who moved through the process of adoption with fewer battle scars and less regret than what is reflected in the literature. Our voices are missing. Our stories, with their lack of deep human loss, may not be as "newsworthy." Or perhaps we are perceived as too far outside the norm—anomalies or oddities. I did and still do feel odd, different, and outside the norm—mostly because I do not feel as regretful as I think I should. My experience does not mirror the normative discourse of teen birthmothers from the 1950s and '60s who placed their babies for adoption. Fessler and Bloch Jones include heart wrenching stories of birthmothers who have "relinquished" and "surrendered" their babies, and it is important that these stories be shared. But it is also important to dispel the myth that all birthmothers have suffered in this way and that their lives are forever ruined. This normative discourse silences, and potentially re-shames, those who had different experiences.

Fessler speaks to the difficulty of moving on and forgetting for mothers in the adoption triangle. Perhaps it is not necessary or even possible to move on and "forget" in order to heal; maybe it is more important to remember, forgive, and let go. Many of the birthmothers in these texts say, "You never forget," and I agree with them. Perhaps part of the "enduring pain" stems from the pressure to forget or the perceived shame associated with choosing to live with, or even embrace, the memories. Frankly, the five days I spent with Dave after his birth are *treasured* memories.

Both Bloch Jones and Fessler speak of the overwhelming number of birthmothers who regret their decisions to "relinquish" their babies. Bloch Jones describes the birthmothers' reactions to relinquishment in terms of depression, anger, fears, flashbacks, phobias, post-traumatic stress syndrome, sleeplessness, and nightmares. Because the emotional problems of birthmothers have "recurred so often and with such commonality" (272), she coined the term "Birthmother Syndrome," for which she describes eight specific symptoms. This is problematic because it pathologizes birthmothers and labels their response to a very challenging and difficult circumstance as an illness. I also strongly suspect that, aside from myself, there is a set of silent birthmothers to whom this condition does not apply. Not one descriptor of Birthmother Syndrome relates to my experience or my emotional state since I placed Dave for adoption.

Being a pregnant teen and making the choices associated with that circumstance was a very painful experience, but it does not forever define who I am and how I feel about my past, present, and future. However, my ability to "move forward" or "carry on" somehow casts an additional layer of doubt upon this act of mothering. I feel shamed once again for continuing my life, post-pregnancy, without anguish and regret. Because I did not experience the *appropriate* amount of shame and blame for being a birth mother, I feel twice shamed.

MOTHERS WHO ADOPT

Like birthmothers, perceptions of mothers who experience infertility and who adopt have shifted over the years. Certainly, these mothers are less hidden or silenced in society; however I (Kerri) believe there are still many problems that need to be addressed. In her 2006 book, Fessler, herself a child who was adopted, states that "by the time [my mother] and my father turned to adoption there was no public stigma attached to those who chose to adopt" (1). My experiences, which are woven with learned shame, challenge this assumption:

> I have come to understand in a palpable, embodied way the powerful constructions of the physical carrying and birthing of a biological child as the "ideal" path to becoming a mother—the right way, the good way, the first choice. Adoption, in contrast, is often viewed as some ineffable and inadequate back up plan. (Kearney and Bailey 153)

Falling short of the ideal and "right way" of becoming a mother may incite feelings of shame or, as in my case, shame may surface when women do not "grieve" appropriately for failing in this regard. In this sense, I was twice shamed—both by the original circumstance and by my reaction to it.

To further complicate matters for mothers like me, we as a society have not yet learned to accept the fertile woman who considers adoption her *first* choice. I include myself in this group. Infertility and divorce raised the circumstances under which I became attuned to other options for building a family, including adoption. From that set of options, adoption was my *first and continuing choice*, even when having a biological child continued to be an option for me when I remarried. That adoption is a second, lesser choice is a dominant theme in contemporary publications (see Tsigdinos; Fessler). There remains a sense that women who choose to adopt should be objects of sympathy, as should the children they mother. In contrast, I want to feel like and be perceived as a "real" mother, because there is unwelcome and unwanted shame associated with being something less than real. However, I find that my greatest resistance to the idea that a mother who adopts is not a real mother surfaces because of an instinctive *mother*-defense of my children. Today, I mother two children who arrived via adoption and one who (surprise) arrived because I did not actively prevent pregnancy. With full acknowledgement and gratitude to their father and their birthparents, all three are wholly my "real" children, and I am completely committed to them, regardless of societal beliefs and expectations. And yet I sense imposed shame lurking just beyond the joyful edges of our lives. I vehemently reject it. It is a battle I have learned to fight.

In 2010, Andrea O'Reilly took a position on the linguistics surrounding adoption. She argued that "the use of the phrase adoptive mother, with its implications that this mother is a sub-stitute mother, has also faded. Socially, culturally, and legally sanctioned, mothers who adopt reject the qualifying connotations of the adjective adoptive" (129). I agree that most mothers who adopt do, indeed, often reject the phrase *adoptive mother*, and I wholeheartedly agree with O'Reilly that the linguistics we use to talk about adoption, or any other topic, are significant in creating meaning. The preferred linguistics around any topic reflects the beliefs and perceptions of the time, in this case a social shaming of being "less than." However, O'Reilly's statement about the fading use of the phrase *adoptive mother* in day-to-day society is, in my experience, well ahead of its time. Many people I am in contact with (representing a variety of parenting paths) still struggle with the terms *real mother* and *natural mother*; as such, they largely do not consider whether *adoptive mother* is an ap-propriate term to use. In some circumstances, I still catch myself occasionally using the term *adoptive mother* while some part of my brain frantically searches for a better phrase. *Adoptive mother* is a term that remains very much in use and, because it linguistically subjugates and shames the mother into someone who has adapted to a lesser status, it influences societal beliefs and expectations. Thus, it is important to continually point out that adoption refers to a legal process that occurs in a limited time and space and binds together a family, much like marriage does. It is not, and should not, be an ongoing label that forever defines a mother's relationship with her child.

I greatly anticipated joining the motherhood club and, in doing so, I have discovered a subgroup of the "social mothering" set. What seems to most tightly bind together these particular women is the imposition of "other"—other than real, other than normal, other than natural. It is a circling of the wagons—a shared defensive of our "other" status, an attempt to reject the societal shaming process—all while we continue with the traditional, critical, and loving tasks of mothering.

CONCLUDING THOUGHTS:
SHARING "OTHER MOTHER" EXPERIENCES

It is very rare in adoption research or popular literature for a birthmother and a mother who adopted to occupy shared mothering space. And yet both birth mothers and mothers by adoption "face a deeply-inscribed ideology of motherhood that defines their experiences and choices as lesser, as somehow frayed around the edges" (Kearney and Bailey 161). Indeed, we discovered that what is also shared in our experiences is feeling *twice shamed*—not getting it "right" the first time and not reacting with the appropriate grief to our failures. In other words, we were *taught* to feel shame, and not just because of the initial *event* (getting pregnant, not getting pregnant, choosing adoption). Rather, shame was a *learned* reaction that eventually trumped our internal beliefs that we were simply okay. In each of our separate positions, it was *not* acceptable to be okay, so our authentic feelings became secrets that we felt obligated to hide. Secrets of mothering are often related to the violation of some broadly accepted social or moral code relevant to a mother's culture, religion, or personal value system, and they are often shame-based (Estés 375). I (Lee) believe it is shame that perpetuates our secrets of mothering. Our inability to voice how we really feel in our life circumstances is related, to some degree, to self-deception and subconscious denial of feeling okay and, dare I say, even happy or content about our choices as mothers. So, as a birthmother and mother by adoption, we share elements of the "other" mothering journey, such as feeling twice shamed.

The experience of feeling twice shamed is likely not limited to birthmothers, women who have experienced infertility, and mothers who adopt. These are simply the stories we can share from our own experiences, situated within a specific set of circumstances, time, and space. However, one of the challenges of providing voice to traditionally silenced groups is the danger that others will hear it as *the* story, the *real* truth, and the uncovered truth for this group of women. In reality, our stories, or others' stories, may represent the majority (or not), but none of our stories can account for the experiences of all women, even those who have walked a similar path. There are also unexpected consequences in drawing conclusions for any group of mothers. For example, the presentation of (all) birthmothers living with never-ending grief and pain provides yet another source of potential blame and shame for mothers who adopt (see Kearney and Bailey). So for every additional perspective we uncover and tell, we risk further silencing others, as well as uncovering a new source of shame for other mothers. We acknowledge these unintended possibilities within our own work.

This should remind us to proceed with caution. We are all inextricably intertwined, regardless of where the current wisdom of society may place us on the hierarchy of mothering—good or bad, natural or unnatural, real or imposter. We choose whether our voices, in this time and place, carry forward traditional, limiting prescriptions of mothering that shame and blame those who are different or release those binds to embrace our goals as mothers. It is our hope that our work contributes to widening the discourse in a way that affirms the vitality and sanctity of diverse mothering experiences.

ENDNOTES

[1]For a more balanced presentation of the myriad reasons parents adopt, see O'Toole; Johnston.

WORKS CITED

Bloch Jones, Merry. *Birthmothers: Women Who Have Relinquished Babies for Adoption Tell Their Stories*. Chicago: Chicago Review, 2000. Print.

Cushman, Linda F., Debra Kalmuss, and Pearila B. Namerow. "Placing an Infant for Adoption: The Experiences of Young

Birthmothers." *Social Work* 38.3 (1993): 264-72. Print.

DeSimone, Michael. *Unresolved Grief in Women Who Have Relinquished a Baby for Adoption*. Diss. New York University, 1994. Print.

Estés, Clarissa Pinkola. *Women Who Run with the Wolves: Myths and Stories of the Wild Woman Archetype*. Toronto: Random, 1992. Print.

Fessler, Ann. *The Girls Who Went Away: The Hidden History of Women Who Surrendered Children for Adoption in the Decades before Roe v. Wade*. London: Penguin, 2006. Print.

Ge, Xiaojia, Misaki N. Natsuaki, David M. Martine, Leslie D. Leve, Jenae M. Neiderhiser, Daniel S. Shaw, Georgette Villareal, Laura Scaramella, John B. Reid, and David Reiss. "Bridging the Divide: Openness in Adoption and Postadoption Psychosocial Adjustment among Birth and Adoptive Parents." *Journal of Family Psychology* 22.3 (2008): 529-40. Print.

Harris, Francesca and Noel Whyte. "Support for Birthmothers in a Group Setting." *Adoption & Fostering* 23.4 (1999): 41-8. Print. [not cited in text]

Janus, Nancy G. "Adoption Counseling as a Professional Specialty Area for Counselors." *Journal of Counseling and Development* 75.4 (1997): 266-74. Print.

Johnston, Patricia Irwin. *Adoption Is a Family Affair: What Relatives and Friends Must Know*. 2nd ed. London: Jessica Kingsley, 2012. Print.

Kearney, Kerri S. and Lucy E. Bailey. "An Adoptive Mother's Reflections on Mothering and Grief: Another Voice from Inside the Adoption Triad." *Journal of the Motherhood Initiative for Research and Community Involvement* 1.2 (2010): 150-164. Print.

Lane, Aprill Fasino. *Infertility Inferschmility*. Los Angeles: Fountain Blue, 2013. Print.

Lauderdale, Jana L. "The Unbroken Cord: The Experience of Infant Relinquishment through Adoption." Diss. University of Utah, 1992. Print.

Miller, Brent C. and Diana D. Coyl. "Adolescent Pregnancy and Childbearing in Relation to Infant Adoption in the U.S." *Adoption Quarterly* 4 (2000): 3-25. Print.

Murray, B. Lee. "An Epilogue of an Autoethnography." *Mothers and the Economy: The Economics of Mothering Conference of the Motherhood Initiative for Research and Community Involvement.* Ryerson University, Toronto, 21-23 Oct 2010. Presentation.

Murray, B. Lee. "Secrets of an 'Illegitimate Mom.'" *Journal of the Motherhood Initiative* 1.2 (2010): 137-47. Print.

Nakano Glenn, Evelyn. "Social Constructions of Mothering: A Thematic Overview." *Mothering: Ideology, Experience and Agency.* Ed. Evelyn Nakano Glenn, Grace Change, and Linda Rennie Forcey. New York: Routledge, 1994. 1-29. Print. [not cited in text]

O'Reilly, Andrea, ed. *Encyclopedia of Motherhood.* Thousand Oaks, CA: Sage, 2010. Print.

O'Toole, Elizabeth. *In on It: What Adoptive Parents Would Like You to Know about Adoption. A Guide for Relatives and Friends.* St. Paul, MN: Fig Press, 2011. Print.

Pietsch, Nicole. "Un/titled: Constructions of Illegitimate Motherhood as Gender Insurrection." *Mother Matters: Motherhood as Discourse and Practice.* Ed. Andrea O'Reilly. Toronto: Association for Research on Mothering, 2004. 65-78. Print.

Rosenberg, Karen F. and Victor Groze. "The Impact of Secrecy and Denial in Adoption: Practice and Treatment Issues." *Families in Society* 78 (1997): 522-9. Print.

Schaefer, Carol. *The Other Mother: A Woman's Love for the Child She Gave Up for Adoption.* New York: Soho Press, 1991. Print.

Scully, Anne-Marie. *Motherhoodwinked—An Infertility Memoir.* Charleston, SC: CreateSpace Independent Publishing Platform, 2014. Print.

Sixsmith, Martin. *Lost Child of Philomena Lee: The Heartbreaking Story of a Mother and the Son She Had to Give Away.* London: Macmillan, 2009. Print.

Sokol, Roy. *Infertility and Adoption: A Husband and Father's Perspective.* Pittsburgh: RoseDog Books, 2012. Print.

Solinger, Rickie. *Wake Up Little Suzie.* New York: Routledge, 1992. Print.

Tsigdinos, Pamela Mahoney. *Silent Sorority: A (Barren) Woman Gets Busy, Angry, Lost and Found.* Seattle: BookSurge Publishing, 2011. Print.

Waits, Kristine Ireland. *Every Drunken Cheerleader: Why Not Me? Wit, Wisdom, and Warmth from Your Fertility Challenged Friend*. Star, ID: Endurance, 2010. Print.

14.
What My Buddhist Son Taught Me About Blame

ROSIE ROSENZWEIG

W HEN I BEGAN WRITING this piece, I had resolved to keep in full view the sad-faced sculpture created by my son when he was a teenager, because I did not want to forget the price my family paid for my internalized mother-blame. I have since placed it in the window to ensure it is clearly illuminated by each morning sun (see Figure 1). I also hope that the insights I record in this essay, which I have avoided writing for so long, will be equally clear. This chapter describes how I learned to effectively cope with blame through Buddhist practices, as well as how I applied these practices in navigating my personal relationships with my son and my own mother. Writing this piece, so many years after the deaths of my parents, brother, and sister described here, has allowed for some healing to take place.

Perhaps my earliest cognizance of mother-blame occurred with my sister's death in 1968. She died of complications from nephritis, a kidney disease that I also contracted after childbirth. At this time, doctors could select patients that would benefit most from the newly crafted experimental dialysis protocol, and I believed that the heads of corporations took precedence over a depressed and toothless 45-year-old woman of teenage twins who talked to her mother numerous times a day in Yiddish. Due to socioeconomic factors, language barriers, and a history of family trauma stemming from the Holocaust, neither my mother nor my sister could access the necessary healthcare to diagnose and treat nephritis during the 1940s and 1950s.

Figure 1.

Even so, I remember blaming my mother for my sister's death; she did not trust doctors and instead resorted to folk remedies to treat instances of illness and injury. This distrust was seemingly passed on to my sister, with whom my mother had fostered an intense relationship. They talked on the phone daily and my mother was seemingly so influential that when she had all her teeth pulled, my sister did the same. This was a relationship that I clearly wanted to avoid, despite my mother's constant demands to communicate more often. My stomach would seize up when I called her each

Sunday and listened to her troubles, all the while feeling powerless to effect any change.

Less than two years after my sister's death, I again blamed my mother when my brother died in his mid-forties after years of neglecting his diabetes. He followed the same pattern of physical neglect that my mother had followed all of her life and allowed no time to even care for a troublesome toothache. He was like the Type A protagonist in the novel *What Makes Sammy Run*, driven to succeed at all costs. Following my sister's death, my mother called my brother's accounting office several times a day and demanded to speak with him while he was meeting with clients. In order to distance himself, he took a vacation to get away but somehow became so distracted by his worries that he sustained third degree burns during a shower. This led to a leg amputation and ultimately to his death. I learned about his death when my mother called and wailed wordlessly in my ear; I was pregnant with my third child at the time.

I believed that my brother's death caused my father to die of a broken heart at age seventy-one. In his male-centered world, his son was the ultimate hope of future progress, and he also supplemented my parents' meager government pension to help support them. My baby daughter was three months old when my father died. As they lowered his coffin into the ground I could not withhold a wail similar to the sounds my mother emitted during that first phone call following my brother's death. With my sister, brother, and father gone, I was now a lone child in the world with my poor grieving mother, who never quite adjusted to life in the "new world" after many members of her Polish family were murdered in Auschwitz. My premature death thus seemed fated; I remember dreaming about my brother's hand rising from his grave, beckoning me to join my family.

When my mother kissed me goodbye after this third family death in two and a half years, her arms winged out and held me so tightly that my sides ached from the crushing bond. I needed to carve out physical and emotional distance from her, as my brokenness was too fresh for any hope of repair. My older children were pre-teens at the time, and I do not believe I was a very attentive or emotionally available mother to them throughout these formative years.

Before these family deaths, I was always home at the end of my children's school day to hear the news of their lives, but this was no longer the case. Instead, I retreated into a dark compartment of my consciousness and became cross when anyone addressed me. The thought of speaking to my own mother created a pain in my solar plexus, causing me to seek solitude whenever I could. I did this by taking long car rides on country roads, secluding myself in whatever corner of the house I could find, and being generally unresponsive. At the time, I needed a panacea from the chaos; I needed extreme quiet to ward off the loud voices of my childhood and my family losses, which seemingly had the potential to bury me alive, both figuratively and in reality. This ultimately took years to abate.

THE HUMAN POTENTIAL MOVEMENT AND
MY MOTHER-BLAME STRUGGLE

One day when my youngest child was five, I became very angry when she massaged my shoulders and asked, "Don't you know, Mommy, that if you are nice to people, they will be nice back to you?" In my mind, this served as irrefutable evidence that I was the "bad mom." I felt that I was perpetuating the legacy of my own "bad mother" who taught me to react to any setback with anger and various extreme emotions. I blamed my mother and myself in equal measure; I compared both of us to the "Perfect Mother" I had created in my mind—some ideally formed Greek goddess—and found us both wanting. I even acquired a metal sculpture depicting a slim mother doting on her children and displayed it where I could see it daily.

However, instead of providing a panacea like this Greek goddess, I frequented a series of therapeutic sessions with what I call the "professional help team." My psychotherapist husband, determined to help me, discovered an experimental approach in the Human Potential Movement, which drew from Abraham Maslow's theory that self-actualization was achievable for everyone. George Leonard, a *Look* magazine editor, indicated that most folks only use ten percent of their brain capacity, and he accordingly teamed up with Michael Murphy to run encounter groups in California to fully foster their patients' innate abilities, creativity, and happiness. Soon enough, my husband and I were off to the Esalen Institute in Big Sur California, where we were encouraged to "get it all out."[1] The "it" in this case refers to any feelings one may be repressing, including anger and blame. The technique for "getting out" was a padded baseball bat called a bataka, which we struck repeatedly against a very large pillow. Psychodrama was the technique of the hour and we applied it in numerous ways, including engaging in dialogue with an empty chair impersonating someone who had wronged us and then answering back in the voice of the perpetrator. Fritz Perls, the father of Gestalt Therapy[2] and resident guru, called this methodology "the hot seat." During one of his numerous workshops, he would invite attendees to come and sit in this hot seat and work through various pressing psychological issues in front of an audience of thirty or more participants. Afterward, my troubles seemed to multiply so that I became increasingly disassociated from my children's needs and always obsessed with my own thoughts, as illustrated in the photograph in Figure 2.

My husband, in contrast, learned the new therapies so well that he returned to become a rather popular therapist in Boston. He frequently lectured to large audiences and it became impossible to simply enter a movie theatre without students rushing up for a moment of conversation. He even organized the Boston Gestalt Therapy Training Group with popular psychologists Erving and Miriam Polster. These were heady times indeed, and they made us believe that we were pursuing the Holy Grail of insight as a much-needed improvement over conventional therapies. Eventually, I also became a trained counsellor in this dramatic methodology, and I designed and led weekend encounter groups at various country locales with singles and couples.[3] However, these fifteen minutes of fame only reinforced the anger and blame still stirring within.

Eventually, I could not take it anymore and finally saw a gentle psychiatrist who encouraged me to work fulltime in my own field. Up until that point, with my homebound immigrant mom as a role model, I thought myself incapable of simultaneously working fulltime, maintaining a marriage, and raising three children.

Figure 2.

Unfortunately, my mother did not have the opportunities to break the economic, health, and cultural barriers that constrained her; otherwise, I believe that her indomitable spirit would have propelled her to a more fulfilling life. In any event, my psychiatrist assured me that I could achieve such a life, and my pursuit of it led me to take a position in an educational collaborative as a librarian, communication specialist, and journalist. During this time, I assembled an eight-page tabloid single-handedly from scratch, including the writing, the production chores, and distribution.

Despite my success and the invaluable support of my psychiatrist, during this time I still internalized the conventional psychological approaches that were inspired by Freud's phallocentric theories.

Such approaches blame mothers for every seeming imperfection in their children's lives; for instance, Freud's "penis envy" postulates that young girls blame and resent their mothers for their lack of penis.[4] Indeed, the father of mother-blame reflected the attitudes of his time, including an opposition to women's emancipation. Blame is, after all, an attempt to feel superior in the face of threatening events, and women's equality was certainly threatening to the early-twentieth-century founders of psychoanalysis. While these beliefs are no longer mainstream, the legacy of mother-blame continues to pervade the psychoanalytic offices of psychiatrists and other therapists.

JUDAISM, BUDDHISM AND MY HEALING JOURNEY

Here I was caught in the warp of an influential Weltanschauung, or worldview, even though going to work fulltime had mitigated some of my insecurities. My next job involved working in the corporate world, and when I was laid off a decade later, I became a Hebrew School teacher. Returning to my religious roots in my studies and regularly attending synagogue provided additional healing, and I took my Judaism quite seriously. Attending weekly services and becoming immersed in the cycle of holidays gave me a supportive community that was essential to my wellbeing. I also attended classes about the weekly Bible portion and its cycle and joined a group called Chavurah, or holy fellowship, whose members supported each other's struggles and accomplishments. I wrote a weekly essay before leaving the synagogue after each class, wherein I recorded the progress of my insights and the stages of my healing. I didn't think I could survive without my religious community, which proved to be one of the pillars of my return to myself. As a result, I became extremely threatened by any other religious path that emerged in my family.

Meanwhile, my thirty-year-old son, Ben, had been living in Nepal and he had found similar healing and release in Buddhist teachings. He eventually returned to the U.S. to pursue a three-year silent retreat at a Buddhist monastery in Wappinger Falls, New York, in the hopes of becoming a monk. Buddhism is still considered a misleading tradition of idol-worship by very religious Jews. In spite of my husband's many attempts to explain the importance of our son following his own spiritual path, I once again fell into the mother-blame trap and convinced myself that I hadn't properly taught him the values and importance of Judaism. I might have been a Jewish teacher for other folks' children but I had obviously failed miserably in my own home, and I believed that my years of depressive grieving had driven my children far from me.

My mother had also just died at the age of ninety, six months after a stroke that rendered her comatose. The loss was quite painful. During the thirteen years before her death, I had resolved to care for her in her widowhood and the experience empowered me as a caregiver. I grieved her death, but I didn't sink into the dark pit I encountered years before with the deaths of my father and siblings. On the heels of all this, my son introduced me to Lama Norlha, the abbot who would be his taskmaster during his three-year training retreat. The Buddhists, many of whom were former Jews now establishing Buddhist centers, were taking over the Catskill Mountains, which had been former vacation sites for many in New York's Jewish community. It was an interesting adventure to visit my son and meet his teachers and friends from Nepal, but I never really took it seriously until his initial training period was over. I regularly sent him loaves of banana bread—one for the head Lama, one for the women's retreat, and one for the men's retreat. At least by feeding my son I could feel like I had not completely failed him, but I still worried about my role in turning him away from Judaism. My failure hit me hard when I was invited to his "graduation" from the three-year retreat of being "off the grid," growing his own food and chopping wood—not to mention sleeping sitting up! It hit me that I had really failed to teach my son the religion of his ancestors, which had helped repair me after my own brokenness.

Interestingly, however, this time it was my son who took to repairing me. Neither the Human Potential Movement nor my decade of psychiatric treatment effected such a radical change in me. This phase of my development did not come easily. When my son initially began his period of seclusion, I remember praying that he would not forget the Jewish lineage that supported and defined me. Now that he was emerging from his three-year retreat,

I feared that he would be lost to Judaism—and to me—forever. I vividly recall the Friday I spent in Wappinger Falls accompanied by my daughters and my grandchildren, all of whom had become more observant in their Judaism. I remember hearing the chanting puja-drone prayer as we waited on a hillside overlooking the Hudson River. The sounds rolling out of the back woods snapped us all to alertness as we heard the flat bleating of long, thin horns and the slow palm-slap of drums. My son, now thirty-three years old and newly named Karma Sherab Gyurmey (meaning Eternal Wisdom), was walking slowly between three monks, followed by six nuns, and with Lama Norlha leading the parade. Each of the ten retreatants wore maroon robes and a tall, triangular red hat with a gold trim on top. We followed them into the main house, parked our shoes, and silently shuffled into a room dominated by hundreds of statues of Buddha, which, for observant Jews, epitomized the sin of idol-worship. Afterward, our family went to the larger neighbouring monastery in Woodstock for another reception and ceremony. The main meditation hall boasted thirty-foot ceilings, a twenty-foot golden Buddha, and a huge staircase where the resident teacher sat. Here women who were older than I was continually bowed down to me because I was now the mother of a guru. Not in my wildest dreams did I ever think I would enter the land of idols with such grandeur.

Little did I know that my son had been planning an intervention during his retreat to help me let go of my harmful mother-blaming beliefs and practices. During the trip back to Boston, Ben spoke seriously about returning to his beloved Nepal with me accompanying him. He realized that he could not continue being a Buddhist if it caused his mother so much distress. The itinerary had already been planned: we would go through France for a meditation retreat with Thich Nhat Hanh, the Vietnamese Zen teacher whose books and tapes Ben kept sending me. He thought that this teacher's gentle approach would be a healthy introduction to Buddhism for me. His desires to spend time with me and help me through my emotional struggle were comforting and seemed to suggest that I was not such a "bad mom" after all. This and my thirst for exploration made me leap at the opportunity to travel half way around the world with him.

MY MEETINGS WITH BUDDHIST TEACHERS

We began our travels in Plum Village, a hermitage with hundreds of plum trees nestled in the wine suburbs of France, which also provided the home base for the Zen teacher. My initial greeting came from a monk dressed in grey robes; upon learning that I was Ben's mother, he immediately picked a pamphlet depicting the image of a rose, smiled, and gave it to me. "For Ben's mother," he exclaimed with enthusiasm. I speedily read A Rose for Your Pocket and learned that Thây, as he was called, had developed a ceremony for the U.S. holiday of Mother's Day, after he learned about it. His Buddhism had taught him to honour me and help me along my own spiritual path, whatever it may be. Thây also explained how every element, event, and feeling is intertwined in what he calls "Interbeing," thus demonstrating how cause and effect "co-arise" and that "everything is a result of multiple causes and conditions."

At this point, something fundamentally shifted within me. It continued during my first meeting with the teacher himself, which had been carefully arranged by my son, since not everyone could gain a private audience with such an esteemed teacher. I entered that meeting literally and figuratively full of baggage, including my backpack, my camera, my notebook, and a tape recorder. Chattering away in the beginning, I was so nervous that I did not realize we were participating in a Zen Buddhist tea ceremony. I continued in this manner until Ben began explaining to the teacher the reason for my discomfort: "You see, one of the early Jewish ancestors was Abraham, who was the son of an idol-maker. One day he destroyed all but one of the idols in his father's shop. When his father came home and asked who did this, Abraham pointed to the last intact idol and said that this idol did it. 'How could that be?' asked Abraham's father. 'He is only an image.' 'Then why do you worship him?' answered Abraham. Since then, because of Abraham, Jews don't bow down to images."

It surprised and pleased me that Ben knew the rabbinical commentary on this point and that he understood me so well. "Yes," Thây said, "people have false expectations that people should behave in a certain way, that children should be a certain way."

264

His voice trailed off as Ben put his finger on my calf, very gently yet very significantly. This was not like the usual rabbinical commentary on the subject. Thây's conclusions awoke me like a Koan-midrash! He had addressed the larger, unspoken issue of making our children follow our own image. I did not expect this turn of meaning on myself. The elemental technique of Buddhism was to let go of attachments to a rigid set of ideas and beliefs. So this is what a Zen insight felt like!

Quiet returned to the room. Caught again by Thây's gaze, I was stilled by his dark brown eyes. His presence was as delicate as a feather floating on a breath in midair, but he was grounded in his lotus posture, holding his hands together in a gesture that resembled a flower. As the time ripened for me to speak, I became even more nervous. I chattered endlessly, describing my night dreams in Plum Village. He listened deeply but made no sound. Mesmerized by his gaze, I was the last to notice that tea had been poured for us, just as I was the last to notice that Thây had already lifted his cup to the palm of the other hand, which served as a saucer. The others had followed their teacher's example and each had raised his or her own cup of tea as they watched me. I looked at my full cup on the table and wondered if I had committed another rudeness in the presence of this venerable teacher. Somehow in this moment the Zen master would teach me how to breathe and how to observe Thây breathing. I would learn how to pause, how to rest in the present moment in silence, and, ultimately, how to meditate. I finally stopped talking and the silence of Thây's hermitage finally began to settle in me for the duration of my long visit to Plum Village.

MY TRIP TO NEPAL

My next meeting with a Buddhist teacher actually took place on a Nepalese mountaintop far above Kathmandu at Nagi Gompa, the monastery of the famed Buddhist Tulku Urgyen Rinpoche. Rinpoche is a bestowed title hierarchically below the Dalai Lama and above the Lama status of Lama Norlha. My son had technically earned the title of Lama because of his three-year retreat, which was a promotion from being a mere monk. Thus he could use his influence to request a meeting with Tulku Urgyen Rinpoche, who was a veteran of numerous such retreats to elevate consciousness. We were let off by the taxi from Kathmandu at the end of a road in the middle of a mountain, with a path leading to an even more elevated peak. There wasn't a building in sight. I stumbled along behind my son, who went from rock to rock like a mountain goat while carrying our backpacks. Seasoned hikers kept passing me on the path. I climbed slowly, knowing that a meeting was subject to the state of the Rinpoche's health as well as his schedule. Physically, mentally, and spiritually, my awareness became glazed as I caught up with Ben, who was deeply involved in a conversation with one of the Rinpoche's attendants. After climbing the numerous stairs to the entrance, we were told that Ben's urgency had won us an audience.

We were then escorted into a small room and found the teacher in maroon robes and a wool hat, leaning against a pillow on an elevated bed. Bowing down, Ben presented him with gifts, including orange juice, which was rare in such hemispheres. The Rinpoche blessed me with a silk scarf around my neck and, after assuming a full lotus position, began what Buddhists call a transmission. He taught me for almost two hours about the Buddhist nature of mind or, as I heard it, the nature of the Divine. A calm enveloped us during this oral teaching and I was told not to repeat to anyone what I had heard or I would dissipate my blessings. Finally, he looked into my mind and asked me, "So, Ben's mother, now look inside. What do you see?" I described a self-perpetuating colourless motion that seemed like a clear mirror. I actually heard him say, "Lahhh sooo," with a sudden rise of inflection. The interpreter said that the Rinpoche felt that Ben's mother could see, but I was requested to look again. The Rinpoche wanted to know what it felt like. He smiled sweetly as he looked at me very deeply. After a long silence, I said, "It feels like home." It was a comfortable and warm place in my mind with no anxiety, threat, or fear. We all shared a lovely silence after what I later learned was the Rinpoche's way of teaching from "personal experience."

Finally, my son asked for personal help with my meditation, which uses breathing as support, and the Rinpoche described numerous ways to experience the unoccupied mind. Eventually we turned to converse about his health and his surgeries and I noticed how aged and frail he looked. I hoped to take these moments with me forever. When I learned some months later that the Rinpoche had passed away, I felt that he still remained an anchor in my meditation and studies ahead, for he had imparted what was called in the Tibetan tradition Pointed Teachings for an Old Woman, which was the preliminary lesson in Buddhist mind training. I would pursue a varied curriculum of study to understand what the Rinpoche called "the original Buddha-mind, which is empty." It took years to digest this through a course of meditation retreats and the study of what can be called Buddhist psychology.

BUDDHIST PSYCHOLOGY AND MOTHER-BLAME MIND HABITS

Buddhist psychology, as taught by Andrew Olendzki, director of the Barre Center for Buddhist Studies in western Massachusetts, was the next stop in my path. When I returned to my Boston suburb, my husband diagnosed me as having quieted the turmoil of my mind, and I was determined to deepen this experience. I was propelled to Barre to continue in Buddhist Psychology. What ensued were many years of bi-annual retreats there, and each time I attended a meditation retreat I would experience further changes, which ranged from mild to extreme. What follows is my own understanding of Buddhist psychology.

Buddhism is based in ethics and letting go of defilements and attachments. This ethical life is grounded in compassion, the mother of all axial religions, which naturally arises from meditation, according to the Dalai Lama. There are obstacles and hindrances that arise in the mind and distort perception. Negative emotions, or kleshas, such as greed, hatred, and delusion, are considered to be poisons that cloud the mind. Skillful meditation can pacify these to make them bearable and eventually lay them to rest. Mindfulness meditation, sometimes called Insight Meditation or *Vipassyana*, can uncover the true nature of the kleshas so that they lose their power to distract the mind. Letting go is the common term for the technique, which is to note the presence of the negativity, or for that matter the presence of any emotion and thought, and then to let them pass by. The Law of Karma, which translates to mean "action," describes how unknown and known causes and conditions bear fruit in future events, causes and conditions. The root cause of anything is basically unknown because of the multitude of factors that can be allowed. Therefore blame and guilt do not exist in Buddhist psychology.[5]

The use of meditation to encourage peaceful thoughts does not focus on the same issues that Western therapy observes. Past experiences, or "stories" as Buddhists call them, are just that—stories. The goal of meditation is to loosen their power to neuroticize us. In past breakout groups, I have heard how retreatants try to allow their "stories" to pass by like mind traffic or movies so that they do not threaten one's wellbeing. Such practices have allowed me to re-interpret the many stories about mother-blame in my life that have coloured my guilt and to understand them as stories rather than truths. Over time I have learned to view their redaction like movies that are distant from my core but still arouse emotions that must be tempered and understood. The stories of my family's deaths were also released into a less hurtful place in my consciousness, and it took a long time to cultivate a healthier view of them. I remember telling a meditation teacher how the pain in my heart was somehow released and how I now viewed it with dispassion and equilibrium. He said that this release was the "beginning of putting it down."

In contrast, twentieth-century psychotherapy approaches mental states from the standpoint of pathology, as demonstrated by the use of the Diagnostic and Statistical Manual of Mental Disorders as "the standard classification of mental disorders used by mental health professionals in the United States" ("DSM"). Andrew Olendzki accordingly states, "One of the criticisms leveled at modern psychology is its tendency to focus on pathology rather than on health" (Olendzki 14). Buddhist psychology, on the other hand, builds on the framework of moral conduct. Olendzki elaborates on Buddhism's "wholesome ethical context," explaining that "it soon becomes apparent that one's ability to see clearly is directly affected by the moral tenor of the mind" (16). Certain states of mind that blur judgment and action are thereby called Kleshas, or poisons. Anger, whose milder cousin is blame, is one such poison. In this way, various forms of anger throughout the years had weighed me down; my depression from deep grieving was anger turned inward and my guilt was a form of self-hatred.

In my numerous retreats with Thich Nath Hahn, I became fond of his remedy in the practice of mindfulness, as well as his use of a mothering metaphor to help envision a solution:

> Holding the baby mindfully, the mother quickly discovers the cause of his suffering. Then it is very easy for her to correct the situation. If the baby has a fever, then she will give him medicine to help the fever go down. If he is hungry, she will feed him warm milk. If the diaper is too tight, she will loosen it.
>
> As practitioners, we do exactly like this. We hold our baby of anger in mindfulness so that we get relief. We continue the practice of mindful breathing and mindful walking, as a lullaby for our anger. The energy of mindfulness penetrates into the energy of anger, exactly like the energy of the mother penetrates into the energy of the baby. There's no difference at all. If you know how to practice mindful breathing, smiling, and walking meditation, it is certain that you will find relief. (*Anger* 34)

The Buddhist practice of cultivating opposites is here exemplified with compassionate meditation, which cools the flames of poisonous anger. Simply put, it is an arduous task to counter such an extreme emotion with a virtuous emotion, and I found this meditative exercise nearly impossible in the beginnings of my practice. During this time I was grateful to meet the Buddhist nun Thubten Chodron for yet another approach. Originally I had pursued an interview with her because I wanted to understand why she became a nun after being born into a Jewish family (see Thubten Chodron, "Jewish Roots"). In the process of our interview we discussed her new book on anger, and I came to understand more about this poison or hindrance to a moral life. She writes:

> While anger is fueled by inappropriate attention exaggerating or projecting negative qualities, attachment is fueled by inappropriate attention exaggerating or projecting positive

Figure 3.

qualities. Attachment is often among the factors giving rise to anger, for the more attached we are to something or someone, the angrier we are when we are denied that. (Thubten, *Chodron Working* 48)

The role of meditation is to cultivate patience, which is a great source of strength during difficult times. This cannot all be achieved overnight, which is why meditation is considered a practice that prepares us for real life situations that can otherwise throw us off course. Thubten Chodron describes how meditation can re-frame our attitudes and recommends "practicing patience in a tranquil environment, not a conflict situation" (Working 53). Remembering the situation that causes the anger with a new perspective can decrease the feelings and provide an opportunity to practice alternative responses. I found her suggestions to be powerfully mind-changing.

For instance, the realization that emotions have a beginning, middle, and end allowed me to become less paralyzed in the

Figure 4.

hopelessness of a "no-exit" approach to trauma. Moreover, I realized that I could bear the feelings because there was an end to them in sight. It was now clear that the Human Potential Movement's practice of hitting a pillow with a bataka multiplies and increases the anger, thereby creating a roadblock to clearing the mind. In fact, the bataka may only reinforce and encourage more anger, rather than allow it to dissipate. The basic Buddhist doctrine of Annica, meaning that all things are impermanent, can help to realize that even trauma has to change and that we can change ourselves in the natural order of life.

FINAL THOUGHTS

In learning all of this, my original mother-blame mind habits, as they are called in Buddhist psychology, changed as well. They had sometimes been multiplied by the prevalent therapies of the '70s and '80s, as well as by the entire structure of U.S. psychotherapy, which is based on the DSM. Now, as a result of these alternative therapeutic approaches, I believe there is a change happening in the way I view my mother, as well as myself. Thây emphasized the need to understand the suffering that mothers endure, in addition to the work that mothers do to nurture their offspring. Compassion is truly a better underpinning to life than blame, be it a projection or a self-infliction. Compassion for one's self is the hardest to appreciate.

I hope to further develop this practice through continuous study (see the statue of the Buddha I keep in my study in Figure 4) with the meditation group that meets in my home, with daily effort, and through the meditation retreats that I attend. Recently, I have reached a state of gratitude for having survived such troubling years with fairly good health and a family that actually laughs together. All three of my children are doing well in their professions and all four grandsons are succeeding in school and life. I have also begun to think more sympathetically about my mother, who was herself a lonely survivor of a murdered family. My son, who recounts his grandmother's history of travelling across Europe and over the Atlantic Ocean in 1927 to reunite with my father in America, recently posted on Facebook a picture of her at my daughter's bat mitzvah in 1983, looking sad and lonely but enjoying the event. Voicing my newly cultivated appreciation, my younger daughter posted a fitting comment: "She survived such a hard life so we could have a better one. RIP Bubbe."

ENDNOTES

[1] For further reading see Rosenzweig, "Rebirth." This article details the various therapies and personalities that I experienced at the Esalen Institute.

[2] Perls, Hefferline and Goodman was one of the early classics that emphasized personal "here and now" experiences against a backdrop of all the influencing factors of one's life, ergo "The Gestalt" as opposed to compartmentalizing one's narrow experiences without context. Erving and Miriam Polster of the Cleveland Gestalt Therapy Institute ran an eighteen-month training in Boston; they emphasized contact with others and a phenomenological-based dialogue with the therapist.

[3] For further reading see Rosenzweig, "A Search." This article describes the insights about community and family that arose for me during the eighteen-month training program with the Cleveland Gestalt Institute.

[4] Sigmund Freud's 1908 paper "The Sexual Theories of Children" developed this theory more fully after hinting at it in his previous writings. See Freud.

[5] For further reading see Dalai Lama XIV. This includes quotes on

all aspects of Buddhism from his writings; most important is this one on the subject of guilt:

Guilt, according to some scholars, is something that can be overcome. It does not exist in Buddhist terminology. With the Buddha nature all negative things can be purified. Guilt is incompatible without thinking as you are part of an action but not fully responsible for it. You are just part of the contributing factor. However, in some cases one must repent, deliberately hold responsibility, have regret, and never commit the mistake again" (179).

WORKS CITED

Dalai Lama XIV. *The Path to Tranquility: Daily Wisdom by the Dalai Lama*. New York: Penguin, 1998.

"DSM." American Psychiatric Association. n.d. Web.

Freud, Sigmund. *Complete Psychological Works of Sigmund Freud*. Volume 9. London: Vintage Classics, 2001. 217-218. Print.

Lama Thubten Yeshe. *Becoming Your Own Therapist: An Introduction to the Buddhist Way of Thought*. Boston: Lama Yeshe Wisdom Archive, 1998. 10-15. Print.

Perls, Fritz, Ralph Hefferline and Paul Goodman. *Gestalt Therapy: Excitement and Growth in the Human Personality*. New York: Dell Publishing, 1951. Print.

Rosie Rosenzweig. "Rebirth at Esalen." *The Boston Herald* 15 Mar. 1970: 20-22, 44-47. Print.

Rosie Rosenzweig. "A Search for Community." *Voices: The Art and Science of Psychotherapy: A Journal of the American Academy of Psychotherapists* (1971-7): 18-21. Print.

Thich Nath Hanh. *A Rose for Your Pocket: An Appreciation of Motherhood* (Revised Edition). Berkeley: Parallax Press, 2008. Print.

Thich Nath Hanh. *Anger: Wisdom for Cooling the Flames*. New York: Riverhead Books, 2001. Print.

Thich Nath Hanh. *The Heart of the Buddha's Teaching: Transforming Suffering into Peace, Joy & Liberation: The Four Noble Truths, The Noble Eightfold Path & Other Basic Buddhist*

Teachings. Berkeley: Parallax Press, 1998. Print.

Thubten Chodron. "Jewish Roots, Buddhist Blossoms." *Thubten Chodron*. 11 Apr. 2005. Web.

Thubten Chodron. *Working With Anger*. New York: Snow Lion Publications, 2001. Print.

Olendzki, Andrew. *Unlimiting Mind: The Radically Experiential Psychology of Buddhism*. Boston: Shambhala Publications, 2010. Print.

15.
"Disabling" Motherhood in 1914 and 2014

Stories of Two Women

ALISON QUAGGIN HARKIN

I N 1998, I BECAME a mother for the third time. When I held my newborn son in the hospital delivery room, he was as beautiful, pink-faced, and warm as his older sister and brother had been. Looking at him, I felt our family was complete. As an experienced mom, I looked forward to enjoying more relaxed mothering than I'd had with my first child, and to some extent with my second. After worrying about and living through multiple infant and toddler developmental stages, ear infections, bumped heads during the learning-to-walk phase, and transitions to preschool and school, I figured I had finally learned enough to ignore so-called expert advice and accept my children's gifts and differences.

Reality proved to be much different from my expectations. During the first year of my son's life, he began to miss milestones—rolling over, sitting up, crawling, standing, taking a few tentative steps—and we entered the world of evaluations, interventions, and various types of therapy. A few years later, these were followed by special education, individualized education plans, and state-funded services such as respite care. The forms and procedures required for each of these, as well as the experience of being out in the community with my son, led to a general interest in disability history and a particular interest in the lives of North American mothers with cognitively disabled children—not only in the present but also in the early twentieth century, when eugenic beliefs and practices were believed to offer an objective "scientific" way to create a healthy, fit population. I sought to learn about the expectations that governed how these mothers cared for their children. How were these

275

women regarded in their communities? What supportive services, if any, were available to them? Ultimately, I wondered how these women's lives might be different from my own.

As I considered these questions and searched for answers, I began to imagine a specific early-twentieth-century mother with a cognitively disabled child—a woman much like myself, but living in a different time. I thought of her as Alice and, because I use narrative methods in most of my research, I decided to write about her.[1] I wove into a short story the information I found on eugenic beliefs and how these influenced the treatment of children and adults with cognitive disabilities. In particular, I focused on the mother-blame and self-blame that resulted when women had "damaged children," supposedly because of their own inherent lack of fitness or proper maternal practices during and after pregnancy. I also began to recognize that such blame did not disappear with the end of eugenics or mass institutionalization of those with intellectual disabilities during the late-nineteenth to mid-twentieth centuries. Blame is still doled out liberally to mothers whose children have cognitive disabilities, the assumption often being that these women failed to take advantage of appropriate prenatal advice or testing. As I continued to write about Alice's life, I considered not only the differences between us—because certainly the lives of people with cognitive disabilities and their families have changed for the better—but also the many points of similarity.

ALICE'S STORY, 1914

Perhaps I should start by addressing the differences between Alice's life and my own. These became evident through the process of writing her story. Alice was born in 1858 into a family of privilege: white, middle class, with a comfortable home in a pleasant town. In her youth, Alice was a good student and quite "bookish." Her parents indulged her enjoyment of reading and writing. After high school, she attended a ladies' college for a year before leaving to marry and devote herself to domestic duties. Although she had dreamed of becoming a teacher and sharing her love of learning, she was frequently told that a woman's greatest achievements were marriage and motherhood. By 1914, Alice has three children; the two older ones, a girl and a boy, are in their late teens and are considered "normal" and healthy in every way. William, the youngest, is not. He is sixteen years old but looks like a twelve-year-old. He has a small, thin body with large dark eyes and a delicate sweep of eyebrows. He is categorized as "feeble-minded," a term that designates all kinds of mental deficiencies. More specifically, if the 1910 terminology of the American Association for the Study of the Feeble-Minded is used, he might be called a "moron," someone considered to have a mental age of eight to twelve years (Trent 162). Others who are designated as feeble-minded may be categorized as "imbeciles," with a mental age of three to seven years, or "idiots," with a mental age of two years or less (162). These definitions have been developed by Dr. Henry Goddard, a prominent American psychologist and eugenicist who is an avid supporter of intelligence testing. Dr. Goddard uses a translated 1908 version of the Binet Intelligence Test to place children and adults into these tidy categories (157). Dr. Goddard is also the director of research at the New Jersey Vineland Training School, an institution and laboratory for studying and managing feeble-minded children and adolescents (156).

Alice knows a little about "educational" and residential institutions for the feeble-minded. She has heard, for instance, that they were founded on the assumption that residents needed to be segregated and controlled for their own good (Trent 109-110). She is also vaguely aware of the growing preoccupation with the creation of "ideal" babies and children. She's even heard of "better-baby" contests, in which infants are "scored" according to various statistical scales (Landsman 72).[2] The larger goal of these contests appears to be the production of children like those that are described in *Rosa Amorosa*, a 1901 epistolary novel by the Australian-born, independent, and educated "New Woman" writer George Egerton.[3] Alice recently borrowed the book from the local lending library. The librarian recommended it, explaining that it was the sort of thing educated ladies and mothers liked. Throughout the book, the narrator Rosa writes to the man she loves, sharing her experiences, observations, and philosophy of life. Alice still has the book—in fact, it's overdue—and one afternoon she notices it while she's dusting the living room bookcase.

Thumbing through the pages, she comes across the following passage, delivered by Rosa: "I never could see any merit in a quiver full of congenital semi-idiots. The man and woman who give one or two beautiful sound-limbed, healthy-souled children to the world are surely more praiseworthy" (104). Rosa even describes such a child in his mother's arms: "[He is] asleep, wrapped in a soft shawl; his lashes [make] a black circle above the exquisite damask bloom of his cheek" (106).

Alice feels a pang of guilt as she reads the text. She believes her own failure is the cause of her youngest child's "deficiency and defectiveness." For these are the terms used by the family's doctor, as well as by William's teachers, to describe him—as if they are truths that cannot be negotiated or disputed. She believes that the locus of the failure lies within her body and moral core—within her very self. She is troubled and wishes to learn more, and so she begins reading other works on heredity and feeble-mindedness. The friendly librarian at the local library suggests a 1912 book written by Dr. Goddard: *The Kallikak Family: A Study in the Heredity of Feeble-Mindedness.*

"It's very modern and scientific," the librarian says. "I've read it. I believe Dr. Goddard's work could help eliminate the problem of mental defectives and the crime they bring with them. Ignorant, immoral, or otherwise unfit women shouldn't become mothers. They're responsible for morons—the worst category of the feeble-minded because they're entirely lacking in moral instincts. I hope you find the book edifying." The librarian smiles and hands over the book. Alice holds it close to her chest, her face hot. She's glad she didn't bring William to the library.

At home, she locks herself in her bedroom and reads about the Kallikaks, a family with two branches. Alice knows that the name is a pseudonym. She learned a little Greek at the ladies' college and knows that *Kallos* means *good*, while *Kakos* means *bad*. The book focuses on Deborah, a resident of the institution where Dr. Goddard works. It seems that Deborah's great-great-great-grandfather, Martin, who fought in the Revolutionary War, fathered a son with a "nameless feeble-minded girl" who worked as a barmaid (Goddard 18, 33). This son was feeble-minded, too, and went on to have other children, as did his children, and so on down the generations of immoral, poor, "insane," and law-breaking descendants. Deborah descends from this side of the family (Trent 163-164). However, Deborah's ancestor Martin also went on to marry a respectable woman, and the children from this "good" side of the Kallikak family grew to become prosperous adults who were considered to be intelligent and morally upstanding (163-164).

Tears prick Alice's eyes. Her fears about her own deficiency as a mother are apparently proven by Goddard's lineage of fit and unfit motherhood—for evidently the mothers of Martin Kallikak's children are the ones primarily responsible for the damage to or success of subsequent generations of children. Alice can hardly bear to read Goddard's phlegmatic statements about the unseen threat of feeble-minded genes, which can be present in healthy and seemingly intelligent members of the population. Goddard describes a female descendant "who seemed to be a normal woman . . . [but] was always peculiar" (22). He adds that the defective progeny who are "morons," whom he sees as the most dangerous group of feeble-minded people because of their propensity to reproduce, should be prevented from doing so through eugenic sterilization (108). Another possibility is "segregation and colonization" (105) in institutions where they can be controlled and taught to do useful, if menial, work.

Closing the book, Alice glances out the open window at the pleasant back garden with its apple trees and summer flowers. William is sitting on a swing that hangs from a bough of the largest tree. She can hear him humming to himself. Pale pink peonies sway in the warm air as Alice wonders how she could have failed so badly at motherhood and why she still cannot identify in her son the morally degenerate "moron" whom Goddard has so clearly categorized. Her sadness and self-blame make the room seem desolate and airless. Alice moves to the window and opens it wider, resting her elbows on the sill as she breathes in the freshness of the garden. She stays there for five minutes, ten minutes, and then loses track of the time—or, rather, has the sense that time has become compressed. Her mind clears. Blame and sadness transform into what she realizes, much later, is a moment of grace, beauty, and even joy as she watches her son gaze peacefully up into the moving leaves of the apple tree.

Turning from the window, though, Alice catches sight of the book in her lap and is once again downcast and full of self-blame. Nevertheless, in one way she is fortunate. At least she cannot see into the future, which holds more heartache: in a year, she will be cajoled into doing the "best" thing for William, which means moving him from home and his special education classroom at the local public school to an institution modelled on Vineland. She will be discouraged from visiting by the superintendent since visits are disruptive to William and his "training," which involves shelling peas and mopping floors in the kitchen. William will sob and cling to his mother during these visits, and the superintendent will explain how they prevent him from accepting and benefiting from his new life. When he turns eighteen, William will be sterilized without his consent, and Alice will learn of this "necessary" procedure after it has occurred and will be told that it is all for the best.

Alice will eventually wonder if her daughter should avoid marriage and motherhood altogether. This is particularly the case seven years later when she reads Margaret Sanger's work about the use of sterilization to prevent "the defective progeny resulting from irresponsible and unintelligent breeding"—although at least Sanger does not argue, as some do, that communities should send such progeny to the "lethal chamber" (32). Then, twelve years later, in 1927, Alice reads a newspaper report about the United States Supreme Court decision in the case *Buck v. Bell*. The Court has upheld the state of Virginia's right to sterilize a young woman named Carrie Buck, who lives at the State Colony for Epileptics and Feeble-Minded, without her consent. She had given birth to a daughter who was conceived when Buck was raped ("Eugenics"). A statement by Justice Oliver Wendell Holmes is included in the report:

> It is better for all the world, if instead of waiting to execute degenerate offspring for crime, or to let them starve for their imbecility, society can prevent those who are manifestly unfit from continuing their kind. The principle that sustains compulsory vaccination is broad enough to cover cutting the Fallopian tubes....Three generations of imbeciles are enough. (*Buck v. Bell*)

Alice recognizes in Holmes's statement some commonly held assumptions, not only about disability and its supposed attendant evils but also about the right to control the bodies of women who are not considered "fit" to become mothers. Alice wonders if everyone would have benefited had her hidden "unfitness" been obvious and "treated" appropriately. She fears for her institutionalized "degenerate offspring" and mourns the drudgery and isolation that comprise his life.

MY STORY AND OBSERVATIONS, 2014

If I could speak to Alice about current attitudes toward disability and tell her the story of my experience as a white, middle-class, married mother in the U.S. today, I think she would be glad to know that the era of institutionalization is gone—although it lasted far too long, with the number of institutionalized people with intellectual disabilities in the U.S. rising to more than 194,000 in 1967 before declining (Berger 68-69). I have no doubt she would be interested to see how legislation, such as the 1990 Americans with Disabilities Act, has in at least some cases led to greater community inclusion of and accessibility for children and adults with disabilities.[4] She might also find, however, that the blaming of mothers for their children's disabilities is still quite prevalent, although it is expressed somewhat differently.

I would begin my narrative by telling Alice about my own son named William. In 2014, William is sixteen years old, although he looks about twelve. He has a small, thin body with large dark eyes and a delicate sweep of eyebrows. Genetic testing has revealed a mosaic pattern defect in his chromosome 8 pair. The condition is rare—so rare that it has not been given a name. Medical and educational reports indicate that the implications of the condition are moderate cognitive disability and autistic spectrum disorder, with fine and gross motor delays. William attends the local junior high school, spending part of the day in a regular classroom and most of the day receiving individualized instruction in the living skills classroom. He is popular with other students and enjoys school.

I also have an older son and daughter, both of whom are considered perfectly healthy and "normal." In addition to being a mother, I also work as an editor and as a university instructor in disability studies, gender and women's studies, and English. Once a month I meet with William's state-appointed case manager to discuss services he or the family might need, such as respite care or assistive devices. He is expected to live at home and within the community, and I am expected to mother and care for him as I do my other children.

At this point in my narrative, I imagine Alice might be surprised at my freedom to work and my ability to have my youngest child live at home—so different from her time when the "science" of eugenics and a desire to eliminate so-called feeble-mindedness necessitated mass institutionalization. Nevertheless, I would tell her that, as in 1914, mothers today are still clearly judged by society at large to be either fit or unfit—and mothers like me who have children with disabilities are often considered to be unfit, and we frequently internalize this sentiment. In Alice's lifetime, North American mothers were expected to prevent feeble-mindedness in their children by exercising "constant vigilance" (Carlson 133). Specifically, "pregnant women were responsible for ensuring a healthy environment, physically and mentally, for the baby in the womb. Mothers of newborns were taught to watch for signs of idiocy" (133). Now, as Gail Landsman explains in *Reconstructing Motherhood and Disability in the Age of "Perfect" Babies*,

> routine availability of prenatal screening for fetal abnormalities in the United States, the development of new reproductive technologies, and the widespread dissemination of expert knowledge regarding the impact of maternal behavior on pregnancy outcome have affected in new and particular ways American women's accountability for the failure to produce "perfect" babies. (16)

Specifically, Landsman describes how health professionals, public health posters, and self-help books detail, step by step, how mothers can and should "do the right things" to produce healthy babies. She refers to *What to Expect While You're Expecting*, for example, which implies that women can come close to "guaranteeing" excellent infant health by eating well during pregnancy (Landsman 25).

While Landsman does not claim that advice about folic acid, smoking cessation, and alcohol avoidance is wrong or unhelpful, she does point out the implication that "the birth of a healthy (i.e. non-disabled) child is within the control of a woman who behaves appropriately and who seeks and complies with professional medical care during pregnancy" (28). Mothers of children with disabilities often experience self-blame and guilt that they are responsible for damaging their child—a feeling that is reinforced by other people's belief that mothers can and should prevent such disabilities (Landsman 31-32). Certainly I have found that my own self-blame is reinforced quite often. I have been asked, for example, whether I followed the Centers for Disease Control and Prevention's advice to take folic acid daily for at least three months before conception (Landsman 24). (No, as the pregnancy was not planned.) I've also been asked if I might have been exposed to certain toxic chemicals that caused William's "problems." (I don't think so.) Likely because I am a middle-class, married white woman, no one automatically assumed that I took drugs, drank alcohol, or smoked during my pregnancy.

While I have occasionally experienced feelings of guilt for not taking folic acid supplements before my pregnancy—even though I know this particular "failure" is not responsible for William's differences—my main struggle has been with the issue of prenatal testing, something that was not available in the fictional Alice's socio-historical context. Although I was an "older mother," I decided not to have amniocentesis or chorionic villus sampling when I learned I was pregnant with William. I am not sure why, except that I knew I would choose to continue the pregnancy regardless of the outcome of testing. I was aware of arguments for testing, including Laura Purdy's on "preventing certain births" in *Reproducing Persons: Issues in Feminist Bioethics*:

When I look into my heart ... I see, I admit, emotions I would rather not feel—reluctance to face the burdens society must bear, unease in the presence of some disabled persons. But most of all, what I see are the demands of love: to love someone is to care desperately about his or her welfare and to want only good things for him or her. The thought that I might bring to life a child with serious physical or mental problems when I could, by doing something different, bring forth one without them, is utterly incomprehensible to me. Isn't that what love means? (58)

Purdy and I apparently have very different ideas about the demands of love and whether the life of someone with a serious disability can include "good things," but I have seen her view more often than mine reflected in others' attitudes. While my obstetrician respected my decision to forgo prenatal testing, simply remarking that I must be "okay with uncertainty," many others—from strangers at the grocery store to professional acquaintances and even some friends—have asked whether medical professionals neglected to advise me that amniocentesis was available, if I was unable to afford it, or if my medical insurance failed to cover it. I still remember the day a client for whom I did editing work met five-year-old William for the first time. She whispered, "Why does he look and act a bit different from most kids?" When I explained how he had been born with a chromosomal disorder, distress and sympathy were evident in her voice: "I'm so sorry. Too bad you didn't have prenatal testing, because then you could have prevented these problems." After a moment, she added, "The government should require prenatal testing for all pregnant women—especially if they're over thirty-five, like you were. Then kids wouldn't have these problems. Everyone could have a perfectly healthy baby." When I replied that many such "problems" could not be prevented because they cannot be "fixed" prenatally, my client appeared puzzled and asked what I meant. I pointed out that often the only option if one learns a fetus has a disability is to decide whether or not to terminate the pregnancy. "Yes, I know," she replied. "Wouldn't you have made the logical choice if you had known beforehand?"

While this particular woman used the phrase "logical choice," I have also heard it referred to as a "rational," "sensible," or even "the kindest" choice. The mother-blame in such statements may not be overt, but it is certainly implied. An ideal child is assumed to be attainable through science and the correct, caring actions of a "fit" and educated mother. This assumption is really not so very different from the expectations for "fit" mothers in Alice's day. In both socio-historical contexts, a "good" mother would have made a different choice than I had made.

Over the past few years, I have learned to tell those who ask about my decisions during pregnancy that I am happy with them and with my much-loved child. Interestingly, when I do so, the conversation often shifts to apparent mother admiration—which is really another form of mother-blame. I have been told, for instance, that I am incredibly strong and heroic and that God sent William to me because He knew I was a very special mom who could care for a child with his special needs. Similarly, at a recent conference on disability, I was reminded by a keynote speaker (as were other mothers who attended) that we are heroines who must never relax our efforts, as "special moms" are supposed to push their "special children" and themselves every minute of every day to make sure they receive the needed resources and become "all that they can be." To put it another way, mothers are expected to take on the "warrior-hero" role that Amy Sousa has described and to carry full responsibility for their children's successes and failures in life (220). Sousa explains:

> [The] "warrior-hero" identity [is] a reformulated archetype in the social construction of a good mother. This archetype places a cultural expectation on mothers to do battle to attain resources and possible cures for their children, ultimately shifting the historical burden on mothers from causing the intellectual disabilities of their children to curing them. (220)

In fact, if we warrior-hero moms do not manage to cure the disability—or at least work tirelessly to find services for our children—"this idealized notion of 'mother-valour' quickly shifts back to mother-blame in which mothers are viewed as 'proximate causes' of prolonged or exacerbated disability" (Sousa 235).[5] Many of my "special mom" friends and I have come to view our children's differences as part of who they are and value their ways of viewing and engaging with the world. We no longer believe we must "do everything" to ensure our children do not challenge others' ideas of healthy or "perfect" children. Even so, while we may tell ourselves we are "fine with it" when others—including some self-identified "warrior" mothers—are surprised by or disapprove of our decisions, we continue to feel the same weight of mother-blame as women in Alice's socio-historical context felt.

FINAL THOUGHTS: TELLING OUR STORIES

As I near the end of my narrative, I have begun thinking about Alice's fictional life once again. Of course, I know that my son and I are more fortunate in many ways; still, I believe that Alice and I could understand each other's sorrows and struggles and share a wish—certainly unfulfilled for her—that "the wider society recognize the worth and worthiness" of our children with cognitive disabilities (Kittay 623). I also believe that Alice would resist and reject certain mothering expectations and blaming practices to the best of her knowledge and ability, as I do. I have my own "moments of grace" with William, as I hear his complicated narratives about friends or school, see him watching the shifting cloud patterns on the grass, or feel him take my arm as we walk to the school bus each morning. They are the private moments that are not subject to others' judgments; they occur when self-blame falls away and I am unencumbered by the need to explain my son's disability or my own mothering decisions. These moments are what have led me to think not only of my own mothering stories but those of other mothers with cognitively disabled children.

I believe that telling these stories, whether they are real or imagined, contemporary or historical, can be a way to resist mother-blame and make visible the hidden and often harmful effects of societal assumptions and expectations. As Susan Zimmermann states in *Keeping Katherine*, her memoir about life with her daughter with Rett syndrome, "We are our stories. Each story is a ripple that adds to the richness of the larger pool of stories. When we tell our stories, we come to realize that ours is part of something greater than we'd ever imagined" (235). Telling life stories is a powerful practice. They give a voice to those who have typically been denied one, and they demonstrate the value of devalued lives. Perhaps they even connect us to those who have had lived experiences more similar to our own than we might at first realize. I hope that Alice—and the non-fictional women who mothered in her socio-historical context—would agree with me.

ENDNOTES

[1] In this essay, I have used two forms of evocative writing that Laurel Richardson describes in "Writing: A Method of Inquiry." One is "the narrative of the self," which is "a highly personalized, revealing text in which an author tells stories about his or her own lived experience" (521). I use this form when I tell my own story. The other form is "ethnographic fictional representations," with which "writers define their work as fiction, as products of the imagination" (521). I use this form when I tell Alice's story. I have also tried to combine "cultural analysis and interpretation with narrative details," which is an important part of Heewon Chang's definition of autoethnography (Chang 46).

[2] These "better-baby" contests were held between 1910 and 1930 at county and state fairs in the United States (Landsman 72). Landsman shares Alexandra Minna Stern's explanation of how "best babies" were chosen: "Being deemed 'the best' required a score as near to perfect as possible on a set of physical, psychological, and physiological scales, most of which were statistically measured according to bell curves" (cited in Landsman 72).

[3] George Egerton's real name was Mary Chavelita Dunne Bright. She lived from 1859 to 1945 (Denisoff and Kooistra 1).

[4] Davis points out that "many areas of the ADA are being rolled back in the courts and in the legislature" (264).

[5] In her recent book *Autism and Gender: From Refrigerator Mothers to Computer Geeks*, Jordynn Jack mentions mother-blaming by "mother warriors" whose children have autism. She gives examples of how these "warriors" actively criticize other mothers who do not try every treatment, therapy, or diet that could conceivably be helpful for their children (84). Interestingly, Jack also describes resistance from some of these non-warrior mothers because "the

warrior mother persona may not only seem self-aggrandizing but also unsympathetic to other mothers" (86).

WORKS CITED

Berger, Ronald J. *Introducing Disability Studies*. Boulder: Lynne Rienner Publishers, 2013. Print.

"Buck v. Bell. 274 US 200. Supreme Court of the U.S. 1927." *Supreme Court Collection*. Legal Information Institute, Cornell University Law School, n.d. Web. 11 Jun. 2014.

Carlson, Licia. "Cognitive Ableism and Disability Studies: Feminist Reflections on the History of Mental Retardation." *Hypatia* 16.4 (2001): 124-146. Print.

Chang, Heewon. *Autoethnography as Method*. Walnut Creek: Left Coast Press, 2008. Print.

Davis, Lennard J. "The End of Identity Politics: On Disability as an Unstable Category." *The Disability Studies Reader*. 4th ed. Ed. Lennard J. Davis. New York: Routledge, 2013. 263-277. Print.

Denisoff, Dennis, and Lorraine Janzen Kooistra, eds. "George Egerton [Mary Chavelita Dunne Bright] (1859-1945)." *The Yellow Nineties Online*, n.d. Web. 30 Oct. 2014.

Egerton, George. *Rosa Amorosa: The Love-Letters of a Woman*. 1901. Forgotten Books, 2012. Print.

"Eugenics. Three Generations, No Imbeciles: Virginia, Eugenics & *Buck v. Bell*." *Historical Collections at the Claude Moore Health Sciences Library*. Claude Moore Health Sciences Library, University of Virginia, 2004. Web. 11 Jun. 2014.

Goddard, Henry Herbert. *The Kallikak Family: A Study in the Heredity of Feeble-Mindedness*. 1912. University of California Libraries, 2014. Print.

Jack, Jordynn. *Autism and Gender: From Refrigerator Mothers to Computer Geeks*. Urbana: University of Illinois Press, 2014. Print.

Kittay, Eva Feder. "The Personal Is Philosophical Is Political: A Philosopher and Mother of a Cognitively Disabled Person Sends Notes from the Battlefield." *Metaphilosophy* 40.3-4 (2009): 606-27. Print.

Landsman, Gail Heidi. *Reconstructing Motherhood and Disability in the Age of "Perfect" Babies*. New York: Routledge, 2009. Print.

Purdy, Laura M. *Reproducing Persons: Issues in Feminist Bioethics*. Ithaca: Cornell University Press, 1996. Print.

Richardson, Laurel. "Writing: A Method of Inquiry." *Handbook of Qualitative Research*. Ed. Norman K. Denzin and Yvonna S. Lincoln. Thousand Oaks, CA: Sage Publications, 1994. 516-529. Print.

Sanger, Margaret. *The Pivot of Civilization*. n.d. San Bernardino: n.p., 2014. Print.

Sousa, Amy C. "From Refrigerator Mothers to Warrior-Heroes: The Cultural Identity Transformation of Mothers Raising Children with Intellectual Disabilities." *Symbolic Interaction* 34.2 (2011): 220-43. Print.

Trent, James W. Jr. *Inventing the Feeble Mind: A History of Mental Retardation in the United States*. Berkeley: University of California Press, 1994. Print.

Zimmermann, Susan. *Keeping Katherine: A Mother's Journey to Acceptance*. New York: Three Rivers Press, 2004. Print.

16.
Loving Miss JBP

Writing/Art as Mothering Practice in a Mother-Blaming Culture

LORINDA PETERSON

If to love (her child) is, for a woman, the same thing as to write, we have in that conjunction a modern, secular equivalent of the word made flesh.
—Susan Rubin Suleiman

When I write, I can shake off all my cares.
—Anne Frank, April 5, 1944

WRITING AND SEQUENTIAL ART have become part of my mothering practice. As a lesbian single mother, I am often devastated by the challenge of raising a traumatized adolescent who was neglected and abandoned in infancy by her biological mother, Anna, and raped by a nineteen-year-old acquaintance when she was fourteen. My fear is exacerbated by physical violence from Anna during our life-partner and co-mothering relationship and by my own traumatic childhood. Cathy Caruth defines trauma in *Unclaimed Experience: Trauma, Narrative, and History* as "a wound on the mind ... a breach in the mind's experience of time, self, and the world" (3). Trauma wounds do not heal themselves over time like wounds on the body. To heal from trauma, survivors repeatedly visit past traumatic events in present time through trauma memory. One way to do this is through writing and art.

This chapter addresses my experience of mother-blaming as a lesbian single mother to my non-biological daughter, Miss JBP, and the power of writing and art to move us forward after trauma. In *The New Don't Blame Mother: Mending the Mother-Daughter Relationship*, Paula Caplan identifies "untapped energy . . . bound up not only in the daughter's mother-blaming but also in the mother's self-blame and self-hate" (38). She adds, "Once we're aware that mother-blaming comes easily and that it distorts our view, we can begin to catch ourselves doing it" (41). This chapter highlights the curious twist on mother-blaming that comes not only from professionals, as seen so often in the literature, but from Miss JBP and from me as we navigate our mother-daughter relationship. I incorporate theory and personal anecdote in my analysis of our complicated situation, defined by trauma, invisible disabilities, and mental health issues. I also consider sequential art—comics and other visual-art series of words and images strung together in journals, on walls and canvases, and on my daughter's body.

Based on my own experience, the struggle in creating trauma comics and in writing this chapter about mother-blaming, is deciding how to write about real people—what to include, what to leave out, how best to tell the story. It is a struggle Susan Olding describes well in *Pathologies*. She writes, "How to tell a true story? If I write it as non-fiction, I get to include all the messy details. I do not have to package it in an artificial plot, I get to say what I see. But how do I prevent myself from flattening the characters, turning real people into caricatures, turning their lives into anecdotes?" (97). The comic form lends itself nicely to writing my stories by allowing the messy traumatic details to be included in illustration, blunting their impact on the reader somewhat by purposely flattening the characters to stick people. It works because I want my audience to see through or past the people. In flattening the characters, they have been moved aside to reveal the issues. The plot is revealed through their gestures. The stick people act out slices of experience filtered through my memory, experiences that are necessary to move the comic narrative forward.

The adolescent years with my youngest daughter, Miss JBP, are tumultuous. She is a quirky fifteen-year-old, recently diagnosed with attention deficit disorder (ADD), oppositional defiance disorder (ODD), depression, and anxiety. She exhibits limited impulse control and engages in risky behaviour, such as leaving home or school without telling anyone where she is going, walking long distances on public highways in sub-zero weather at night, and sexting nude pictures of herself to a boy she barely knows.

She lives in fight or flight mode, and I become over-vigilant with fear for her safety.

Our days are chaotic as I try to keep her from spilling so far outside herself that she does not know where she ends and others begin.

They are challenging. Any single day dares me to create order where it appears there is none.

Recording experience, not only from my perspective and my body but also from my daughter's, is a way to authenticate life events that would otherwise drive us apart. Incorporating images in narratives about mothering, especially in cases of trauma, can

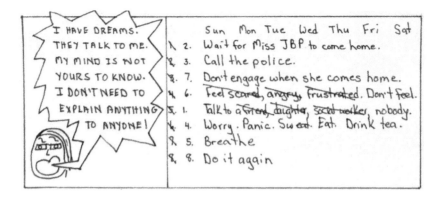

help tell stories that cannot be fully articulated in words. In her introduction to *Drawing from Life: Subjectivity in Comic Art*, Jane Tolmie explains, "An image of abuse reaches out and makes—often coerces—emotional connections, forcing a public acknowledgement of private trauma, re-making a closed world of shame into an open book" (ix). She describes an "aesthetic of affect, not an inevitable or natural emotional side effect but a deliberate result of artistic decisions: the image of ... an encounter grounded in power inequalities [that] is in turn thrust onto the audience" (ix). In my less-is-more approach to comics, audience is a necessary component for interpreting the trauma story. Audience is invited to both experience affect and grapple with complex issues like the ones Tolmie describes. In trauma comics, the physical can be displayed on the page and through it, the emotional and psychological must be portrayed.

Comics can help deconstruct the existing patriarchal ideal of motherhood, making room for mother-centred experience by incorporating stories that provide a focus on the spoken language mothers use to describe specific mothering practice. In *Understanding Comics*, comics artist and theorist Scott McCloud suggests, "Comic panels fracture both time and space, offering a jagged staccato rhythm of unconnected moments" (69). They offer a different spatial reality and possibilities for a different kind of order. Hilary Chute claims, "Comics can express life stories, especially traumatic ones, powerfully because it makes literal the presence of the past by disrupting spatial and temporal conventions to overlay ... past and present" (109). My aim in creating trauma comics is to step back from the arena of moral judgment and away from what Alice Walker calls the narrowed and narrowing view of life that often wins in our society (5).

By revealing intricate relationships in my comics, I hope to weave a narrative path through some sensitive terrain that still seems little-understood by experts and not well represented in the literature. My comics are an attempt to understand certain lived experience. Walker describes appreciating art or life as "connections made, or at least attempted, where none existed before, the straining to encompass in one's glance at the varied world, the common thread, the unifying theme through immense diversity, a fearlessness of growth, of search, of looking, that enlarges the private and public world" (5). She was describing a larger world and a larger history, but I think the allusion applies to my way of looking at the microcosm of my experience. Without an appreciation for the complexity of the story's structure, the tendency might be to annihilate, lop off parts of people and chapters of their lives, to make them in our image or to reject them. Child abuse and domestic violence are never justified, but they are products of a social system that places extreme burdens on mothers collectively and places small value on some of the individuals in that group, especially those who struggle to survive.

My mothering experience, like some comics literature, facilitates a journey through time and space, where events do not always make chronological sense or adhere to expectations. Caruth says, "The history of ... traumatized individual(s) is nothing other than the determined return to the event of destruction" (63). As Miss JBP and I weave a path through present time, our experience is often rooted in recurring memories and references to the past, what Jill Bennett refers to as trauma memory. Bennett locates trauma memory in the struggle to illustrate a collision between common memory, the language that enables narrative memory to be understood from the past, and sense memory, the memory that registers the physical imprint of an event and is always in the present (25). This collision means putting an outside and an inside into contact to enact a process of seeing feeling, and creating sensation , similar to what Tolmie describes as *affect*. Art creation allows trauma to flow through bodies and spaces, therein creating what Bennett calls a "mode of 'traumatic time'" (12). Sense memory is of the body. Writing and art give voice to the ways Miss JBP and I experience ourselves through our traumatic past. A handprint is a handprint, but a pattern of handprints covering a bathroom wall is something different, as I show later in this chapter.

In *Rootprints: Memory and Life Writing*, Hélène Cixous explores language as a tool for embodiment and transformation in the act of creating. Her writing practice connects to both her inner and outer worlds. When deliberating on why she writes, Cixous says, "I write ... with an incessant drive for re-establishing the truth, justice.... We do not think with justice. The world is not just" (11). Miss JBP also knows the world is not just. She struggles to connect who she is inside her body with what happens in the world around her, to find a way to fit in. Miss JBP was born to two mothers, one—her biological mother, Anna—lives with bipolar disorder and addictions. Miss JBP's early life was both women-centered and violent. By the time she was a year old, Anna and I were separated, and I had custody of Miss JBP. On a good day, Anna was sober when I dropped off Miss JBP for a visit and still sober when I came to pick her up.

As a writer, I ask myself how my mothering role impacts my writing. Does the fact that this is my story, and that I identify and empathize with each of the characters, colour the scenes I choose to portray? Am I capable of depicting a fair and balanced account of what actually happened? Is this really a true story? Do the answers to any of these questions matter to the story's telling? Mother-blaming is irrational and, in my story, I want to blame Anna for the life narrative she penned herself, the one that does not include Miss JBP. I want to blame her for this more than I want to blame her for Miss JBP's genetic predisposition to ADD, ODD, and bipolar disorder or the way the outside world perceives her. I want to blame Anna for how her absence is at times more real to Miss JBP than my presence and how we fall into uncomfortable silences between words trying to understand it. I want to blame her because I am doing all the mothering. This is not an act of courage; it is a necessary set of actions that challenges my sense of self most days. Most of all, I want to blame Anna for how Miss JBP does not fit nicely into my story, so I constantly find myself re-writing. But I do not blame her. I just keep writing.

When discussing writing and mothering in *Of Woman Born*, Adrienne Rich says, "For me poetry was where I lived as no one's mother, where I existed as myself" (31). In contrast, writing with Miss JBP has become a way for us to connect as mother and daughter. We use writing to communicate when tension between us is too great to speak out loud and feelings push through our bodies asking us to make sense of them. When Miss JBP was seven years old, we penned our first sequence of collaborative writings. Being also visually gifted, she illustrated each story with coloured pencil. I designed that short collection to help Miss JBP develop printing skills and address the blame teachers placed on me for her left-handed untidiness and her lack of printing pizazz. The writing was a way to do this creatively while sharing quality mother and daughter time in our busy lives. But the project initiated focus on shared experience, the way we interpreted our lives in the present with reference to our pasts. On August 2, 2005, six months after our last contact with Anna, Miss JBP ended one story, saying, "And it was lots of f ~~Fon~~ fun and we lived happily ever after." At the time, we had pushed Anna, her drunkenness, her verbal abuse, and physical violence, deep down inside us. Miss JBP drew the picture below to go with that story.

Miss JBP and I lived in the country, miles away from Anna, but I kept the doors and windows locked. I feared Anna and blamed her for the effort it took to hide my fear from Miss JBP and from the world. In our writing on August 3, Miss JBP ended the story with, "I felt skard." In the context of writing this story, she means "scared." I blamed Anna for Miss JBP's fear too. In the misspelling, though, Miss JBP revealed a truth she would later work out on her body, cutting and scarring herself to make pain visible.

Simultaneous with the writing practice, Miss JBP initiated collaborative painting in acrylics. She preferred this way of expression over written language. Her visual vocabulary was much more developed at seven, and there was no right or wrong way to create. We simply chose a canvas and got to work. Writing and painting over the years became a way for me to keep my finger on her pulse. I needed to know one mother's love would sustain her. In the early years of the new millennium, patriarchy prevailed; same-sex families, invisible disabilities, and mental illness were often tolerated but still not widely accepted.

Miss JBP and I are "inextricably bound together through the story of a trauma" (Caruth 102). When she was thirteen, she contacted Anna on Facebook. Although this was planned on her part, Miss JBP did not talk to me first. The action was so sudden and unexpected that I had no time to anticipate the strength of my reaction, the only reaction my body permitted, consumed by all the danger of the past violence but in present time. I was not ready for Miss JBP's surprise and alarm at my reaction. I realized too late how her contact with Anna would change the pattern of our lives.

Neither Miss JBP nor I had seen Anna for six years following a

final act of violence, ending a co-mothering experience between Miss JBP, Anna, and me. The event also ended our relationship with Miss JBP's biological half-sister, Skye.

Although Miss JBP's contact with Anna was broken, biology did not end; bodies do not work that way. We are culturally conditioned to look for who we are in the story of our biology, paying particular attention to who we come from. Ironically, although I have been the nurturer, I am not the mother professionals and peers blame for Miss JBP's disabilities or the one they write into the family "herstory." Our genetic stories begin and end with our biological families. As a young adolescent, Miss JBP fought to experience them, and I fought to protect her from them. I feared their violence and the possibility that Anna would reject Miss JBP again. Although I was not ready to face the impact that re-connection would have on her life, or on mine, I blamed myself for Miss JBP's struggle and I blamed Anna for causing the struggle by never attempting to re-connect with Miss JBP.

After contacting Anna, Miss JBP began hearing voices inside her head. She was diagnosed with anxiety-induced psychosis and depression. The diagnosis started a long journey through medication aimed at helping her find a more peaceful place within herself.

Experts concluded that Miss JBP's inability to communicate with me about the past kept her from bringing her memory of Anna's violence into contact with her feelings about it. They tacitly blamed me for the wall that went up between my youngest daughter and me after she contacted Anna.

At this time, Miss JBP and I came together again through collaborative writing. We used separate journals to maintain control

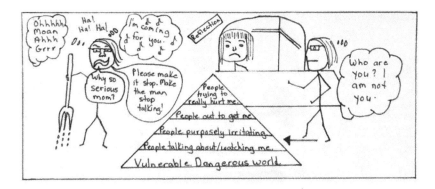

over our places in the mother-daughter relationship. We agreed on ideas or issues, and we created images. Then we wrote about the images. The writings in this series are dialogues with ourselves. In discussing them afterwards, neither of us could break through the shields protecting us from the memory of violence that we recognized in each other, even though we did not own it. As a writer, and as a mother, I am often lost and directionless, thinking back to move forward, trying to navigate both a senseless world and meaningless language. On April 3, 2012, Miss JBP wrote, "I am voiced with silence as I stand." And I wrote, "I am hopeful that words are enough to sustain me between times, and explanations that falter fade away over time." It appeared that words had failed us both. But between the two collaborative attempts at age seven and age twelve, Miss JBP and I created collages of words and images cut from magazines and hung them around the house to remind ourselves of the creative moments. We played with magnetic poetry on the refrigerator, leaving poems and messages for each other. We sculpted from clay, creating amorphous figures and tiny lifelike characters of mother bears holding their babies. We drew in pastels, markers, and charcoal. Her creative practice was born; she believed in the power of writing and art.

My writing practice began in childhood with a story about a flying house. I grew up in a home with an alcoholic father suffering with mental health issues. He was not physically violent, but my mother fought to make him stop drinking. She worked to raise five children and support them on a low income. In my child's mind, I blamed my mother for the unhappiness in our family. I wanted her to leave my father alone, or to leave him. I wanted her to find a different way, but she was a woman of her time and she stayed with my father until all her children left home.

I struggled with homophobia and my own lesbianism as a teenager in the '70s without parental support. I married, gave birth to three children, and was divorced by twenty-two. I came out as a lesbian at twenty-eight and enjoyed a loving relationship for ten years while raising my three older children. Then I met Anna and walked knowingly into her difficult life thinking I could somehow make a difference. Over my lifetime, I came to depend on my ability to turn thoughts and feelings into language. I learned to believe myself. My key challenge as Miss JBP's mother is learning to believe her. In the wisdom of adolescence, and through her ADD/ODD lens, she holds me responsible for her behaviour and its consequences. Far from contributing to success in her personal narrative, she sees me as the reason she is not successful. She resents the ways she is not like me and her difficulty in discovering who she is. In the age-old debate with nature at one extreme and nurture at the other, Miss JBP blames me for who she is because I raised her, and I blame Anna because she possesses the only known genetic marker. On the good days I know the story exists somewhere along this continuum and that mother-blaming contributes little to the narrative.

In my search for a way to find purpose and move my life forward, I began creating trauma comics with Miss JBP and me as two of the avatars. My mothering journey with my youngest daughter parallels our journey through comic art. We become actors of our life experiences, and such experiences do not always make sense. In comics, as in life, we move through time and space like puppets without strings in calculated suites of movement, taking our cues from each other in a curious dance. Agency moves back and forth between us in life, and agency moves back and forth between our comics' characters, carrying the narrative forward. In creating comics I am putting myself inside a shifting space/time continuum and inside my characters' different personas. I am also travelling into the comic's formal structures of frames and gutters that both allow for order and accommodate the shifts, so although the stories defy space and time, they still make sense and are believable. The comics are not meant to recreate trauma but to illustrate how trauma creates meaning. As trauma art, comics produce affect, and through affect comics continue to produce meaning after the events they represent are over. In Tolmie's words, the comics are a form of "feminist art activism, art that deliberately self-defines as a form of creative emancipation" (xvi). My and Miss JBP's stick people forms in the comics become metaphors representing traumatic life experiences at the boundaries of representation. The characters are intentional; their purpose is defined by their actions.

For Cixous, purposeful living and writing work to facilitate change or metamorphosis. Words, writing, and language are bound up with love and the process of transformation, from one state to another. They are "of the body" (28). After the rape, Miss JBP took Cixous's of the body writing literally. As the person closest to her, I became her provider, her prison guard, her enemy, her emotional punching bag, the object of her hatred, the person who tried to love her most, and her loudest advocate. Communicating with her became difficult if not impossible. Text messaging became her

weapon against me, her avenue for verbal and emotional bullets, well aimed and devastating.

Miss JBP began writing messages on her body with Sharpie markers. She wrote secret words and phrases concealed by clothing and scrubbed away over time, then replaced by more words. In therapy with me, she recounted the story of her rape—how she froze and could not fight back. In relinquishing power, she relinquished her known ways of experiencing herself, and she escaped by retreating inside her head. Her mind protected her. She did the right thing to keep from being beaten or killed but the rape left an invisible wound she tried to heal.

Miss JBP wrote messages on her friends' bodies and they wrote messages on hers. When the language was ready, and the tiny transformation from one phase of healing to another was complete, words appeared uncovered on her hands, or she wore short-sleeved shirts to reveal words and images on her arms. In Caruth's interpretation of trauma, she traced the story of the rape through recurring words, moving beyond what she could know, to bear witness to the trauma wound. Her "words [were] passed on as an act that [did] not ... awaken the self, but rather passe[d] the awakening on to others" (16). Soon, Sharpie markers and words on Miss JBP's body were not enough. They washed away without leaving scars. Cixous refers to scars as the stories and what remains when the events are over (16). Miss JBP needed the stories. She needed to go deeper and bring the wound from her mind back to her body. In her need to re-live the experience, she began cutting into her hips, her arms, her thighs, and her calves. She concealed the wounds, keeping them secret until she was ready to let them go; she nurtured her scars. She came close to cutting too deeply into her wrists, leaving one scar that will never fade. While she cut she was engaged in risky sexual behaviours. She refused to eat and had trouble sleeping. She tried to heal trauma's wound with an overdose of medication. She survived. She cut or ran away if I left her alone. She did not talk to me if I was there. Miss JBP's behaviour became so risky and dysfunctional that she was admitted as an inpatient in the local adolescent psychiatry ward for assessment the summer after her fifteenth birthday. While there she made hostile phone calls to me. She also recorded every detail of her life, every day. Months after she was released, she told me about the rape. Then the cutting stopped.

After writing on her body, Miss JBP began creating from her body on larger canvases—first her handprints in acrylic paint on her bathroom walls, the palms with no paint, gaping open and empty, like mouths that could not scream. She was looking for language. She was also defacing my home in an act of defiance. She pressed handprints onto canvas, white skeletal digits on a black background with sparkles of colour showing through.

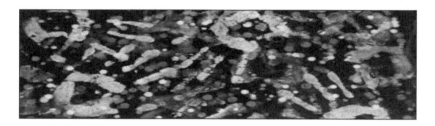

The handprints are still on the wall and on the canvas. They are testaments to her attempts at experiencing herself in new ways. In calmer moments she painted pastoral scenes, then she created an explosive canvas divided by a thick black line down the center with so much passion flowing off its edges that red seems to drip down the wall where it hangs. She created canvases of words— some her own, some borrowed—in flamboyant colours, and she wrote poetry. Perhaps she sums up her struggle best when she says, "Read between the lines./ Know that even though your flesh is marked, it is only as permanent as you make it./ ... Know that your beauty is not perfection./ But simply a painting that cannot be copied" (Brown-Peterson).

Based on my experience mothering Miss JBP, I agree with Andrea O'Reilly that "mothering is a profound experience of powerlessness and power" (96) and also with Cixous's claim that "suffering and joy have the same root" (12). As I work on this paper, Miss JBP has been living away from home for four weeks. She has no explanation why. She no longer blames me, and I do not blame myself. For a full year I regularly called police to find her and bring her home. They sometimes blamed me and assumed I was her reason for running. Mostly they blamed her for taking them away from

more urgent duties and tried to convince her to stay home.

At times I found her and brought her home. But I have stopped. I know she is staying with her boyfriend's family. She is off her medications and she does not attend school regularly. She is frequently sick. I connect with her to make sure she is safe, usher her to appointments, and replace her eyeglasses and her cellphone. I reassure her that I love her and that she has a home with me when she is ready to live here. We are estranged for now, mother and daughter, working on our relationship from different perspectives. We negotiate space in our lives for each other, drawing new boundaries; the ordinary between us changes on any given day.

Miss JBP is still writing her way through change in a personal journal, and I am still creating trauma comics. We share when we can. She tells me she wants to come home but she's afraid the running cycle will start again, and I know she is deflecting her running to me. I tell her she may not be ready to come home. I'm learning that I cannot re-write Miss JBP's story and that the part my youngest daughter plays in my life-narrative is becoming less about me and more about her. Tolmie writes, "Self-expression gives you power over your own memory and your own sense of self/subject" (xviii). Miss JBP and I cling to that power for survival. The body works that way, finding meaning not in *what* we live but in *how* we live it, in how we experience ourselves. Hilary Chute claims, "Embodiment in comics may be read as a kind of compensation for lost bodies, for lost histories. Comics resurrects, materializes" (113). Miss JBP and I have created new stories for ourselves through sequential art, re-interpreting and piecing together parts of our past that were torn apart without our permission, looking for closure in the process. I may not like the new stories any better than the old ones. In mothering, as in writing and art, love and language will let us down at times and often there is no one to blame.

WORKS CITED

Bennett, Jill. *Empathetic Vision: Affect, Trauma, and Contemporary Art*. California: Stanford University Press, 2005. Print.

Brown-Peterson, Jacobi. "Lines." Unpublished poem

Caplan, Paula. *The New Don't Blame Mother: Mending the Mother-Daughter Relationship*. New York: Routledge, 2000. Print.

Caruth, Cathy. *Unclaimed Experience: Trauma, Narrative and History*. Baltimore: The John Hopkins University Press, 1996. Print.

Chute, Hilary. "Comics Form and Narrating Lives." *Profession*. The Modern Language Association of America, 2011. Print.

Cixous, Hélène. *Rootprints: Memory and Life Writing*. New York: Routledge, 1994. Print.

Frank, Anne. *The Diary of a Young Girl*. Toronto: Random House, 1993. Print.

McCloud, Scott. *Understanding Comics*. New York: Harper-Collins, 1994. Print.

Olding, Susan. *Pathologies*. Peterborough: Broadview Press, 2008. Print.

O'Reilly, Andrea. *Rocking the Cradle*. Toronto: Demeter Press, 2006. Print.

Rich, Adrienne. *Of Woman Born: Motherhood as Experience and Institution*. New York: W.W. Norton and Company, 1986. Print.

Suleiman, Susan Rubin. "Writing and Motherhood." *Longman Anthology of Women's Literature*. Ed. Mary K. DeShazer. New York: Addison-Wesley Educational Publishers, 2001. 621-37. Print.

Tolmie, Jane. Introduction. *Drawing from Life: Memory and Subjectivity in Comic Art*. Jackson: University Press of Mississippi, 2013. vii-xxiii. Print.

Walker, Alice. *In Search of Our Mothers' Gardens*. New York: Harcourt, 1973. Print.

Contributor Notes

EDITORS

Vanessa Reimer is a PhD candidate in York University's Graduate Program in Gender, Feminist and Women's Studies. She is co-editor of the Demeter Press anthology *Mother of Invention: How Our Mothers Influenced Us as Feminist Academics and Activists* (2013). Her research interests include feminist studies in religion, girlhood studies, and mothering.

Sarah Sahagian is a PhD candidate in Gender, Feminist and Women's studies at York University, where she is currently finishing her dissertation on the mothering of inter-ethnic children. Her writing has appeared in such publications as *Chasing Rainbows,* a popular anthology on gender fluid parenting; *The Huffington Post*; *Bitch Media*; *Gender Focus*; the pop culture website *Comments Enabled*; and the *Journal of the Motherhood Initiative*. Sarah is also the co-editor of the Demeter Press book *Mother of Invention: How Our Mothers Influenced Us as Feminist Academics and Activists.*

CONTRIBUTORS

Kaley M. Ames is a master's student in Interdisciplinary Studies at York University. Prior to beginning her degree, Kaley was a political staffer at Queen's Park, where she worked at the Ministry of Finance and caught the bug for campaigning. Fiercely passionate about change at the political and academic level, Kaley hopes to combine both to pursue a career in legislative reform and political lobbying for women's issues, as well as her PhD.

Berit Åström, PhD, is a Senior Lecturer at the Department of Language Studies at Umeå University, Sweden. Having published on rape in crime fiction and on transhistorical cultural fears concerning breastmilk, she is currently working on representations of motherhood. Her most recent publication is "The Symbolic Annihilation of Mothers in Popular Culture: Single Father and the Death of the Mother," forthcoming in *Feminist Media Studies*.

Aurelie Athan, PhD, is a member of the faculty in the Department of Clinical Psychology at Teachers College, Columbia University, and co-founder of the Women, Sexuality, and Gender Project. Dr. Athan is also the Director of the Maternal Psychology Laboratory, which studies the transition to motherhood as a developmental niche within the female lifespan trajectory.

Jennifer L. Borda (PhD, Penn State University) is Associate Professor of Communication at the University of New Hampshire. Her work focuses on how discourse and ideologies about women, work, and identity have been constructed and challenged in the mass media. She is co-editor (with Anne T. Demo and Charlotte H. Krolokke) of the forthcoming anthology *The Motherhood Business: Consumption, Communication, and Privilege* and author of *Women Labor Activists in the Movies: Nine Depictions of Workplace Organizers, 1954-2005*. Her research also has been featured in a number of academic journals, including *Text & Performance Quarterly*, *Feminist Media Studies*, *Women's Studies in Communication*, and *Communication Quarterly*.

Talia Esnard is an Assistant Professor of Sociology at the Centre for Education Programs at the University of Trinidad and Tobago. Her main research interests include gender and entrepreneurship, poverty and entrepreneurship, mothering and entrepreneurship, entrepreneurial education, and educational leadership.

Marie Hansen, MA, is a Clinical Psychology doctoral student at

Long Island University Brooklyn. She received a BA in Women's Studies from Stony Brook University and a Master of Arts in Clinical Psychology from Teachers College, Columbia University. Marie's scholarly interests include psychoanalysis and premenstrual syndrome, postpartum psychosis, and biopsychosocial approaches to women's reproductive health.

Alison Quaggin Harkin is a University of Wyoming lecturer in Disability Studies, Gender and Women's Studies, and English. She has a BA in English from the University of Toronto and an MA in Cultural Studies and Educational Studies from Athabasca University. Currently, she is a PhD candidate at Tilburg University.

Kerri Kearney is an Associate Professor at Oklahoma State University in the area of Higher Education and Student Affairs. She holds an MBA and an EdD. Through her work, she prepares individuals to lead at institutions of higher education or function in related research or policy roles. She teaches and advises students almost exclusively at the doctoral level. Her research, teaching, and service agendas focus on the broad area of other mothering issues (fostering and adoption) with a distinct emphasis on college students who are alumni of foster care, the role of emotions in human transition (both inside and outside of the organizational environment), issues related to organizational behaviour, and visual or arts-based methodologies in qualitative research.

Tasha Muresan, MA, is a graduate of the Department of Clinical Psychology at Teachers College, Columbia University. Tasha's main scholarly interests include Jungian psychology and female psychosocial development across the lifespan. Accordingly, her graduate thesis explored motherhood archetypes through folklore and fairy tales. Alongside her scholarly work in both maternal and positive psychology, Tasha is preparing for doula certification and developing a small collection of children's stories and illustrations.

Lee Murray is currently an Associate Professor at the College of Nursing, University of Saskatchewan. She is also a Clinical Nurse Specialist (CNS) in adolescent mental health, in particular, suicidal adolescents and adolescents with developmental disabilities. Dr. Murray's clinical practice, research, and teaching are in the areas of adolescent mental health, individual and group counselling, interprofessional practice and leadership, and school health in the context of the role of a mental health nurse in schools. She also has a great interest in and curiosity regarding "mothering." To satisfy this curiosity, she uses autoethnography as a methodology to explore the normative discourse of mothering in the context of her own experiences as a mom.

Linda Pershing is Professor of Folklore and Cultural Studies at California State University San Marcos. The founding faculty member of the Women's Studies Department there, her scholarship and teaching focus on the politics of culture, women, gender, and peace movements, and feminist analysis of folklore and popular culture.

Lorinda Peterson is a PhD student at Queen's University. She also holds a master's and an undergraduate degree from Queen's. She is currently focused on motherhood studies at the intersection of theory and practice, and on the comics form as an appropriate vehicle for rendering traumatic experience visible. Other research interests include trauma memory and maternal performativities in comics art. Dr. Jane Tolmie is her supervisor.

Heather Reel is a graduate student in the Human Rights Studies program at Columbia University. She holds an MA in Developmental Psychology from Teachers College, Columbia University, where she is also a current member of the Maternal Psychology Laboratory. Her scholarly interests include the psychological, sociocultural, and historical dimensions of mothering under duress, developmental perspectives on motherhood and early childhood, and rights-based analyses of institutional care and adoption.

Catherine Robinson engages in interdisciplinary research within sociologies and social geographies of place, embodiment, and emotions. Her work has focused on the felt experience of the body and of place within the contexts of homelessness and trauma and is currently broadening to include examinations of feeling, technology, and selfhood in the context of intensive motherhood and breastfeeding struggle. Catherine is a Senior Lecturer in the Faculty of Art and Social Sciences at the University of Technology, Sydney.

Rosie Rosenzweig is a Resident Scholar at Brandeis University's Women's Studies Research Center. She is the author of *A Jewish Mother in Shangri-la*, which explores her journey to meet her son's Buddhist teachers in America, France, India, and Nepal. After interviewing over forty women artists, she is currently writing a book about creativity.

Tracy Royce is a feminist writer, poet, and sociology graduate student at the University of California, Santa Barbara. Her scholarly and/or creative work has appeared in numerous places, including *Archives of Sexual Behavior*, *The Fat Studies Reader*, *Gender & Language*, *Modern Haiku*, and *Mother of Invention: How Our Mothers Influenced us as Feminist Academics and Activists*. She lives in Los Angeles with animator Rob Renzetti and their naughty rabbit, Zigzag.

Sally Stevens, PhD, is the Executive Director of the Southwest Institute for Research on Women (SIROW) and a Distinguished Outreach Professor in the Department of Gender and Women's Studies at the University of Arizona. Dr. Stevens conducts collaborative process and outcome research in the area of health disparities, substance abuse, mental health, criminal justice, sexuality, and innovations in education. Much of her work is community-based with a focus on gender and culture, and those living in the U.S.-Mexico border region. Her research is informed by ecological perspectives and feminist theory and methodologies. Dr. Stevens has received funding from the numerous federal, state, and local public and private agencies. Contact: sstevens@email.arizona.edu

Jenna Vinson, PhD, is an Assistant Professor of English at the University of Massachusetts Lowell. She is currently researching contemporary representations of teenage pregnancy that produce and sustain limiting understandings of women. Her work also investigates the persuasive strategies some young mothering women use to resist these representations. Her articles have appeared in journals such as *Feminist Formations*, *Kairos: A Journal of Rhetoric, Technology, and Pedagogy*, and most recently *Sexuality Research and Social Policy*. Dr. Vinson became a mother when she was seventeen and her work is very much inspired by her experiences raising her two children. Contact: jenna_vinson@uml.edu.

Fang-Tzu Yen is an Assistant Professor at National Defense Medical Center, Taiwan. She has been conducting fieldwork with Kam people in China for years, with a special focus on the politics of reproduction among indigenous women. Apart from her doctoral dissertation, she has published a series of papers, including "The Impact of Gender and Hierarchy on Women's Reproductive Health in a Kam Village, Guizhou Province, China" in 2006 and "Reproductive Politics in Southwest China: Deconstructing a Minority Male-dominated Perspective on Reproduction" in 2009.